LLOYD GEORGE, WOODROW WILSON AND THE GUILT OF GERMANY

Lloyd George, Woodrow Wilson and the Guilt of Germany

An Essay in the Pre-History
of Appeasement

A. Lentin

LOUISIANA STATE UNIVERSITY PRESS
BATON ROUGE

First published 1985 in the United States of America by
Louisiana State University Press
Baton Rouge

Library of Congress Catalog Card Number 84-081766
ISBN 0-8071-1231-3

Designed by Douglas Martin
Photoset in 10/12 Linotron 202 Plantin
by Alan Sutton Publishing Limited
Printed and bound in Great Britain by
The Pitman Press, Bath

Contents

Illustrations

Acknowledgments

For permission to consult or quote from unpublished material, my thanks are due to: Mr and Mrs W. Bell (Dawson Papers); Mrs Mary Bennet (Fisher Papers); the University of Birmingham and the Earl of Derby (Chamberlain and Derby Papers); the Master and Fellows of Churchill College, Cambridge, Lord Hankey and the Lady Vansittart (Hankey and Vansittart Papers); the Clerk of the Records, the House of Lords Record Office, Mr A.J.P. Taylor and the Beaverbrook Foundation (Lloyd George Papers); Mrs E.H. Colville and the Librarian, Lambeth Palace (Davidson Papers); Lord Cunliffe (Cunliffe Papers); Mr M. Gendel and the Master and Fellows of Trinity College, Cambridge (Montagu Papers); Lord Hardinge of Penshurst and the Rt. Hon. Julian Hardinge (Hardinge Papers); Professor Agnes Headlam-Morley (Headlam-Morley Papers); Professor D.E. Moggridge and Lord Kahn (Keynes Papers); the Provost and Fellows of King's College, Cambridge and the University of Texas (letter from E.M. Forster); Professor A.K.S. Lambton (Cecil Papers); the Marquess of Lothian (Lothian Papers); the Warden and Fellows of New College, Oxford (Milner Papers); Mr H.D. Miller, M.P. (Buckmaster Papers); Dr A.L. Rowse (letter to the author) and Messrs Warren Murton and Co. (Bryce Papers). Thanks are also due to Mr Bruce Arnold, Lord Boothby, Mr David Buxton, Dr Piers Brendon, Dr Angus Calder, Dr Catherine Cline, Dr Henry Cowper, Mr P.N. Furbank, Mr Magnus John and Mrs Sabine Phillips, and to Mr Peter Boulton and Mrs Susan Martin, of Leicester University Press. Above all I wish to thank Mr Thomas Camps, Professor John Ferguson, Professor Arthur Marwick, Mr A.W. Purdue and Mrs Wendy Clarke.

TO SIMON
quo nihil carius

Introduction

The Lost Peace

If on our conscience we had had no errors,
   No follies, or injustice; if we'd thought
That through a hell of death and pain and terrors
   We'd reach the earthly paradise we sought;
If we had always justified the littler
   Against the greater to our own despite,
We should have been quite wrong to talk to Hitler;
   But as, in fact, we hadn't – we were right.

From 'If' after Kipling, published in *Truth*, 12 October 1938, on the occasion
of the Munich Agreement and enclosed in a letter from Barrington-Ward to
Arnold Toynbee, 24 October 1938 (Toynbee Papers)

It was because of this feeling that Germany had not been justly
treated that so many people in England failed to realise the true
nature of the National Socialist movement.

Philip Kerr, Marquess of Lothian, letter, May 15 1939 (Lothian
Papers)

The tragedy of the lost peace retains its power to move, if not to
pity and terror, then at least to continual wonder. It opens with
the Armistice of November 1918: terms amounting in effect to
unconditional surrender, crowned, half a year later, by the victorious
Treaty of Versailles. As Britain's statesmen gathered in Paris to
debate the constraints to be imposed upon a prostrate and exhausted
foe, and even urged concessions, Churchill, as Minister of War,
stressed the totality of their achievement. 'The Germans', he pointed
out, 'had given up their fleet and their army. They were prepared to
dismantle fortresses and to give up their guns. They were giving up
their colonies. Poland had been carved out of their territory. They had
offered to pay five thousand million pounds. . . . Already it was the
greatest triumph in the history of the world.' Twenty years later, the

settlement of 1919 stood revealed as a mere truce: successfully defied, gradually undermined, finally overthrown and nearly reversed. How, one asks again, did it happen? How, above all, could the victors have allowed it to happen?

Various elements, of course, contributed. A natural revulsion against the horrors of war and a determination never again to resort to it until all other methods of resolving international disputes had been exhausted; imperial preoccupations and fear of Italy and Japan; consciousness of the need to re-arm, and so forth. But in seeking to comprehend why British opinion acquiesced, while Germany, at first clandestinely and then with ever-increasing boldness, threw off one by one the shackles of defeat, one is drawn back repeatedly to the residual and fundamental phenomenon of a bad conscience about Versailles and a predisposition to sympathize with German complaints of injustice. Retracing what might be called the psychological pre-history of Appeasement – for Appeasement was as much a state of mind and feeling as a policy – one is struck by a powerful undertow of disenchantment among the British delegates at Paris. 'We do not need to apologise for our victory', protested Clemenceau, when this mood began to make itself felt. But 'apologetic' was precisely the temper which took root in the British consciousness even before the Treaty was signed.

The Cabinet itself, summoned by the Prime Minister to Paris to approve the final drafts, was sceptical, critical, and, as Lord Robert Cecil complained, 'very unhappy about the Treaty.' 'We have got everything we wanted,' he said, 'far more than we ever wanted, in terms of material possessions. Yet we are all miserable.' The prevailing unease was confirmed and shared by the equable Herbert Fisher: 'We all condemn the Treaty and agree that it should be modified,' he noted. 'My own view', he wrote to Gilbert Murray, 'is that passion still runs too high to get a really enduring settlement now; but if a Treaty *tel quel* is signed, there will be an appeasement, and by degrees readjustments and modifications.' Such prognostications on the part of his colleagues hardly suggest official confidence in the document to which the Prime Minister was about to affix his seal and commit the nation.

The younger delegates in particular, trustees, after all, of the post-war future, were the most poignantly affected by Versailles. For them, for the most part liberals in the widest sense, peacemaking soon lost the aura of a crusade for right and justice, which had fired their early enthusiasm and illuminated their preparatory labours. The magnificent, golden vision of a 'Wilson Peace', a *Pax Americana*, faded into what seemed a nightmare of compromise and contrivance, the tawdry object of shame and regret. 'A terrible outcome of all our professions', lamented General Smuts, who spoke of Versailles as the 'Carthaginian Peace' – a phrase to be taken up with much effect by John Maynard Keynes.

Symbolic of this perceived discrepancy between the promise and deed of Versailles was article 231, the notorious 'war-guilt clause', whereby Germany's plenipotentiaries were compelled to subscribe to the following proposition:

> The Allied and Associated Governments affirm and Germany accepts the responsibility of Germany and her allies for causing all the loss and damage to which the Allied and Associated Governments and their nationals have been subjected as a consequence of the war imposed upon them by the aggression of Germany and her allies.

Few sentences in history can have been as fraught with consequences. Of all the 440 conditions of Versailles, onerous, irksome and shameful as they seemed to the mass of German opinion, none provoked such instant, vehement and lasting resentment. To Germans of almost every persuasion between the wars – to Ebert and Stresemann no less than to Hitler, who formally repudiated it in 1937 – the war-guilt clause remained the ultimate symbol of unacceptability. Long before the rise of National Socialism, it served to brand the Treaty as a whole with the stigma of a *Diktat*, a document signed under duress and lacking moral validity. Far from reconciling Germany to a sober consciousness of her role in the origins and course of the war, article 231 helped to nurture all that was worst in the German character, accentuating feelings of self-pity and fostering an exaggerated spirit of aggrieved pugnacity against Versailles and all its works.

The recrudescence of German nationalism, however, need not and could not of itself have proved fatal to the peace, had it not been accompanied by a corresponding crisis of will among the victors. In Britain, the immediate effect of Versailles was to gratify a temporary and far from universal mood of self-righteousness, a temper well reflected in the war-guilt clause and in Lord Curzon's presentation of the terms to the Upper House. 'The bringing home to Germany and its rulers', he stated, 'of their responsibility for having inflicted on the world the sufferings and calamities of the last five years fundamentally distinguishes the Treaty of Versailles from any previous peace treaty.'

Such sentiments, though genuine, were transient, and quickly veered to an opposite and brooding sense of Versailles as an incubus, a *damnosa hereditas*, particularly with the return from Paris of the younger delegates and the consequent spread of their misgivings. Thus, while the immediate view of Versailles from London was of a settlement severe but just, by the early 1920s, increasingly the whole Treaty came to be regarded as tainted. In the 1930s, this distorted and essentially morbid image came so to obsess the mind and cloud the judgment that public opinion was unable, until almost too late, to appreciate the challenge, not merely to the settlement of 1919 but to the verdict of 1918. As late as 1942, with Britain again under arms, a rare apologist of the Treaty, in a work significantly entitled *The Treaty of Versailles: Was it Just?*, observed: 'most British people have come to take it for granted that the Allies' handling of Germany has been simply monstrous; and this assumption, with the bad conscience attending it, has been Hitler's most powerful ally.' Surveying the phenomenon of Appeasement a quarter of a century later, Mr A.J.P. Taylor confirms the diagnosis. 'Guilty conscience', he agrees, 'was undoubtedly the strongest factor.'

In probing the origins of this debilitating and near fatal *malaise*, in seeking to understand the transformation, in British eyes, of the 'Wilson Peace' into the 'Carthaginian Peace', a study of the interplay of circumstances, policy and personality behind the inclusion of the war-guilt clause may serve to shed further light on the reputation – and hence the fate – of the Treaty overall. A chronological account of this aspect of peacemaking must focus on decisions taken at the highest level in London and Paris during the half year between cease-fire and Treaty. It must follow the strivings, desperately serious, of Woodrow Wilson, for the promised peace of right and justice, and indicate the no lesser insistence of Georges Clemenceau on a peace of security and restitution. Above all, such an essay must attempt to trace the unfolding contribution of David Lloyd George, a protagonist in this as in so much of the Conference; to penetrate or divine his concerns and his objectives; to unravel or to infer the motives and the methods of that remarkable politician, then – in that fateful interval between war and peace – at the height of his fame and the furthest ambit of his influence.

In attempting this brief account, the present writer had no particular axe to grind. I agreed with those who found the Treaty unrealistic because it fell between two stools, being both too harsh to conciliate Germany and at the same time too weak to restrain her indefinitely. But my opinion of Versailles was beside the point. What mattered was how contemporaries saw it, since contemporary opinion, if I am right, was what served in the last resort to seal its fate. My aim, then, was to suggest how Versailles came to seem as it did by explaining how it came to be as it was. I sought rather to understand than to judge. The policies of Wilson and Clemenceau, though ultimately incompatible, were clear and comprehensible; and in reconsidering them from the perspective of reparation and war-guilt, I had little to add and much to reaffirm. The President, for all his faults and his detractors, remains a tragic hero of the Conference. His vision was noble and enduring, and his defeat, as Smuts said, was the world's. The demands of Clemenceau in the matter of reparations were more moderate than is commonly supposed. They were also, originally at least, founded upon unquestioned legal right. Less clear to me in this context were the expectations of the Prime Minister, both those which he aroused and those which he entertained, and their relation to the peace of Europe. As I examined the documents and transcribed their contents, increasingly it seemed to me that the record speaks for itself. It was also borne in upon me that the essence of what happened at Paris, the particular human decisions that are the subject of this enquiry, were – despite the by-play of time and chance – 'acts or omissions thoroughly expressive of the doer', in the words of A.C. Bradley (*Shakespearean Tragedy*, 1904), 'characteristic deeds'; and that 'the centre of the tragedy, therefore, may be said with equal truth to lie in action issuing from character, or in character issuing in action.'

Chapter 1

Armistice

If the 'leaders' of democracy in this and other countries do not lose their balance in the midst of this orgy of thankfulness, the silent dead, lying in the holocaust of the labyrinth and elsewhere, may reap their reward in the peace of the world for perhaps two generations. As Your Majesty well knows, ambition, vanity, tyranny and a 'swelled head' are not the characteristics of Monarchs only, as it is the fashion of the moment to suppose, but are equally the privilege of statesmen and journalists and other leaders of that curious superstition which men call democracy.

Lord Esher to King George V, 12 Nov. 1918

You have filled the bill as Jupiter Pugnax. You are now before the footlights as Jupiter Victor.

Edwin Montagu to Lloyd George, 1 Nov., All-Hallows, 1918 (Montagu Papers)

In the spring and summer of 1918, Germany came close to winning the war. Fresh from her conquest of Russia, she threw the weight of her forces into a final bid to overwhelm the British and French, before the Americans should reach Europe in sufficient numbers to turn the scale against her. At the end of March, preceded by the most massive artillery bombardment in history, the Ludendorff Offensive smashed suddenly through the Allied lines. For the first time since 1914, the seemingly interminable stalemate of the western front was broken, as the storm-troopers raced towards Amiens. At the end of May, they were once more on the Marne. A month later, the *Kaiserschlacht*, the 'Kaiser's Battle' that promised to bring the Germans to Paris and the war to an end, opened with an attack on Rheims and the fall of Château Thierry. As gigantic shells, fired from German howitzers 50 miles away, rained down on the capital, the French Government made ready to evacuate.

But the Allied armies regrouped, held firm, stemmed the onrush, and began, yard by yard and at agonising cost, to advance. By August, it was clear that Ludendorff's strategy had failed. While the Allies, now effectively aided by America, pushed steadily eastward and prepared for the campaign of 1919, the Germans realized, with the sudden and successive collapse of their allies, Bulgaria, Turkey and Austria-Hungary, that victory was no longer a possibility. Germany herself, by shortening her lines in the west, by making a tactical withdrawal to the Rhine, might, for a time, hold out; she might postpone defeat; she could not escape it. Early in October, at the insistence of the High Command, the German Government appealed urgently to President Wilson for a cease-fire. A month later the war was over.

With benefit of hindsight, it was often regretted that the Allies failed to complete their victory in classic and unambiguous tradition, by advancing into Germany and dictating terms at Berlin. The fateful myths of German invincibility and the 'stab in the back' might thereby have been stifled at birth. Lloyd George himself, with characteristic clairvoyance, for a time urged such a policy. After careful and compelling deliberation, however, more humane counsels prevailed. Wars, as Marshal Foch explained, are fought for specific objectives – '*On ne fait la guerre que pour ses résultats.*' The Germans, by agreeing to Wilson's demand for 'absolutely satisfactory safeguards and guarantees [of] the present military supremacy' of the Allies, had conceded these objectives in full. To persist, in the face of this compliance, with an advance into Germany might be to provoke a hard resistance in defence of the homeland. Operations therefore could and should be brought to an immediate end. To the British and French Cabinets, their armies still hard-pressed and suffering appalling losses from an enemy retiring in good order, the argument was irresistible. Thus it was that, when the cease-fire commenced on 11 November, the German army still stood foursquare on French and Belgian soil. Not one Allied soldier had penetrated the territory of the Reich otherwise than as a prisoner-of-war. 'They fought well,' said Foch of the enemy. 'Let them keep their weapons.' At Berlin, German, not Allied, divisions marched past the Brandenburg Gate to the blare of martial music and the acclamations of the crowd, their helmets decked with oak-leaves, returning, in the ominous words with which they were hailed by President Ebert, 'undefeated from the battlefield'.

Whatever Ebert, Ludendorff, or others, then and later, might claim, however, the terms of armistice spoke for themselves. The abrogation of Germany's treaties of victory, the renunciation of her each and every conquest, the immediate evacuation of Belgium and France, withdrawal from Russia, the cession of Alsace-Lorraine, the internment in British ports of the High Seas Fleet, the surrender of all submarines, aircraft and vast quantities of weaponry, the relegation beyond the Rhine of all German divisions and the entry into the Rhineland of Allied armies of occupation, with bridgeheads across the river, the continuance of the blockade: the acceptance of such terms, which the British Cabinet itself considered harsh and humiliating, is proof enough that Germany's rulers acknowledged the full measure of her defeat.

Defeat, however, was not surrender. 'A nation of seventy millions suffers, but it does not die,' affirmed the chief German plenipotentiary at Compiègne; and the existence of the Armistice also bears witness to the fact that Germany laid down her arms in reliance on precise and categorical assurances regarding the eventual peace settlement to be concluded. It was to be a peace in express conformity with the Fourteen Points of President Wilson. These celebrated Points, first enunciated in a speech to Congress in January 1918, and refined and clarified in subsequent pronouncements, were of a quality new to the chancelleries of warring Europe. They called for a settlement freely negotiated between equals. They postulated a peace 'without victors and vanquished', a 'peace of justice', a peace containing 'no annexations, no contributions, no punitive damages'.

Ever since the outbreak of war, it had been Wilson's lasting hope that he might mediate between the belligerents; even after America's own entry, he still strove to maintain an attitude of studious and lofty objectivity. In this there was nothing nerveless or anaemic, as his critics complained. He was no less firm or decisive in the cause of victory. Nor was he blind or indifferent to the excesses of Imperial Germany. They moved him, on the contrary, to a righteous anger. Not only the fact of war itself, which he deplored with an almost fastidious horror, seeing the instruments of nineteenth-century Progress turned to hellish purposes, but also the manner in which it was waged by Germany, provoked him to incredulous revulsion. The violation of Belgian neutrality, the deportation of civilians, the use of poison gas, the sinking of the *Lusitania* and the strategy of indiscriminate submarine attack that had forced America herself into the war, the unconcealed, the smirking rapacity displayed at Brest-Litovsk – however much exploited by allied propaganda, such policies spoke for themselves. In Wilson's eyes, they reflected the character of a government, as he put it, 'throwing to the winds all scruples of humanity or of respect for the understandings that were supposed to underlie the intercourse of the world'. 'We cannot "come to terms" with them,' he protested. 'They have made it impossible. . . . We do not think the same thoughts or speak the same language.'

At the end of the war, these things were fresh in his mind. In their retreat across France and Belgium, the German armies left a trail of wanton yet purposeful and systematic devastation. Without military justification and without mercy, towns and villages, already pitiably battle-scarred, were looted and razed by order of the High Command. Cattle and industrial plant were removed to Germany. Gutted houses and farmsteads, dynamited factories, torn-up railway-track and flooded mines awaited the advancing Allies. Ruin on such a scale had not been seen since the depredations of the Thirty Years War, and seemed almost to warrant the opprobrious synonym customarily bestowed on the Germans by the British press – 'the Huns'. Haggard civilians and prisoners-of-war had their own tales to tell of arrant misrule. Even as the German Government, aware that the war was lost, was plying the President with urgent requests for cease-fire, the British mail-boat *Leinster* was torpedoed in the Irish Sea, with the needless loss of 400 civilians. 'Brutes they were when they began the war,' the normally soft-spoken Balfour exclaimed in the Commons, 'and, as far as we can judge, brutes they remain.' The President was no less outraged than the British Foreign Secretary, and the tone and content of his communications with Berlin appreciably stiffened.

The overthrow of the German monarchy now became for him a precondition of peace. It was not merely that 'no autocratic government could be trusted to keep faith'. The President, as an American, an historian and a Democrat, cherished a positive faith in the native virtue, the instinctive, residual goodness, of the People, and its inherently peaceful aspirations. Once autocracy was made to yield to responsible government, once coercion was replaced by consent, and once peoples were free to determine their own destiny, they would, he fervently believed, be naturally impelled towards honest and healthy co-operation. He had, he affirmed, 'no quarrel with the German people'. He paid generous tribute to their peacetime achievements. He wished to see them resume a worthy, though not a dominant place, in the comity of nations. Once they threw off their present masters and produced a government responsive to the popular will, they would, he pledged himself, be accorded 'full, impartial justice'. 'We are ready', he insisted, 'whenever the final reckoning is made, to be just to the German people, deal fairly with the German power, as with all others. There can be no difference between peoples in the final judgement, if it is indeed to be a righteous judgement. To propose anything but justice, even-handed and dispassionate justice, to Germany, would be to renounce and dishonour our own cause'. He warned that there must be 'no discrimination between those to whom we wish to be just, and those to whom we do not wish to be just.'

In this crucial respect – its overriding character of justice – the treaty would differ fundamentally from earlier settlements. It would be something other than simply the imposition of the will of the victor, should reflect more than merely another respite in the arbitrary ebb and flow of the Balance of Power. The President was resolved that the peace to be concluded, by virtue of its zealous and manifest fair-mindedness, should bring about such a harmony of interest and sentiment, of mind and spirit, between the nations, as to liquidate the conditions which had produced and prolonged this most terrible of wars. The Fourteen Points called for 'absolute freedom of the seas, . . . the removal, so far as possible, of all economic barriers, . . . the absolutely impartial adjustment of all colonial claims', and the implementation of the principle of national self-determination. Above all, as the linchpin and consummation of the peace, there should be founded a League of Nations, 'for the purpose of affording mutual guarantees of political independence and territorial integrity to great and small states alike'. Nations would coexist in peace, submitting their differences to arbitration or judicial settlement, absolute in the renunciation of force. Instead of the sinister web of secret agreements, which had, he felt, served to embroil so many nations in the war, there should be 'open covenants of peace, openly arrived at', diplomacy conducted 'always frankly and in the public view'.

The President's aims thus looked beyond the immediate defeat of Imperial Germany. They were conceived and presented as a cure for those deeper rivalries and ills which predated and underlay the present conflict. At the heart of the causes of the war, he believed, lay the violation of a simple, self-evident principle: that nations, no less than peoples, should be free to determine their own affairs. He spoke of 'an imperative principle of action' that should inspire and guide the peacemakers in their deliberations; 'and that principle', he declared, 'is plain. No people must be forced under sovereignty under which it does not wish to live.' 'The peace of justice', to which he covenanted himself, should thus reconcile the principle of national self-determination with the principle of international order; it should combine 'the principle of justice to all peoples and nationalities, and their right to live on equal terms of liberty and safety with one another, whether they be strong or weak'.

Despite the unusual distinction of style, and the novelty of such pronouncements at such a moment, there was, in the President's principles, little that was inherently new. Therein lay the historic strength of their appeal – in the promulgation at that time of those ideals. They harked back to man's most rooted aspirations, to the prophetic vision of a world in harmony and to the classical equation of the law of nature and of nations. They recalled the medieval hope of a Christian Republic and the philosophers' schemes for perpetual peace. They linked the brightest hopes of nineteenth-century liberalism with the most recent proposals of the Hague Conferences. They looked to a community of states which, though sovereign, national and independent, would be, as the President said, 'governed in their conduct towards each other by the same principles of honour and of respect for the common law of civilised society that govern the individual citizens of all modern states in their relations with one another'.

Such was Wilson's 'programme of the world's peace . . . the only possible programme, as we see it.' It was a programme worth fighting for; it was the only programme worth fighting for. It transmuted a sordid imperialist war into a war of liberation. Nothing less than the promise of these goals, he believed, could allow him 'to continue this tragical and appalling outpouring of blood and treasure'. America's part he conceived of in terms of a crusade, casting his fellow-countrymen in the role reserved by Jehovah for the Children of Israel – as a light to the Gentiles. 'We have', he declared, 'no selfish ends to serve. We desire no conquest, no dominion. We seek no indemnities for ourselves, no material compensation for the sacrifice we shall freely make. We are but one of the champions of the rights of mankind.' America's mission, he proclaimed, was 'to redeem the world and make it fit for free men like ourselves to live in'.

If, in these ringing affirmations, this confident perfectionism, there was a certain priggishness, a hint of Calvinist condescension, an unmistakable tone of exclusiveness, a touch even of revivalist arrogance, it will be remembered that these were after all exceptional times. European statesmen might scoff in private at the President's Utopian outpourings; might discern, in his insistence that the

United States be termed an 'associate' rather than an 'ally', of Britain and France, a certain conscious self-distancing, a touch of 'holier than thou'. There were reasons for his stand-offishness. When the Bolsheviks in 1918 divulged the various secret treaties which had been concluded between the Allies under pressure of war, there was revealed, in the unblushing rapacity, the *sacro egoismo*, of some of the states enlisted in the Allied cause, and the candid realism, however excusable, with which the *Entente* catered to it, more than a suggestion of the old diplomacy, of cynical deals behind closed doors, of what the President loftily reproved as 'the great game, now forever discredited, of the balance of power', of an imperialism which differed in degree but not in kind from that of the Central Powers, and was starkly at variance with official professions of Allied war aims. To those who believed or hoped that the struggle in which they were engaged stood for something higher than naval supremacy or imperial aggrandisement, that element in the President's utterances of a vibrant self-righteousness, inseparable from all great upward strivings, was cleansing and reviving. To a world enmeshed in hideous and, as it often seemed, meaningless conflict, it answered in every civilized land the promptings of what Wilson called the 'heart and conscience of mankind'. When his declared aims were nothing less than 'a new international order, based upon broad and universal principles of right and justice – no mere peace of shreds and patches', it was the very millenarianism of such pronouncements that raised and quickened the spirit and gladdened the heart. When he spoke of 'making the world safe for democracy', for every seasoned politician who smiled at 'Professor Wilson' and his Rousseauesque naïveté, hundreds were moved and uplifted by the vision of man and nations regenerate. If Wilsonism seemed in part to fly in the face of history and human nature, there precisely, in its promise of a clean break with the past, lay its attraction. What, after all, was the alternative?

Though transcendent and universal in its appeal, Wilsonism was a creed essentially Anglo-Saxon in origin, its roots in Jeffersonian democracy and Gladstonian liberalism. It struck an immediate chord in liberal England. To the Asquithians, to the radicals, to Conservative idealists like Lord Robert Cecil, to serving men and women, and to the young, it offered a prospect at once idealistic and familiar. It was not only young hopefuls, like Harold Nicolson of the Foreign Office, who thrilled to the call at the time of the Armistice, believing that they stood at the dawn of a new age. Lord

Curzon himself, Lord President of the Council, presenting the cease-fire terms to the Upper House, was so caught up in the prevailing mood as to declaim from Shelley's apocalyptic lines

> The world's great age begins anew,
> The golden years return . . .

Even so detached an iconoclast as Bernard Shaw hailed the President as the Man of Destiny, embodiment of the 'mystic force of evolution'.

What was new about the President's principles, however, was not so much their inherent moral and intellectual compulsion – though seldom have they been so eloquently or so movingly proclaimed, and seldom were they more generally welcome than at that time of weariness and hope – but the fact that their realization seemed to be an actual possibility. Woodrow Wilson was not only an intellectual and an avowed progressive, a former President of Princeton University, a man of civilized tastes, of patent enlightenment and proven beneficence: he was chief executive officer of the world's most powerful state. America had come late into the war. Her military participation had been slight compared with that of the Allies; but her contribution to victory, in terms of her immense reserves of manpower and equipment, of industrial might, of food supplies and of mercantile credit, was unsurpassed and decisive. Europe was utterly dependent on her for food and finance. The New World having been called in to redress the balance of the Old, the President appeared to stand in a uniquely advantageous position to enforce the principles which he proclaimed and to impose 'the peace of justice' which he promised. If America's material preponderance and political authority did not of themselves inspire ready acquiescence among the Allies, it lay within his power to exert stronger pressures, whether by deploying or withholding the vast resources at his disposal. Nor did the President appear to shrink from exercising, if need be, such formidable prerogatives: 'agreeably, if we can; disagreeably, if we must'.

The President's war-aims were lofty; they were difficult, perhaps impossible of attainment. What was certain was that they were binding upon the Allies. The Prime Ministers of Britain, France and Italy had not accepted them lightly, although, until the very last days of hostilities, they had barely considered them at all. Before then, they had been preoccupied with the business of war and the promotion of their own national interests. It was true that Britain and France, at least, had not entered the war with a conscious view to gain; but the prospect of Germany's defeat offered obvious opportunities for settling old scores and realizing wider ambitions. Having been forced, in the hour of need, to endorse the shopping-lists of their more mercenary allies, they were not disposed to renounce, in the dawn of victory, some share in its fruits. Among these, for Britain, the elimination of Germany as an imperial and economic rival loomed large. The Government, Bonar Law announced in July, was committed to a post-war policy of imperial preference. There would be no question, declared Balfour in August, of returning to Germany her captured colonies.

Nothing, for his part, disturbed the President so much as this resurgent tide of national ambitions. It was what he had most feared and deplored since 1914. It was the tragedy of total war, he perceived, that appetite increased with what it fed on, to the point where all compromise was excluded: that Germany would not countenance moderate terms unless beaten beyond hope of recovery, while the prospect of victory was unleashing among the Allies passions difficult to stem and likely to sow the seeds of future strife. It was against the fostering of such ambitions and the assertion of such commitments by the Allies, quite as much as against the ruthlessness of Imperial Germany, that his thoughts and speeches were principally directed as the war drew to its close. In September, he wrote of 'the very deep anxiety I have that the whole temper of the nations engaged against Germany should be a temper of high-minded justice'.

The Imperial War Cabinet had studied, with a mixture of anxiety and contempt, the various encyclicals from the White House. For three years, while the British Empire struggled for survival, the President had encumbered them with moral exhortations and remonstrances, while boasting, as it seemed, that America was 'too proud to fight'. Even after America's entry, his public declarations still seemed to them to draw too little distinction between Germany and the Allies. With victory now imminent, they watched with anger and alarm as he suddenly took matters more and more into his own hands, and seemed about to dictate, on his sole authority, the terms of peace. Incensed at Germany's astuteness in suing directly to the President, at the President's entering unilaterally into *pourparlers*, and at the preponderant place in these assumed by the Fourteen Points, they demanded consultation, explanation and urgent pause for thought; and asked 'that the President would send Colonel

House over at the earliest possible moment'.

The personality of Colonel House may be accounted among the most significant forces in the shaping of the peace. With no official position in the Wilson administration, this Texan politician exerted an influence in American foreign policy second only to the President's. He was not a diplomat by training, but he possessed an impressive combination of diplomatic skills – integrity, far-sightedness and firmness allied to practicality, precision, speed and tact – and he enjoyed the ear and the unreserved affection of the President. The talents of the two men were complementary. The President's radiant idealism was filtered and concentrated by House into sharp, clear directives, while losing nothing of its original inspiration. The Colonel admired and venerated Wilson, 'the Governor', as he affectionately called him. The President had the warmest possible regard for House. There existed between them an implicit and unique understanding. 'Mr House is my second personality,' Wilson confided. 'He is my independent self. His thoughts and mine are one.' During the war, as the President's 'Special Representative' in Europe, House had done as much as any man could to promote Wilson's plans for mediation, or at least to make them known in the right quarters, and had made himself liked and trusted by the Allies. As the war drew to a close, it was to him that the President turned to smooth and clarify the path ahead. Immediately on receiving Germany's appeal for armistice, the President had sent for him: and the American replies to Berlin, drafted by the President with House at his shoulder, followed the Colonel's sage advice, and while requiring Berlin's unqualified acceptance of the Fourteen Points, also stipulated for those military safeguards which would 'make a renewal of hostilities on the part of Germany impossible'.

The Allies were well pleased with the military terms; but the question of the Fourteen Points found them perplexed and impatient. 'Have you ever been asked by President Wilson', said Clemenceau to Lloyd George, 'whether you accept the Fourteen Points? I have never been asked.' 'I have not been asked either,' replied Lloyd George. Whereupon both Prime Ministers expressed their determination that there should be no room for misunderstanding. Far from being glossed over in the turmoil of events, as Balfour, for example, later suggested, the nature and role of the Fourteen Points was most carefully elucidated. No one present at the discussions with Colonel House was in any doubt or error as to the profound significance of the proceedings. Lloyd George himself began by asking the Colonel to confirm his own 'interpretation of the situation . . . namely, whether the German Government were counting on peace being concluded on the basis of President Wilson's Fourteen Points and his other speeches'. House replied that 'this was undoubtedly the case', whereupon Lloyd George pointed out that 'unless the Allies made the contrary clear, they themselves, in accepting the armistice, would be bound to those terms. Consequently, before they entered into an armistice, they must make it clear what their attitude towards these terms was.' The Foreign Secretary concurred: 'If we assented to an armistice without making our position clear, we should certainly be bound.' Clemenceau too 'agreed that this was the case'. At this, Colonel House was subjected to a searching interrogation concerning the meaning of the Fourteen Points.

Since much of this account hinges on the relation of the Fourteen Points to the issue of reparations, it is necessary to turn for a moment to this important question. Two of the Fourteen Points provided for the restoration of occupied territory. Point Seven stated that 'Belgium, the whole world will agree, must be evacuated and restored'; Point Eight that 'all French territory should be freed and the invaded portions restored'. The meaning of 'restoration' emerged from a special *aide-mémoire,* drawn up, with Wilson's assent, for the Colonel's use in the present negotiations. This commentary drew a distinction between France and Belgium. Belgium was to be a special case, 'distinct and symbolic'. As the state whose neutrality had been wantonly violated in 1914, she should receive *restitutio in integrum*: full compensation both for damage suffered in consequence of invasion and for all costs incurred by her in resisting it. 'Without this healing act,' the President had declared, 'the whole structure and validity of international law is forever impaired.' With France, the case was different. Though the destruction inflicted in the occupied north-east departments was immense, Germany's invasion in 1914 was not in itself unlawful. German liability to France, therefore, should be confined to the cost of making good the physical damage.

The Fourteen Points, it was noted, made no provision for British losses. Britain had suffered relatively little from direct attack on her civilians. Air-raid damage or the occasional shelling of some east coast resorts, though alarming, was not even remotely comparable to the desolation wrought in France. Sinkings by submarines, on the other hand, had caused enormous losses in civilian shipping. How damage of this category might be recovered was therefore the subject of an Allied memorandum, drafted by Lloyd George's secretary, Philip Kerr, and presented by the Prime Minister to Colonel House. The memorandum contained a qualification to the Fourteen Points: 'The Allied Governments feel that no doubt ought to be allowed to exist' as to the demands to be made of Germany. By the President's stipulations in regard to 'restoration', they understood that 'compensation will be paid by Germany for all damage done to the civilian population of the Allies and their property by the aggression of Germany by land, by sea and from the air'. The purpose of this reservation, then, as Lloyd George explained next day to the Imperial War Cabinet, was to enable Britain to advance claims in respect of losses in merchant shipping, analogous to France's rights to territorial reparation.

On 4 November, Colonel House, with the agreement of Clemenceau and the Italian Prime Minister, Orlando, cabled Lloyd George's memorandum to the White House for ratification. On receiving it, Wilson at once signified his approval. He instructed the Secretary of State, Robert Lansing, to notify House immediately of his endorsement, and at the same time to forward the memorandum to Berlin, confirming American acceptance of the reservation. In a covering note, Lansing was to announce the willingness of the Allies, subject to the reservation, 'to make peace with the Government of Germany on the terms of peace laid down' in the Fourteen Points, and to state that Marshal Foch was authorized to communicate the conditions of cease-fire. It was in response to this document, known thereafter as the Lansing note or Pre-Armistice Agreement, that the German Government forthwith despatched plenipotentiaries under flag-of-truce to Marshal Foch at Compiègne. It was there, six days later, in the saloon of the Marshal's *wagon-lit*, that the Armistice was signed.

What, then, were the terms relating to reparations? The Pre-Armistice Agreement itself is not absolutely precise; but the stipulation of 'damage done to the civilian population' clearly excludes by implication the costs of waging the war. This crucial point is abundantly confirmed by Lloyd George himself. On 3 November, while the question was under discussion, he told the Belgian Prime Minister that he thought it 'would be a mistake to put into the Armistice terms anything that will lead Germany to suppose that we want a war indemnity'. Three days later, he informed the Imperial War Cabinet that 'a war indemnity had been ruled out, because, beyond full reparation, Germany would have no means of paying further'. The Prime Minister, relying on an official Treasury estimate from J.M. Keynes, explained that 'the total reparation which might be claimed would, he believed, amount to somewhere between a thousand and two thousand million pounds'. The Allies were bound, and knew that they were bound, by the terms of the Lansing note. They understood that it formed an integral and indissoluble part of the Armistice. They agreed that it contained a clear and firm proposal, defining a salient condition of the future peace treaty; and that, once accepted by Germany, it became a solemn and irrevocable commitment, a *pactum de contrahendo*. As a lawyer, no one knew this better than Lloyd George, as he again confirmed 20 years later in his *Memoirs*: 'I was definitely of the opinion that we were committed by the Armistice terms not to demand an indemnity which would include the cost of prosecuting the war.'

The Prime Minister, at the time of the Armistice, stood at the very pinnacle of his fame. Under his leadership, the nation had come triumphantly through the most awesome challenge in its history. 'British prestige', noted Colonel Hankey, Secretary to the War Cabinet, 'is higher than it has ever been before. So is Lloyd George's.' At the Lord Mayor's Banquet on 9 November, the Prime Minister received a hero's welcome, the entire company standing unceremoniously on chairs, yelling and waving as he advanced along the aisle of the Guildhall. 'I was standing by Arthur Balfour,' recorded the Archbishop of Canterbury, 'and I remarked with amusement of this demonstration to a man who ten years before was regarded in the City as unutterable; and Balfour's reply in the din was shouted into my ear: "Well, the little beggar deserves it all!"' Two days later, shortly before eleven in the morning, Lloyd George stepped out into Downing Street, to inform an expectant crowd that the war was over. The spontaneous joy to which London abandoned itself as Big Ben tolled the hour is legendary: public buildings disgorging themselves into Whitehall; taxis and lorries commandeered, frenzied merrymakers clambering onto running-board or roof; a general cacophany of hooters, tambourines, singing, cheers, laughter and tears; later, in the House of Commons, the Prime Minister, having solemnly recited the terms of Armistice, moving an adjournment to St Margaret's, Westminster, 'to give humble and reverent thanks for the deliverance of the world from its great peril'.

The rejoicings were not unmixed. William Morris Hughes, the Prime Minister of Australia, who was in England at the time, was seriously aggrieved. Although a member of the Imperial War Cabinet, he had not been present at the pre-Armistice discussions, nor had his views been sought. He realized at once, and sooner than most, the implications of the Lansing note, and he made it his business to bring these home to the public in no uncertain terms. In a succession of impassioned speeches, in letters to the press as well as in memoranda to the Prime Minister, and personally in the Imperial War Cabinet, he pointed out that Britain had forfeited her right to a war-indemnity, and complained of the consequences for the Empire. Whatever Britain might claim by way of reparations, the Dominions, having suffered no civilian damage as such, were not, apparently, entitled to anything. Australia would not stand for it, he protested. Australia, having entered the war from the start and shared the heat and burden of the day, had at least as much right to be heard as President Wilson. On 7 November, addressing the Australia club, he renewed his attack. 'I object to these terms of peace', he protested amid cheers, 'because they do not provide for indemnities.'

Hughes was not liked in the Imperial War Cabinet. His deafness and his aggressive manners, allied to his dogged persistence, were not endearing characteristics. He 'had long been a bore', observed Geoffrey Dawson, editor of *The Times*, 'and was becoming a nuisance.' Steps were taken to quieten him. Leo Amery, Assistant Secretary to the War Cabinet and a fervent advocate of imperial unity, was deputed by Lloyd George 'to explain to Hughes that nothing had really happened and that we were still quite free to enforce whatever peace terms we wished'. The Prime Minister was diplomatic but disingenuous; and Hughes was not satisfied. Lloyd George himself intervened. He wrote to Hughes on Armistice Day to impress upon him that the Allied reservation had been 'specifically raised in order to safeguard issues which might conceivably be prejudiced by President Wilson's terms'; and drafted a communiqué stating that the purpose of the reservation had been 'to avoid the possibility of a misunderstanding from the outset'. What he meant by this is not clear. Perhaps it was not meant to be. It failed to silence Hughes.

Questions were raised in the Commons. On 12 November, Sir Joseph Walton complained of the huge burden of Britain's war-debt. 'And yet', he said, 'in looking through the terms of the Armistice, I do not see any mention of indemnities.' What, precisely, were Britain's rights in the matter? Were they really restricted to civilian damage? Mr. Houston asked 'whether, in view of the crimes committed by Germany against civilisation and humanity, the Allied Governments are prepared to accept such terms of reparation and atonement, or whether they are determined, in addition to the compensation to civilians for damage done, to make Germany pay in full' the cost of the war? Bonar Law, as Leader of the House, replied that it was not possible for him to comment. Brigadier-General Page-Croft raised the same point a week later, receiving the same inscrutable answer. 'The question', said Bonar Law, 'must be left to . . . the Government, which represents the nation.' And there, for the moment, with this somewhat ominous official reticence, the matter rested, when Parliament was dissolved on 25 November.

Disquiet, however, continued to be fanned by the press, particularly the Northcliffe press. Lord Northcliffe's feverish energies had lately been put to effective use in the post of Director of Propaganda in Enemy Countries. The Germans themselves paid him tribute; and though doubtless it was more flattering to their self-esteem to ascribe defeat to the fiendish wiles of the British press baron than to the perseverance of the British army, Northcliffe did not dispute the claim. He too indulged the belief that he himself, in large measure, had won the war for Britain. Nor, in the transition to peace, was he disposed to relinquish the methods that had brought him before the public eye, and made him seem, in his ability to make or break the careers of public men, a force akin to Warwick the Kingmaker. Had his publicity not helped to propel Lloyd George himself, first into the Ministry of Munitions, and then into Downing Street?

At the end of the war, Northcliffe was increasingly obsessed by dreams of his personal destiny and of a yet greater role in affairs. In the words of the official *History of the Times*, he 'was now approaching the very climax of the megalomania which settled upon his mind at intervals after December 1916, when his critics had compared him first with the Kaiser and then with Napoleon'. By August 1918, he aspired to see a new government set up, with himself as Lord President of the Council. He pressed his demands unavailingly upon the Cabinet. Frustrated, he warned that he would not support a new Lloyd George government unless a list of its prospective members were submitted for his approval. Again, his wishes were ignored. Northcliffe responded with a blistering press attack on the Secretary of State for War, Lord Milner, who had ventured to express in public views favourable to a moderate peace. Sir Edward Carson denounced this as a disgraceful abuse of press power and questioned Northcliffe's motives. 'For what? In order that Lord Northcliffe may get into the War Cabinet, so that he may be present at the Peace Conference?'

Such indeed was Northcliffe's latest ambition. It seems that he believed he had been offered a place. It may be that, in order to temporize, Lloyd George had suggested that Northcliffe might make himself generally available in Paris, and that Northcliffe took the Prime Minister to have offered him a place in his delegation. At all events, he determined to clarify the position. He stormed into Downing Street. The encounter was brief and explosive. Lloyd George expressed surprise: 'There must be some misunderstanding.' Northcliffe insisted. The Prime Minister shook his head. 'He had obviously expected otherwise,' Lloyd George recalled, 'and he flared up at me, like Vesuvius in eruption.' The Prime Minister had a rich sense of humour: 'I told him to go to hell!' Perhaps power had really gone to Northcliffe's head; perhaps he had fallen victim to his own propaganda and had come to believe his own newspapers. The Prime Minster was no more likely to appoint him to the Peace Conference than to the See of Canterbury.

Or was he? It was generally agreed that you never could tell with Lloyd George. On 24 November, in discussion with Milner and Hankey, he was still pondering what to do with Northcliffe. He canvassed 'the alternatives of keeping him quiet by bringing him to the Peace Conference, of taking no notice of him, or of attacking him'. In the event, he rejected the first, entrusting press coverage to his friend, Sir George Riddell; he then attempted the second, until, as will be seen, circumstances finally induced him to adopt the third. From now on he had no more determined or insensate enemy than Northcliffe. And Northcliffe knew that Prime Minister Hughes, like himself, was, as he said, 'in a dangerous mood and likely to make trouble'.

Three days after the Armistice, a general election was announced. Already in the summer, with victory in sight, Lloyd George had made up his mind to go to the country at the first opportunity. Despite the controversy that has raged ever since about the propriety of his decision, he was well within his rights, both constitutionally and politically. The existing Parliament had sat since 1910. The issues on which it had come to power were outdated. The franchise on which it was elected, consisting of some three-fifths of the adult male population, had been almost doubled in 1918 by the introduction of manhood suffrage and the enfranchisement of women over 30. The Prime Minister was entitled to seek a fresh mandate if he wished, and there was nothing untoward in his choosing, like all Prime Ministers, to do so at the moment of greatest political advantage.

16

The election was certainly of peculiar personal concern to him. His sudden elevation to the premiership in 1916 had stemmed from the pressures of war: from the recognition, especially by the Conservatives in the Asquith Coalition, of Lloyd George's unique personal merit and of a worsening military situation and the need to wrest power from the complacent and dilatory Asquith. The new Prime Minister rose superlatively to the challenge. His firm and confident grip, his stamina and enthusiasm, his bold, decisive leadership, his quickness and grasp of strategy, his flair for new men and ideas, his readiness to try unconventional methods that brought success, or at least action, his inexhaustible resilience, never more tested than in the supreme crisis of the Ludendorff Offensive, the bustling zest, invigorating and sustaining, of his executive energy, and the tonic joviality of his perennial good spirits – all this made Lloyd George the ideal war leader. It also raised him, for the duration, to presidential, almost dictatorial heights. Cabinet government, reduced to a directorate of five – the War Cabinet – under the immediate control of the Prime Minister, assisted by a private secretariat and unfettered by party ties, suggested a form of personal rule. Parliament, on the whole, was approving and obedient.

With the coming of peace, however, political differences threatened to obtrude themselves once more and to bring to the surface the Prime Minister's essential vulnerability. Lloyd George, a Liberal, was dependent on Conservative support. When Asquith left the Coalition, some 160 Liberals had followed him across the floor of the house, leaving behind them 100 Liberal supporters of the new Government. Though the Asquithians sat on the opposition benches, however, they did not regard themselves as an opposition, but as independent supporters of a temporary coalition, and looked forward to post-war reunification under Asquith. Lloyd George, for his part, favoured remaining at the head of the Coalition, preferably with Asquith's support, but if not, then without it. In September, he offered Asquith the Lord Chancellorship, but Asquith declined to serve under him. In October, Lloyd George struck a bargain with Bonar Law, whereby the Conservatives would continue to support him as Prime Minister.

The Tory backbenchers were not, at first, enthusiastic. They had welcomed Lloyd George as a war-leader; but old suspicions now revived of the pre-war radical, the rabble-rouser of Limehouse, the author of the People's Budget, the emasculator of the House of Lords, the advocate of Irish Home Rule. The whiff of Marconi continued to hang about him. Nor was his reputation enhanced by the sale of honours to obvious undesirables, or by his amused connivance in this trade. From such instinctive antipathy, the Conservative leaders brought the party round to a more appreciative view of Lloyd George. 'We must never let the little man go,' Bonar Law declared emotionally on Armistice Day. 'His way and ours lie side by side in the future.' The appeal was aimed less perhaps at party ideals than at party interests. For while the Conservative leaders were far-sighted enough to perceive in Lloyd George the instrument wherewith to revive the long-term fortunes of the party, as practical politicians they were also awake to his immediate attractiveness at the polls. For the side which backed him, 'the man who won the war', at the height of his popularity, must be a winner. 'Remember this,' as Bonar Law told a Conservative gathering the next day, 'that at this moment Mr Lloyd George commands an amount of influence in every constituency as great as has ever been exercised by any Prime Minister in our political history.' The Conservative party machine was accordingly activated in support of approved candidates, consisting of Conservatives and Lloyd George Liberals. Those selected received a letter, signed jointly by Lloyd George and Bonar Law, inviting them to stand as Coalition candidates. Asquith, with patrician disdain, compared these invitations to wartime ration-books, thereby immortalizing the proceedings as 'the Coupon Election'.

The Prime Minister's electoral pact, however, concerns us here only in so far as it helps to shed light on his foreign policy and the overriding question of the peace. Lloyd George's attitude to Germany, as originally enunciated, appeared reasonable and moderate. In an important address on war-aims in January 1918, anticipating by only a few days the Fourteen Points speech of President Wilson, he called for German withdrawal from occupied territories and 'reparation for injuries done in violation of international law'. He specifically renounced any claim for indemnity: 'This is no demand for war indemnity,' he declared. 'It is not an attempt to shift the cost of warlike operations from one belligerent to another.' In the autumn, with victory in sight, he continued to advocate 'a peace that will lend itself to the common sense and conscience of the nation. . . . It must not', he warned, 'be dictated by extreme men.'

His election programme maintained, at first, this statesmanlike level. On 12 November, addressing a pre-election gathering of Liberals at Downing Street, he issued a resounding statement of intent: 'You may depend upon it', he predicted:

there will be vigorous attempts made in certain quarters to hector and bully and stimulate, to induce and cajole the Government to here and there depart from the strict principles of right, in order to satisfy some base and some sordid, and if I may say squalid, principles of either revenge or avarice. We must [he concluded, to loud applause] relentlessly set our faces against that; and if we go to the country, it will be the business of every candidate to have regard to that.

These declarations won for the Prime Minister not only the express endorsement of his own Liberal supporters, such as Herbert Fisher and Churchill, but also of Asquith, who publicly commended them as an unexceptionable statement of Liberal principle. The President himself sent a telegram expressing his 'sincere congratulations'. They failed, however, to stir the imagination of the electorate, or at any rate to satisfy the press, particularly the Northcliffe press. The campaign was said to be uninspired and unresponsive. Hughes, who had not ceased his agitation, was roused to fresh protest. On 14 November, he again spoke out publicly. Was it realized, he expostulated, that while France and Belgium would be recompensed, the Dominions were to receive nothing? His complaints reverberated in the press. 'The Huns must pay,' warned the *Daily Mail*. 'What, by the way, is the policy of the Coalition on this matter of indemnity?' asked the *Morning Post*. Lloyd George's answer was in the making.

At a meeting of the Imperial War Cabinet on 26 November, the Prime Minister launched a remarkable initiative. Hughes had reiterated his standard complaint that the Armistice imposed 'an invidious distinction . . . between a country like Belgium, or even England – and Australia'. Bonar Law then observed that England too looked like emerging the loser, unless her war-costs, totalling eight billion pounds, were recoverable. He referred to the Treasury estimate of two billion pounds as the maximum that could be demanded of Germany, and said that he disagreed with it. At this point, the Prime Minister produced his suggestion. He proposed the formation of a special Cabinet Committee 'to consider', as he said, 'the question of an indemnity'. The proposal was unanimously approved.

It was a startling change of policy; but no one present objected to it as such, or, indeed objected at all. No one seemed disturbed at the open deviation from the principle so carefully discussed and ratified only three weeks before. That the significance of the Pre-Armistice Agreement was present in their minds is clear from Hughes's admission that 'a fair reading of President Wilson's proposals would show that they did not include any suggestion as to an indemnity'. The decision was not taken in some fit of absent-mindedness. Perhaps they saw the role of the Committee as no more than exploratory. Certainly the Prime Minister seemed, at this stage, to view its brief as somewhat academic. 'What he wanted to find out', he said, 'was whether we could get an indemnity out of Germany without doing ourselves harm', a matter which he appeared to regard as doubtful. Or perhaps he valued the Committee chiefly as a device to placate Hughes and keep him out of harm's way, since he now proposed him as its chairman.

Hughes at first demurred. 'I much prefer to remain free so I can criticise,' he said, with characteristic candour. 'Well, that is not quite playing the game here,' observed Lloyd George; pressed by the Cabinet, Hughes reluctantly agreed. The Committee on Indemnity, as it was officially designated, was to include two further members of the Imperial War Cabinet: Walter Long, the Colonial Secretary, and Sir George Foster, the Canadian Minister of Finance. The remaining appointees were, at Hughes's suggestion, the economist W.A.S. Hewins; Herbert Gibbs, an influential City banker, and Lord Cunliffe, lately Governor of the Bank of England. All except Foster were well-known Tories and well-known protectionists. The Committee's terms of reference were, as Foster revealingly noted, 'to report as to what might be imposed over and above reparations'.

The Committee began its deliberation two days later, and after only one day, produced a figure of 24 billion, that is to say, 2400 million pounds – 12 times the sum recommended in the Treasury estimate. What was the basis of its calculations? Hughes admitted that the Committee had few statistics at its disposal, and that what evidence it did have was 'of the vaguest character'. Lord Cunliffe readily confessed that his knowledge of Germany was inadequate. On the other hand, said Hughes, 'everything is practicable to the man who has strength enough to enforce his views, and we have that strength'. The Committee favoured indemnity: therefore it recommended indemnity. It believed, as a matter of common justice, that Germany ought to pay: so it reported that Germany could pay. Also in their minds were Britain's trading prospects, overshadowed by her colossal war-debt to America. Would not British trade, said Gibbs, be 'completely ruined by American competition', unless this burden were shifted, rightly shifted, in their view, onto the Germans? As Cunliffe put it, 'it is rather a choice of who is to be ruined, we or they'.

'On the whole,' observed Hewins, 'I think we had better ruin them.'
'I think so,' agreed Cunliffe.

The figure, then, was reached on no more scientific a basis than wishful thinking. At the first meeting, Keynes, who was present with adviser-status, was asked to state the total cost of the war to the Allies. He volunteered an estimate of 20 billion pounds. The next day, Cunliffe proposed an indemnity of 20 billion. The figure, he admitted, was 'a shot in the dark', based on casual conversation in the City. 'It is very rough,' he insisted, 'and if anybody went for *forty* billions, I should not disbelieve him.' Foster was under no illusion as to the character of the Committee or the value of its recommendations: 'The oddest committee I ever served upon. . . . all guesswork and sentiment. . . . all personal impression and desire – evidence there is none. . . . Except as an opinion, there was no force behind it.' Hughes and Walter Long pressed the importance of a quick decision, whatever it might be. 'A meeting of the Cabinet is to be held,' said Hughes, 'and I apprehend we shall be asked to present a report because the matter is urgent.' Walter Long put the matter still more bluntly: 'We have an election coming on,' he reminded them, 'and this is one of the questions which is exercising the public mind far more than any other. Every day, men who hope to be members of Parliament, who are now candidates, are pledging themselves to proposals about which they know absolutely nothing.' This was the real point. Whether or not the Committee on Indemnity was conceived primarily as a harmless talking-shop for Hughes, it had become a crucial element in the election campaign, as the Prime Minister now made plain.

That same day, at Newcastle-upon-Tyne, he sounded the new note to the electorate: 'There is absolutely no doubt about the principle, and that is the principle we should proceed upon – that Germany must pay the costs of the war up to the limit of her capacity.' It was true that he hedged the statement about with cautions as to the extent of that capacity and warned against endangering British exports; but the commitment was made, or so at least it appeared. The statement of intent caught the headlines: the qualifications were muted.

This was more to the liking of the press. *The Times* greeted it as 'the first touch of realism in the campaign'. Northcliffe, however, soon perceived the characteristic ambiguity of the Prime Minister's pledge. He pronounced himself 'not satisfied with Lloyd George's speech'. On 6 December, he threw down the gauntlet in an open telegram to Downing Street: 'The public,' he asserted, 'are expecting you to say definitely the amount of cash reparation we are going to get from Germany. They are very dissatisfied with the phrase "limit of her capacity",' which, as he pointed out with truth, 'may mean anything or nothing'. Lloyd George took up the challenge immediately, though he did not yet directly answer it. In his reply, cabled *en clair* the next day, he riposted: 'Don't be always making mischief.'

Demands for indemnity were pouring in from constituency agents across the country. C.P. Scott believed that Lloyd George was carried away by the popular wave. 'George,' he noted in his diary, 'who at the start meant very well (he spoke to me of his determination to stand for a just peace with obvious sincerity) has gone downhill under stress of the election!' Morally downhill; politically uphill. Lloyd George was not engulfed by the wave or swept off his feet: a smooth and nimble surf-rider, he sped along its crest. He was not the first to raise the hue and cry for indemnity, but ônce alive to its popularity, he led the chorus in full throat. 'Public opinion', he told his colleagues on 2 December, 'demanded that we should obtain from Germany as much as we possibly could. The question arose, therefore, as to how much we could get. The general public was commonly under some illusion in this matter.' How would the Prime Minister enlighten the new and inexperienced electorate? His answer came the next day, when, having received an interim report from the Hughes Committee, he informed the Cabinet that 'it was proposed to ask for indemnity as well as reparation'. General Smuts was shocked to learn of this change of policy, and wrote to warn him that it might 'place the Government in a very difficult position, and you may find yourself committed to much more than you desire to be'.

Lloyd George was in no mood for caution. 'He talked of nothing but the election,' noted a fellow-guest at a luncheon party, ' – of what cries went down with the electorate and what did not – and speculated what the results would be.' 'He seems to have a sort of lust for power,' noted Hankey, 'ignores his colleagues, or tolerates them in an almost disdainful way, and seems more and more to assume the mantle of a dictator.' In throwing his authority behind indemnity, he knew what he was about, and that

> There is a tide in the affairs of men
> Which taken at the flood leads on to victory.

If the initial impetus behind the Committee on Indemnity had been Hughes, Lloyd George had now taken the lead in forcing the pace of its deliberations. Foster was alarmed at the direction these were taking. He spoke frankly to his colleagues of their 'very cursory' and 'very insufficient' estimate of German capacity. 'No grounds are stated,' he said on 9 December. 'What grounds can be stated? We have not a sufficient ground of knowledge, and we have not made a deep enough investigation upon which to base a calculation of that kind.' Cunliffe himself concurred, with equal openness: 'I agree entirely with Sir George Foster as to the difficulty in obtaining evidence of Germany's power to pay. I said so to begin with.' 'It is impossible to get such evidence,' Hewins interjected. 'It is impossible,' echoed Cunliffe.

What was the Committee to do? Electioneering was in full swing. The Government's campaign, after over a fortnight, was entering its final phase. Polling was five days away. With demands for indemnity still flooding in, the Committee's report was impatiently solicited from Downing Street. 'Mr Lloyd George must have some resting ground for his feet,' said Hughes, 'and if we are uncertain, then he is launched into a sea of uncertainty.' On 10 December, the eve of a campaign in the West Country, the Prime Minister again sent word to the Committee. His tone was peremptory. 'Dear Mr Hughes,' he wrote, 'when may the Cabinet expect to receive the report of the Committee on Indemnities? Will you kindly let me know. The messenger will await an answer.' It was under direct pressure from the Prime Minister, then, that the Committee finally made up its mind. Its report, hastily drawn up and signed, in Foster's case only under protest, was rushed to the Prime Minister just before his train left for the west. The recommended indemnity, he read, should comprise 'the total cost of the war to the Allies', now computed at around 25 billion pounds.

Next day, at Bristol, Lloyd George renewed his Newcastle pledge. He seized vigorously on the point on which Northcliffe had sought to throw him. 'Why have I always said "up to the limit of her capacity"?' he asked. 'Well, I will tell you at once. It is not right for the Government to raise any false hopes in the community, and least of all is it right on the eve of an election. You have no right to mislead your public at any time, and I', he insisted, to cheers, 'am not going to do so now, whatever the result. . . . Let me give you the facts.' The Treasury advisers, he explained, had been doubtful about German capacity. However, 'we appointed a very strong committee some weeks ago. . . . You will be glad to hear that they take a more favourable view of the capacity of Germany.' 'Who is to foot the bill?' came the timely interjection. 'Germany should pay the bill,' replied the Prime Minister. 'We have an absolute right to demand the whole cost of the war from Germany. We propose', he concluded, to loud cheers, 'to demand the whole cost of the war.' Northcliffe was pleased: the *Daily Mail* described this as 'the best speech of the campaign'. It was certainly a masterpiece of popular oratory in its engaging display of moral rectitude, alternating with businesslike frankness and an overall air of effusive confidentiality – the suggestion of admitting the public to privity in affairs of state, while in fact giving little away. There was a difference, after all, between demanding the cost of the war and securing payment. But the immediate effect was the same. It flattered the public's self-esteem. It justified and gratified their expectations. It set the seal on the new policy.

This policy was graphically amplified by Sir Eric Geddes, First Lord of the Admiralty. At his adoption meeting, Geddes had disconcerted his supporters by voicing some scepticism as to German capacity, and warned of the dangers if reparations should come in the form of goods, undercutting British exports. The party agents put their heads together, and Geddes was constrained to issue a *démenti*, promising that he would shortly 'make my view abundantly clear'. On 9 December, he made up for his lapse. 'Someone', he said, 'suggested that he was a pro-German or weak-kneed. . . . If he was returned, Germany was going to pay restitution, reparation and indemnity, and he personally had no doubt that they would get everything out of her that you could squeeze out of a lemon, and a bit more.' The metaphor provoked laughter and cheers; and Geddes expanded it the next day into the immortal pledge to squeeze Germany 'until the pips squeak'.

Lloyd George claimed later that the indemnity pledge was 'held no less definitely by responsible statesmen of all parties'. This was not so. Bonar Law, Churchill and the Attorney-General, F.E. Smith, all warned publicly against indulging in extravagant hopes of German capacity. Asquith, under persistent heckling, agreed that Britain was entitled to 'the uttermost farthing' of reparation, but reminded the electorate that 'a place must be found for our old enemies, as well as our old friends'. He stressed the need for 'good faith' and 'wisdom' in negotiation, 'a clean peace', 'a peace that did not contain in itself the seeds of future quarrels'.

A question no less in the public mind than indemnity was the fate of the ex-Kaiser. The Northcliffe press, to be sure, had branded him as the incarnation of Anti-Christ; but the Kaiser himself, by his bombastic language and grandiose gestures, had long established himself in popular imagery as the embodiment of arrogant bluster, now at last come deservedly to grief. The young men who hustled his effigy like a guy through the cheering streets on Armistice night regarded the fallen war-lord with half-affectionate contempt as a figure of fun – 'Kaiser Bill', gone to ground and 'a better 'ole' across the Dutch frontier.

The King was embarrassed by the public expressions of disrespect for his wayward but royal cousin. Not so the Prime Minister. When the proposal to put the Kaiser on trial was raised in Cabinet on 5 November, Lloyd George was surprised and disappointed to find his colleagues mostly sceptical. He was sorry, he said, 'to find any hesitation in the Imperial War Cabinet'. 'Lloyd George wants to shoot the Kaiser,' noted Sir Henry Wilson, Chief of the Imperial General Staff. A week later, Curzon pressed the matter of popular feeling. 'Public opinion', he wrote to Lloyd George, 'will not willingly consent to let this arch-criminal escape. The supreme and colossal nature of his crime seems to call for some supreme and unprecedented condemnation.' *The Times* agreed. 'The test for the simple elector', it declared on 29 November, 'is clearly the position of the Kaiser.' The item reappeared on the agenda of the Imperial War Cabinet next day, when a dramatic entry was staged by F.E. Smith. Splendid in legal robes, he carried the day with a passionate plea for the Kaiser's arraignment. Lloyd George endorsed the Attorney's speech enthusiastically. The Kaiser, he said, 'ought to be tried for high treason against humanity'. At a meeting between Lloyd George and Clemenceau on 3 December, the trial, together with the indemnity, was agreed as a non-negotiable term of peace. Not that the decision was unopposed. Sir Robert Borden, the Canadian Prime Minister, Lord Milner and Churchill were all against it. So was Bonar Law. According to Hankey, he warned the Prime Minister: 'George! If you take my advice, you won't touch it.' But a matter which had caught the popular imagination was not something from which Lloyd George could readily abstain.

The country was indeed at this time swept by a sudden, vehement cry for revenge. Lord Stamfordham, the King's Secretary, might deplore that 'the majority of people appear to have lost their balance about the Kaiser'; but the popular reaction was natural and understandable. Victory, for the nation at large, had come unexpectedly. After the first delirium of joy and relief, remembrance of loss quickly supervened, particularly among widows and mothers, sisters and sweethearts, newly bereaved and now often newly enfranchised. The war had brought suffering of a scale and intensity which the harshest pessimist could not have prophesied, and for which Britain, after a century of peace and progress, was, psychologically speaking, peculiarly unprepared. The interminable casualty-lists, the row upon row of beardless faces in the 'Roll of Honour', the rattle through a thousand letter-boxes of the same War Office telegram – all this produced a stunned sense of disbelief at the annihilation of so much youth and promise. When, with the peace, people began to come to terms with what had happened, it was not to be expected that they would rise overnight to the serenity of saints or sages. Even if they wished to forget, the press would not let them. As a Cambridge newspaper put it: '*Somebody has got to be hanged!*' The obvious scapegoat lay at hand, skulking in Holland. Was he to live out his life in honourable retirement, while a million Britons lay dead in Flanders? Not in the opinion of George Barnes, Labour's representative in the Cabinet, whose son was among them. 'I am for hanging the Kaiser,' he declared at the hustings.

Against such clarion-calls, the slogans of orthodox Liberalism sounded thin. What were 'good faith' or 'wisdom' compared with squeezed lemons or squeaking pips? What was free trade to 'hanging the Kaiser' or Welsh disestablishment to 'searching their pockets', or 'a clean peace' to either? If the Asquithian slogans looked like faded banners from a vanished past, the Asquithians themselves, in contrast to the brimming vigour of the Prime Minister, looked tired, played-out and ineffectual. Asquith's own war-record left him with an air of bland and fumbling indecision that was not an electoral asset. He was also hampered by a reluctance to seem to criticize, for party or personal advantage, a programme which, originally at least, professed a Liberal allegiance. He might protest; he would not oppose. 'The outcry of orthodox Liberalism leaves me unmoved,' wrote one voter. 'They had their chance; for more than two years the direction of the war was in their hands, and the country is not likely to forget it or to be tender towards the record of their failure.'

The Asquithians, naturally, but not only they, were appalled at the Prime Minister's electoral tactics. To Lord Bryce, these were 'profoundly disheartening'. 'Simply disgusting', noted Sir Henry Wilson. The Archbishop of Canterbury agreed that they were 'beyond measure mischievous'. 'The people', lamented the former Lord Chancellor, Lord Buckmaster, 'are being fed on the delusion that the burden of the war is going to be lifted from their back and put upon Germany. It is such an easy election cry to shout: "Make the Germans pay."' 'Punishment for the Kaiser and Make Germany Pay!' exclaimed C.P. Scott in the *Manchester Guardian*. 'Thus are the nations to be regenerated.' The former War Minister and Lord Chancellor, Haldane, wrote in his diary: 'I hate this election. Lloyd George always lives for the moment and never thinks of the lessons of the past.' He noted 'the wild expectations which are being flourished before the public. . . . The country is being whipped up into the worst possible mood for a wise settlement at home and abroad.' 'Last day of election-eering,' wrote Milner on 13 December. 'God be praised! The atmos-phere has been very fetid during the past ten days.' Lord Stamford-ham, noted the Archbishop, 'is simply disgusted with Lloyd George and his ways. . . . The absurd vote-catching claim of a hugh indem-nity, apart from reparation, can only do mischief; and he has met no thoughtful people, apart from Government, who really advocate the trial of the Kaiser.'

There were those too in the Imperial War Cabinet itself, who also viewed with disquiet the Government's pledges at the hustings, and sought to draw back. At a Cabinet meeting on Christmas Eve, Barnes, Borden, Milner and Churchill spoke out roundly against indemnity. Milner and Churchill warned of driving Germany into Bolshevism by overweening demands. Of the Committee on Indemnity itself, Foster and Walter Long were openly sceptical of the figure recommended in their report. Borden declared that he was 'not prepared to concur in it'. Going to the heart of the matter, he reminded them that the President would shortly be among them. The 'Fourteen Points spoke of reparation and nothing else and thus by implication excluded indemnities . . . If President Wilson should put this contention for-ward to the Prime Minister and Mr. Balfour, what answer could they make?' Bonar Law suggested that 'they could point to the great deal of feeling which prevailed in this country on the subject'. Walter Long agreed. In his view, while 'no-one could give any information really worth having as to Germany's capacity to pay, [it] would create a very awkward situation if the Government did not press its full demands'. He proposed, however, the important rider that 'this would be without prejudice to fuller information disclosing reasons for mod-ifying that demand'. The Cabinet agreed. Britain should press for indemnity, subject to ascertaining the subsequent facts of German capacity, these being the 'controlling considerations'.

Such were the considerations that chiefly agitated the Imperial War Cabinet in the last days before Christmas. Not that it was in any way abnormal to determine tactics and prepare the ground for the Conference, to ensure that British interests were protected, and to agree that – whether the sums due be called 'indemnity' or 'reparation' – 'the most important question', as Amery put it, was 'to make sure that whatever the amount Germany does pay, we should get our fair share'. Nor was it unnatural to authorize the Prime Minister to enter the Conference unhampered by detailed instructions, free to negotiate according to his own best judgment, in a spirit of enlightened opportunism.

And yet Government policy was not what it had been at the Armistice. The Prime Minister was now claiming, apparently unblinkingly, that 'he did not think it could be argued that President Wilson *had* ruled out indemnities'. The spirit of these discussions filled one Cabinet-member at least with foreboding. The Secretary of State for India, Edwin Montagu, sat silent and dismayed in the Cabinet-room. He wrote to Balfour:

> I do not think at any period of my incumbency of any office I have been so much depressed. . . . There we were, the trusted of the Empire, the custodians of the future, the translators of victory, the instruments of lasting peace. And what was our attitude? It seemed to me that we were apprehensive of the arrival in our midst of a really disinterested man who might, although we all hoped that he would not, want to apply the principles for which he had fought, actually might (O heaven forbid) really have meant what he said on more than a hundred occasions! What was to be the effect of his coming upon us, who did not dare confess this morning that, flushed with victory, we meant to insist upon terms of peace which had no justification in our war aims, and which were based, not on brotherly love, on the healing of wounds, or international peace, but on revenge on our enemies, distrust of our Allies and a determination for swag.

It would have been a mark of statesmanship to have included in the peace delegation a man of the calibre of Asquith. Asquith, it was true, had proved unequal to the challenge of war; but his pre-war record and his personal qualities, his integrity, his detachment, his calm sagacity and balance, could have made his presence at the Peace Conference a lodestone for the forces of moderation. Churchill and Fisher were strongly in favour of his inclusion. So was the King. 'You served for many years in Mr. Asquith's Government,' he urged in a letter to Lloyd George, 'and know his worth as a lawyer, a statesman and a man of clear, dispassionate judgment.'

Lloyd George resented these royal promptings. In conversation with Hankey, he was 'very hostile about Asquith, and annoyed with the King for wanting him to be at the Peace Conference'. Was not the King's recommendation of Asquith un unspoken reflection on himself? The King admitted as much. 'He hardly concealed his own personal mistrust of Lloyd George,' noted Hankey, 'and his liking for Asquith.' But the King looked beyond mere personalities. Urging Hankey to use his influence with Lloyd George, he added: 'Lloyd George will say that the King wants Asquith to go to the Peace Conference because he is his friend. But the truth is, I want him to go for the good of the nation, for the good of Lloyd George himself, and to make for unity.'

Shortly after the Armistice, Asquith himself had called on Lloyd George in his room at Westminster. Their colloquy was polite but inconclusive. While confirming his reluctance to take Cabinet office, he would be glad, Asquith told the Prime Minister, to serve on the British delegation. His knowledge of international law and finance might be of use at the Conference, he suggested, neither Wilson nor Clemenceau, he understood, being expert in those important matters. At this, Lloyd George, looking, we are told, 'a little confused', mumbled something about 'considering the proposal', glanced at his watch and stooped to pick up some books that had fallen to the floor. The interview was over. The petitioner withdrew. A lesser man, or perhaps a greater, might have tried again; but Asquith lacked the inclination or the temperament to beg favours of the man who had supplanted him. Rebuffed, he bowed imperturbably out of the contest. No later summons issued from Downing Street. Shortly afterwards he shared in the electoral massacre of the Liberal Party, and recedes, henceforth, to the side-stage of these events.

The same electoral wave that carried away 'the last of the Romans' swept Lloyd George back into power, with a landslide majority of 262. Armed with this unprecedented and incontrovertible suffrage, he left for the Conference in high spirits. Exuberant on deck, as the channel-steamer headed out of Dover harbour, he pointed up at the cliffs and the castle beyond. 'That's the place for the Kaiser's trial!' he exclaimed.

Chapter 2

Peacemaking

We have used great words, all of us; we have used the great words 'right' and 'justice', and now we are to prove whether or not we understand those words and how they are to be applied to the particular settlements which must conclude this war.

Woodrow Wilson, Address at Buckingham Palace, 27 Dec. 1918

We are going into these negotiations with our mouths full of fine phrases and our brains seething with dark thoughts.

Edwin Montagu to Balfour, 20 Dec. 1918 (Balfour Papers)

O n 4 December 1918, Woodrow Wilson embarked for Europe. With him aboard the *George Washington* he took as high-minded a company as can ever have crossed the Atlantic since the voyage of the *Mayflower*. Predominantly young, scholarly, sanguine and idealistic, the American delegation had been preparing for this argosy of peace ever since the United States entered the war; whole libraries, in heavy oak packing cases, crammed the hold: the bulkheads groaned, the stanchions strained under the collective weight of their erudition. As the *George Washington* neared her destination, the delegates were summoned to the saloon, where the President opened his mind to them. It was the scholar's dream of action, a noble extension of the graduate-class at Princeton, privileged to assist in the gravest conceivable mission, undertaken by the world's most powerful state, addressed by a man, their mentor, smiling, deliberate, lucid, earnest, who seemed to combine, in intellectual distinction, in lofty idealism, in inspiring eloquence and in political strength, the fabled attributes of the philosopher-king. He was bringing to a waiting continent principles which, as he had said, were those of 'forward-looking men and women everywhere, of every modern nation, of every enlightened community. They are the principles of mankind, and must prevail'.

How, indeed, could they fail, backed by the overwhelming might of the United States? Politicians in Europe, it was true, were up to their Old World tricks. The President, as he informed his listeners, had just received a cable from Colonel House, warning him that Lloyd George and Clemenceau had met in London to agree on 'a definite programme'. 'Apparently they are determined to get everything out of Germany they can, now that she is helpless. They are evidently planning to take what they can get, frankly, as a matter of spoils, regardless of the ethics. . . . Now,' declared Wilson, 'we are absolutely opposed to any such plan. A statement that I once made that this should be a 'peace without victory,' I believe holds as strongly today in principle as it ever did. It is impossible in this day to make a peace based upon indemnities; it must be a peace of justice to the defeated nations, or it will be fatal to all the nations in the end.' The President expressed his intention, if Lloyd George and Clemenceau persisted 'in this sort of programme', to withdraw from the Conference, to return to the United States, 'and in due course, take up the details of a separate peace'. That was his strategy if the worst came to the worst. He did not believe that would happen, if he took a firm line. 'I think that once we get together, they will learn that the American delegates have not come to bargain, but will stand firmly by the principles that we have set forth; and once they learn that that is our purpose, I believe we shall come to an early agreement.'

It was in this sanguine and determined frame of mind that Wilson alighted on the shores of Europe, to be greeted by a succession of popular celebrations of such unmeasured and overwhelming rapture, such frenzied and spontaneous acclaim, as may properly be compared with some great religious revival. It was, indeed, as the symbol of deliverance and rebirth that they cheered him, that first Christmas since the war, those vast, delirious, full-throated crowds in Paris and Rome. Even in staid, wind-swept Dover, schoolgirls in smocks strewed rose-petals in his path along the station platform; and Charing Cross was a sea of cheering, exultant faces. The soft-mannered Princetonian was astonished and not a little delighted at his reception. He was probably correct, in a general way, in associating the goodwill of the multitudes with his plans for their future. At that particular moment, humanity, with all its hopes, if not quite hanging breathless on his fate, did regard him as something akin to the Prince of Peace, without inquiring too precisely into the meaning of peace. It was unfortunate, however, that the loud Hosannas and what the President called, wonderingly, 'the dumb eyes of the people', should confirm his belief in the existence of a mystic and indissoluble communion between himself and the world-spirit of Democracy.

Lloyd George, who had made searching inquiries into the President's character, was taken aback, when the two men conferred on Boxing Day, by his determined stance against indemnities. In vain he exerted the famous Welsh charm. Wilson was immovable – 'stiffer', Lloyd George informed the Imperial War Cabinet, 'than on any other question.' 'He had failed to make any impression on the President. . . . They were up against a really hard resistance from President Wilson.'

On the other hand – as Hughes was quick to remind the Prime Minister – it might seriously be called into question whether the President actually possessed the political authority which his authority of manner suggested. Whatever the acclamations of the European crowds might or might not betoken, the mid-term congressional elections of November 1918 had returned a Republican majority to both Houses, a clear enough indication that Wilson was by no means as secure in his mandate to negotiate as Lloyd George was in his. This impression was confirmed by rumblings of discontent from the United States, hovering like albatrosses in the wake of the *George Washington*. Even before Wilson crossed the Atlantic, ex-President Roosevelt had publicly asserted that the Allies were entitled to impose whatever peace they chose. He denied, with brutal trenchancy, that Wilson, his Points, his Principles or his Particulars, 'have any shadow of right to be accepted as expressive of the will of the American people'. For all that Wilson might set his face against indemnity, therefore, Lloyd George, for his part, had not the slightest intention of taking no for an answer.

In Paris, Lloyd George and Balfour were given private apartments in the fashionable Rue Nitôt. Here, after a day of strenuous negotiations, the Prime Minister could relax in relative seclusion, enjoying the services of a French chef and the soothing ministrations of Miss Stevenson. Occasionally, sounds of discordant revelry disturbed the night, as he burst suddenly into song, vigorously intoning Welsh hymns with every appearance of fervour, or essayed the latest dance-steps, footing it gaily across the parquet flooring to the cheerful ragtime strains of a pianola or gramophone; both instruments, not altogether uncharacteristically, 'sometimes playing different tunes simultaneously'. On the floor above, the Foreign Secretary's musical tastes were more decorously indulged in the form of classical soirées. At one of these recitals, the soloist asked whether anyone objected to

German *Lieder.* 'I don't,' replied Balfour equably. 'I will take them as part of the reparations that they owe us.'

The rest of the British delegation was housed in the Hôtel Majestic, on the Avenue Kléber. 'A vast caravanserai,' complained Milner, 'not uncomfortable, but much too full of all and sundry, too much of a "circus" for my taste.' The lobby, stairs, and corridors of the Majestic were indeed continually astir with the to-ings and fro-ings of pleni-potentiaries, civil servants and journalists, a constant hubbub of conversation amid the clatter of tea-cups and the rhythm of dance music. 'All the world is here,' noted Geoffrey Dawson. 'It's like a gigantic cinema-show of eminent persons.' In the restaurant, at any given time, might be seen, for example, Dominion delegates, like General Smuts, strolling arm in arm with his ailing chief, General Botha, or Prime Minister Massey of New Zealand; Foreign Office luminaries, like Lord Hardinge, the Permanent Under-Secretary, and the influential Assistant Under-Secretary, Sir Eyre Crowe; or their underlings, the sagacious Headlam-Morley, or the young Harold Nicolson; Treasury officials, like Maynard Keynes; Milner himself, surrounded by Dawson, Philip Kerr, Lionel Curtis and other members of his 'kindergarten'; Lord Robert Cecil, enthusing over the League of Nations; Bonar Law, newly arrived by air to report on the situation at Westminster; George Barnes, 'seeing life in Paris for the first time', or F.E. Smith – now raised to the woolsack as Lord Birkenhead – 'flanked by a bottle of champagne'.

In the lobby might also be seen the delegates appointed to present the British case for reparations. They were none other than Hughes and Cunliffe of the Indemnity Committee and also Lord Sumner, an eminent Law Lord. This triumvirate could not be described as conciliatory. Born and bred a Welshman, schooled in the rough-house of Australian politics, Hughes combined the quick tenacity of his race with the blunt forcefulness of his adoptive country. He made a passionate and uncompromising advocate of indemnity. As for Cunliffe and Sumner, Thomas Jones, the Cabinet Secretary, regarded them as 'both stony-hearted men'; and Headlam-Morley considered them 'the two bad men of the Conference'. They are 'always summoned when some particularly nefarious act has to be commit-ted'. By the younger delegates, they were irreverently dubbed 'the Heavenly Twins', both because they were almost inseparable during the Conference and invariably perambulated the Paris boulevards together, and, more particularly, because of the astronomical sums which they insisted could be extracted from Germany.

None of the three attempted to deduce German liability from the Lansing note. Their basic argument was simply: winner takes all. This principle was the basis of British civil jurisprudence; it also appealed to common sense. Hughes invoked general principles of justice. Sumner, echoing Lloyd George's Bristol speech, claimed that the Allies had 'an absolute right to demand the whole cost of the war', notwithstanding the Lansing note, which merely constituted 'bases of discussion'. 'The reimbursement of war costs', he declared, 'is the constant practice of international law. No particular clause, either in the Fourteen Points or in the Armistice, excludes this reimbursement.' These contentions were denied, calmly but robustly, by the chief American delegate, a young international lawyer named John Foster Dulles. Dulles insisted that Germany's liability was exclusively defined by the Lansing note – 'a document at the foot of which are the signatures of Mr. Wilson, M. Orlando, M. Clemenceau and Mr. Lloyd George.' It represented, he pointedly reminded Sumner, not a 'basis of discussion, but the terms of peace'. 'Our bargain', he concluded, 'has been struck, for better or worse. It remains only to give it a fair construction.'

Any such limitation was, of course, anathema to his British colleagues. To compound their difficulties, the Americans brought matters to a head with a most untoward proposal. Instead of wracking their brains over the interpretation of the Lansing note, 'they should ask the representatives who had signed the document exactly what they had meant'. This would have placed the Prime Minister in a position of acute embarrassment. How could Lloyd George possibly commit himself on the meaning of the note? How could he endorse Wilson's interpretation without abandoning the case for indemnity? How could he oppose Wilson's interpretation, without provoking an open rift? Did he, truth to tell, even remember exactly what he *had* meant at the time? Was Kerr, who had drafted the note, any wiser as to whether it 'was intended to exclude indemnities or not'? 'This of course is a matter of first-class importance,' agreed Kerr; but appeared unable to shed any further light on it.

The Prime Minister was saved, however, from any such contretemps. 'Our reply', Sumner reported, 'was "No!"' An immediate excuse lay to hand in the temporary unavailability of all four signatories. Wilson, Lloyd George and Orlando had each returned to face a political crisis in his own country. Clemenceau was recovering from an attempt on his life. 'Besides,' as Sumner continued, 'they have given us our instructions, so we know their intentions.' As for

1. Lord Sumner (William Orpen, 1919): 'As for Sumner . . . some very able lawyers can be very cruel men' – Lord Robert Cecil.

seeking further direct testimony, then, the British attitude, he assured the Cabinet on 25 February, 'was that it was idle to do this, as they were quite certain that Britain had never intended to give up her right to the inclusion of the cost of the war'. Lloyd George agreed. Certainly, whatever the Lansing note might or might not have meant, 'the British Cabinet stood by the demand that reparation should include indemnity', and it was resolved that the delegates 'should not recede from the attitude adopted'.

Within days, therefore, of the opening of the Reparations Commission, there was deadlock. In the words of a *compte rendu* drawn up for Colonel Hankey, 'the American delegates announced that they were not prepared to assist in the preparation of any report that included "cost of war", while Mr. Hughes announced that he was not prepared to present any report which did not'.

There was a clash of personalities as well as of principles. Hughes's Antipodean abrasiveness and Sumner's judicial pomposity were not to Dulles's taste; his New England didacticism offended them. Sumner, accustomed to the polite deference of counsel, did not relish being instructed in the rudiments of the law of contract or being informed, with 'calculated rudeness', that the Commission was wasting its time; and reacted testily to the American stance as 'an unpardonable *bêtise*'. Hankey notified Lloyd George that the two delegations 'do not work together at all, and are unsympathetic to one another'. 'You yourself', he suggested, 'will have to take this matter up with Colonel House, with a view to some agreement on broad lines.'

But Lloyd George could make no headway with the Colonel. Wilson was on his way back to the United States, to attend the final sessions of Congress. In his absence, House, his master's parting admonitions fresh in his ears, took a strong line in support of Dulles. Deliberating tactics with the American delegation on 24 February, he proposed that if the French and British 'still insisted on carrying out a project which was contrary to the wishes of the President and contrary to the pledge which had been given to Germany before the signing of the Armistice, we should then state that we wash our hands of the whole business, and that for our part we would absolutely refuse to ask for any indemnity from Germany'. He then cabled his recommendation to Wilson aboard the *George Washington*.

Wilson supported House to the full. In his reply, transmitted the same day, he declared:

I feel that we are bound in honour to decline to agree to the inclusion of war costs in the reparation demanded. The time to think of this was before the conditions of peace were communicated to the enemy originally. We should dissent, and dissent publicly if necessary, not on the ground of the intrinsic injustice of it, but on the ground that it is clearly inconsistent with what we deliberately led the enemy to expect and cannot now honourably alter simply because we have the power.

This simple, unequivocal stand put an end to Allied demands for war costs as such. If the matter had rested there, the story might have ended differently. But resolute though the President appeared, he was to find in Clemenceau and Lloyd George two formidable antagonists, by no means so easily to be put down.

At this point, an important misconception ought to be disposed of. Professor Temperley, in his standard *History of the Peace Conference*, suggests that the construction of the Lansing note called for considerable legal expertise and that the solution of the problem was open to debate. The question, he contends, 'was obviously difficult and admitted of legitimate divergence of opinion'. This is a doubtful proposition. Genuine differences might arise over details; but as for the substance of the note, no impartial scrutiny can surely yield anything other than the literal and natural meaning maintained by the Americans from the first.

It would in any case be wholly artificial and misleading to portray the Conference as though it were merely the scene of some animated but academic disputation between rival schools of jurisprudence. 'Divergences' there were indeed; but they were political, not legal. The Conference was not a lawyer's moot, but a trial of strength, an arena of conflicting interests, ambitions and wills, national and individual, where the future of Europe was fought over by the politicians – the 'frocks', as Henry Wilson called them – no less earnestly than it had lately been contested by the military. In the matter of reparations America sought nothing for herself, while the Allies were out for spoils. It was true, as Clemenceau often objected, that America could afford to be idealistic. There was little pressure on Wilson for the recovery of war-costs. Protected by the Atlantic, enriched by the war and attracted by the prospect of further gain held out by the reconstruction of Europe, the United States was immune to the particular obsessions of the Old World. She was not, of course, without preoccupations of her own. Whether he contemplated the spread of Japanese influence in the Pacific or the threat of naval competition with Britain, the President was no less jealous of *his* country's interests than was Clemenceau or Lloyd George. Even in regard to reparations, he set his face firmly against the one option that might have resolved the whole tortuous problem – a waiver of the enormous war-debts owed to America by the Allies – which might in turn have enabled them to moderate their demands on Germany. Idealist though he was, he was realist enough to be quite unwilling to forgo America's advantage as the world's leading creditor in order to let Lloyd George and Clemenceau off the hook and pull their chestnuts out of the fire. His sentiments, though not his language, anticipated those of his successor, Coolidge: 'They hired the money, didn't they?' 'Each will defend his own interests,' as Clemenceau was wont to observe. The question for the Peace Conference, then, was not whether national interests would be considered, but in what spirit they would be considered and how far there would be weighed in the scale of priorities – honour, good faith and statesmanship. The fact that Wilson might be more dispassionate towards Germany than Clemenceau or Lloyd George does not affect the simple truth that the Lansing note was no less binding on them than on him.

Wilson's veto, however, placed Lloyd George in an unenviable predicament. The Coupon Election had returned the Coalition to power in a victory of stunning proportions. The Asquithian Liberals were smashed; and Lloyd George found himself heading an overwhelming and unassailable Conservative majority. The very magnitude of that majority was a liability. It served to emphasize his isolation from his former allies and his dependence on his former oponents. To most people, the election might be seen as a personal plebiscite, 'designed', as Lord Hardinge put it, 'entirely to make Lloyd George into a species of dictator'. At first sight, he appeared to enjoy an unrestricted personal mandate to conclude a sensible peace in accordance with his original manifesto and his own better instincts and judgment. In reality it was otherwise. On the morrow of the election, Lloyd George awoke, like Gulliver, to find himself tied down, an uncomfortable prisoner of the slogans that he had promulgated with such success at the hustings, and of the party which had profited most from that success. 'George thinks he won the election,' said Walter Long to his neighbour at a dinner. 'Well, he didn't. It was the Tories that won the election, *and he will soon begin to find that out.*'

Such was the mood of growling belligerence that greeted the Prime Minister from his own back benches as he entered the House of

Commons at the start of the session of 1919: a bluff, no-nonsense mood, not disposed to let Germany or Lloyd George off lightly. The House, recalled one of its few Asquithian members, was 'the most sentimental, the most uncontrolled and the most passion-driven'. Not that immoderate passion was confined to the Government side. With the reduction of the Asquithians to an extraordinarily meagre rump of two dozen 'Wee Frees', as they were called, the voices of moderation on the Opposition benches were also thin. On 11 February, Sir Donald Maclean himself, Asquith's substitute as Liberal leader in the Commons and in effect Leader of the Opposition, rose to remind the Prime Minister of his more punitive election pledges; not, as might be supposed, in a spirit of reproof, but to demand an assurance that they were not being neglected. Lloyd George replied affably that 'an able Commission' was at work on the question of 'responsibility for the war' and 'breaches of the laws of war', while another 'singularly able Commission' was studying the question of indemnities. Cunliffe, Sumner and Hughes he described as 'singularly able men'. The Government, he promised, would act upon their report.

This was not enough for Brigadier-General Page-Croft for the right-wing National Party, who spoke of the 'overwhelming feeling in the country' and the 'disquieting rumours abroad'. He raised the spectre of Britain's war-debt. 'What have our people done,' he asked, 'what have our fighting men, above all, done, that they should go down to their grave burdened with this colossal debt, when, after all, they have won the position to dictate terms to our enemies?' The question was a fair one, and deserved, surely, a candid answer. The Government, replied Lloyd George, 'stand by the election pledges that they gave', He was pressed again. 'The Government stand by every word of that pledge,' he repeated. 'The House had heard with great relief', said Lieutenant-Colonel Guinness, 'that there is no foundation for all those newspaper statements.'

It is a measure of the mistrust in which Lloyd George was held by the backbenchers that his assurances failed to carry total conviction. It was true, as Colonel Gretton said, that they were 'much more definite and much more satisfactory than those which had gone before'. Nevertheless, he gave a significant warning that the House would be on the look-out for backsliding. 'Any deviation', he said, 'will cause the downfall of any Government of this country, and a most lively expressed indignation amongst our people.'

The Parliament of 1919 has gone down as one of the most insular, reactionary and benighted in the annals of Westminster. Learned comparisons have been made with the post-Waterloo Parliament of 1815 and even with the restoration Parliament of 1660. More familiar, legendary indeed, is the description of the Government benches which Keynes attributed to Baldwin – 'a lot of hard-faced men who look as if they had done very well out of the war.' J.C. Davidson, parliamentary private secretary to Bonar Law, also noted the 'high percentage of hard-headed men, mostly on the make'. They were not all war-profiteers, to be sure; but a casual onlooker in the Visitor's Gallery might be forgiven for supposing otherwise. The landed interest and the learned professions were conspicuously lacking on the Government benches, which resembled nothing so much, it was said, as the Associated Chambers of Commerce. It was, thought Nicolson, 'a House of Commons possessed of a *Daily Mail* type of mind'. It was certainly a predominantly middle-aged House, with a distinct air of choleric dissipation: it was noted that the stocks of champagne in the cellars of the House were consumed in a single session. Davidson complained of the 'to my mind unscrupulous characters which are to be found in the present House'.

'Unscrupulous character' was by any standards a fair description of the Independent member for South Hackney, the editor of *John Bull* – Horatio Bottomley. Bottomley was a swindler and a fraud. He was cunning and bold to a degree and a practised demagogue, not without a certain raffish and even generous bonhomie, redolent of cigars and the turf. His stout and somewhat reptilian appearance, curiously suggestive of Mr Toad, masked a deft and cynical exploiter of the public's gullibility, never more susceptible than in the heyday of the yellow press. Even as he took his seat in the Commons, 'the People's Bottomley', as he styled himself, was inducing thousands of his readers to invest their savings in his fraudulent scheme for the sale of 'victory bonds'. Those who had doubts, kept them to themselves; more than once, facing charges of grave financial irregularity, he had personally defended himself in the courts with a skill and eloquence that won the wary respect of Bar and Bench.

In 1919, Bottomley was at the height of his influence. He was popular in the services and adulated by his lower middle-class readership for his wartime recruitment rallies, the impeccable stridency of his anti-German utterances and his genuine exposures of bumbledom and profiteering in high places. *John Bull* had been among the first and loudest publications to raise the indemnity cry. 'We'll have an indemnity,' it roared, 'if it takes a thousand years to pay it.' Bottomley also cherished political ambitions. In Parliament, he assumed the role of self-appointed tribune of the people, dubbing himself 'the unofficial Prime Minister'. To the real Prime Minister and Bonar Law, he was a squalid embarrassment, with an unerring eye for the weak spot, and a cunning, caustic and fluent tongue. Bottomley, wrote one member, 'expressed with accuracy the views of the majority in that post-war Parliament'. The names of Lords Cunliffe and Sumner, he told the House on 12 February, cut no ice with him. He demanded an answer to a question 'on which, I assure the Leader of the House, no amount of parliamentary skill, no depth of eloquence, or appeal to the loyalty of his followers, will ever enable him and his Government, should they desire it, to evade. That is, the payment by Germany of the cost of this War'. His speech, *The Times* reported, was 'evidently to the taste of a crowded House'.

Lloyd George was left in no doubt of the mood of the Commons. The figures bandied about by Hughes, Cunliffe and Sumner, were, as he knew, 'a wild and fantastic chimera'. He regretted the whole thing, or, at any rate, the way it had turned out. 'That stunt about indemnities from Germany that *they* started during the election', he observed blandly at a London dinner-party, puffing meditatively at a large cigar, 'was a very foolish business.' He left the indemnity crisis in London to face the indemnity crisis in Paris, where, as Philip Kerr wrote to him, 'things are now reaching the stage when your presence has become indispensable'.

Both Clemenceau and Lloyd George accepted that to recover anything at all, they would sooner or later have to treat Germany as a bankrupt and settle for a percentage only of their claims. But these were home-truths that could not be admitted at home. The wildest expectations of German capacity had been wantonly aroused; the highest demands would therefore have to be made, even if they could never be met. But yet the higher the total demanded, the greater must be the eventual discrepancy between that and the figure actually recoverable. How was such a discrepancy to be explained away?

It was brought come to Clemenceau that, paradoxically, France actually stood to gain by waiving her claim to war-costs altogether. If they confined their demands to reparation, the French could claim the lion's share, or indeed, as Lloyd George warned his Cabinet, 'any figure they cared to name'. Given the vast and for the moment incalculable extent of damage in the war-zone, 'it would be difficult to dispute the claim'. Thus French demands alone 'would probably absorb the whole of the amount it was possible to obtain from Germany'. On the other hand, the nuances of such a refined statecraft would not be appreciated by the National Assembly: having been promised both reparation and indemnity, French opinion would never grasp the advantage of abandoning the shadow for the substance.

Lloyd George was affected by analogous considerations of political face-saving. In his case, however, it was absolutely indispensable to insist on war costs, since, as he reminded the Cabinet, 'British claims for reparation, apart from indemnity, were exceedingly small'. If Germany was only able to pay for reparation, he told House and Clemenceau, 'Britain would be left out altogether'. All the spoils would go to France and Belgium, and 'he could not sustain himself with his people'. Returning to Paris on 6 March, he made no secret of his dilemma to Colonel House. Immediately on his arrival, he made use of the President's absence to buttonhole the Colonel and impress upon him the dire political straits in which he stood. He had, he reported later to the Empire delegation, 'gone to a considerable amount of trouble over this question during the last few days, particularly in the direction of getting the Americans to agree to the British point of view'. Where Hughes and the 'Twins' had got nowhere, however, merely irritating the Americans and making them 'very antagonistic', Lloyd George, in his best *ad hominem* manner over luncheon, 'had had several conversations with Colonel House on the subject'.

The Prime Minister, in the course of these tête-à-têtes, was engagingly, almost embarrassingly frank. House noted:

> He was especially interested in the question of reparations, and said that if I would help him out in this direction, he would be extremely grateful. By 'helping him out', he meant: to give a plausible reason to his people for having fooled them about the question of war costs, reparations and what not. He admitted that he knew Germany could not pay anything like the indemnity which the British and French demanded.

He knew the figures being bandied about by his delegates to be 'perfectly absurd', and the delegates themselves to be, as the Colonel put it, 'largely incompetent'. Cunliffe's estimate of 25 billion pounds, Hankey had told Lloyd George, was 'a figure not calculated on any particular scientific basis, but one drawn rather by that particular instinct on which, I am told, high financial authorities in the City often work'. Nevertheless, noted House of Lloyd George and

Clemenceau, 'in order to meet public opinion, which they have misled in their several countries, they intend to insist upon an amount that they know they cannot collect'. Lloyd George 'wanted the amount named to be large, even if Germany could never pay it, or even if it had to be reduced later. He said it was a political matter in which the English were greatly interested, and he did not want to let the Conservatives "throw him" on a question of such popular concern'.

Colonel House experienced a certain wry amusement at these confidences. While he could not approve, there was, in Lloyd George's unblushing candour, something inherently disarming and risible, something akin to the cheerful amorality of the Artful Dodger. 'I was amused and struck', he wrote of the leaders of the two great European democracies, 'by the cynical way in which they discussed their people. Both of them practically confessed that they knew Germany could not pay anything like the sum they had in mind to suggest, and that it was merely done to meet the expectations and desires of their constituents.' House could hardly approve; but as a natural politician he was keenly alive to the reality of their dilemma. He appreciated that there were two genuine and interlocking problems: a problem of substance and a problem of appearances. The first was to set a round total and agree its apportionment among the Allies. The second was to present this in such a way as not to outrage public opinion in France and Britain, and, at the same time, without violating American principles. It was only fair that part of the spoils should go to Britain. How the proportion was settled was basically a matter of indifference to America, provided that Wilsonian appearances were maintained. He thought he saw a way out, Lloyd George reported to his delegation. 'Colonel House had said that if the exaction could be so framed as to exclude the cost of the war, the United States would stand aside.' This raised an attractive possibility. 'We should be able, under such a scheme, to include the capitalised cost of our pensions in our claim.'

As for the amount, it was decided to approach the problem from another angle and by other means. Rather than persevere in fruitless argument about what Germany ought theoretically to pay, it was agreed that what was needed was for the three leaders to decide privately on a figure which she might reasonably be expected to pay and to lend it their united political backing. But what figure? To leave the cutting of this Gordian knot to the deadlocked Reparations Commission was manifestly futile. There was no conceivable possibility, as Edwin Montagu observed to Lloyd George, of 'bridging over the divergences of view between the Americans and the rest of the Allies as to whether the cost of the war is or is not to be an item in the bill of costs. . . . However long they wrangle, this divergence of view will remain'. It was agreed between Lloyd George, Clemenceau and House, who had lately met Montagu and was impressed by him, that the question of figures should be re-examined by an unofficial subcommittee of three, to consist of Montagu himself for Britain, the American, Davis, and Loucheur, a French moderate. The subcommittee should meet behind the back of the official British delegates – '*dans la coulisse*', as Loucheur put it, ' – *dans le plus grand secret*' – and should work out a final sum for ratification by the Big Three.

It was a device that appealed intimately to House, the very stuff of politics. In the plenary sessions at the Quai d'Orsay, which were the President's domain, he sat back admiringly amid the formal rhetoric, the solemn, thrilling speeches, the snapping press-bulbs and the polite applause. It was rather in the muted confidence of lobby or lounge, the coffee-table tête-à-tête, the delicate weaving of implicit understandings and the divination of short-cuts, that the Colonel's talents were most happily employed, and where, he felt, the real business of the Conference took place. His quiet humour, his tact, his sharp intellect, his ready common sense, his clubmanship, his trustworthiness, found satisfaction in the reflective appraisal of a ticklish problem and the gradual elaboration of a solution; the balancing of diverse and tangled interests, the reconciliation of *raison d'état* and public opinion, of principle and fact, the careful avoidance of an open clash, the final gratifying drawing together of the threads.

If, in the manifold business of diplomacy, there exists a school of *l'art pour l'art*, Colonel House may be described as its devoted amateur. He loved a settlement as a bibliophile loves a first edition: the informal ritual of the armchair colloquy, the invitation to treat proffered with the open box of cigars, the proposal tendered with the striking of a match, terms ruminated amid ascending curlicues of smoke, a query analysed with the spreading of his delicate fingers and satisfied with soothing arabesques of the hand, a deal concluded with a flick of the ash. Not that, in his addiction to backstairs diplomacy, the Colonel ever did anything underhand. On the contrary, he was, after the President, perhaps the most honourable man in Paris. When Mrs Wilson expressed doubts about him, her husband replied firmly: 'I would as soon doubt your loyalty as his.' His coded messages to the *George Washington* kept the President fully informed. It was just that, without being in the slightest way disloyal, House was in no special hurry for the President's return. Difficult and important ground-work, he felt, might be cleared in the interim, obstacles smoothed over. He saw himself, so to speak, as the chief engineer of the Conference, who, in the watches of the night while his captain sleeps, takes a quiet stroll on deck, enjoying the throb of the well-oiled turbines beneath his feet and the inner confidence of the man who knows that the progress of the great liner depends in the last resort on him.

While schemes of compromise and settlement were being canvas-sed in low voices and panelled corners, the *George Washington* herself was once more approaching the French coast. Leaning on the rail in the chill March air, the President peered anxiously into the mists ahead. Occasionally, on returning to his suite, he permitted himself a small dram of whisky. Notwithstanding his recent signature on the bill concerning prohibition, he might be pardoned this rare indulg-ence. There was much, beside the equinoctial Atlantic gales, against which he might legitimately seek to fortify himself. How often the view has been expressed that it would have been better had the President stayed at home; that in the unequal struggle with Clemenceau and Lloyd George, he was foredoomed; that he might have maintained the integrity of his principles more effectively away from the web of compromise into which they inveigled him; and that his first and most fatal error was in leaving the United States. Such were the forebodings of Lansing and House – and such the counsel which they diplomatically but anxiously tendered to him.

Wilson himself had pondered these alternatives. If he rejected their advice, it was not merely out of pique, not just a reluctance to admit that he was not the equal of Lloyd George and Clemenceau, or the desire to arrogate to himself the lion's share of peacemaking. His insistence on returning to Paris also stemmed from well-founded apprehensions: a legitimate fear that Colonel House was too prone to compromise on important issues in his absence; a conviction that the defence of his principles and his duty to America's war-dead required nothing less than his own active presence. He must, he would see the thing through. Addressing the tiered ranks of his supporters in the Metropolitan Opera House, on the eve of his departure, as the band blared out '*Over there!*', he smilingly assured his audience that indeed, in the words of the song, 'I won't come back, till it's over, over there!'.

He also returned in the knowledge that his political position in America was unsafe. The presidential elections fell due in 1920, and already the opening salvos of the campaign were being lobbed. They were damaging. It was not only that after two terms of a Democratic presidency under Wilson, the Republicans were out for victory and had scored heavily in the congressional elections; and that Senator Lodge, his old Republican rival, had become chairman of the Senate Foreign Relations Committee, lending to his criticism of Wilson's policy a wounding vein of personal antagonism. There was also a fundamental national unease at the implications of that policy, a post-war reaction against foreign entanglements, and a spreading hostility to the idea of yet greater responsibilities which the President sought to thrust upon his countrymen. Isolationism was abroad in the land. On the eve of Wilson's re-embarkation, a resolution, sponsored by Lodge, openly disavowed the Covenant of the League of Nations as contrary to the Monroe Doctrine and American neutrality. The resolution was signed by 39 Republican senators. It would require only 33 votes to defeat a treaty of peace.

To Wilson, defeat was unthinkable. He understood, so he believed, he truly represented the will of the American people. He would rouse its deep, generous instincts against the machinations of senatorial faction. The League, he told his New York audience on the day of the Lodge resolution, must be indissolubly 'intertwined' with the Treaty. It was intended as a ringing statement of his resolve and a call to idealism; to his critics, it sounded suspiciously like a threat. The rumblings continued to mount. The President heard them with scorn rather than with apprehension. Nevertheless, he was in haste to finalize the terms of peace before opposition could take further root. Reaching Paris on 14 March, he went immediately into conclave with Clemenceau and Lloyd George. These meetings, attended only by the three heads of state with their interpreters and advisers, mark the period when the future of Europe was in effect dictated by a triumvirate – the Big Three. Orlando took little part in discussion, and was in any case soon to quit the scene.

Lloyd George too was discontented with the slow progress of the Conference. Already it had dragged on into its third month, with little visible result. Press and Parliament were increasingly restive. Hankey, Smuts and Kerr warned him that the *ad hoc* unsystematic approach so far adopted was not leading to a good overall peace. Lloyd George shared the general impatience. It was time, as he saw it, to cut through the President's dilatoriness, the delays and distractions of the League of Nations on the one hand, and on the other to resist the obstinacy of Clemenceau and the annexationist demands of Foch, and to indicate the kind of terms which Britain would and would not endorse. On Sunday, 23 March, leaving Paris for the rural seclusion of Fontainebleau, the Prime Minister, discoursing freely with Kerr, Hankey, Montagu and Henry Wilson, took a hard, deliberate look at the Conference and produced a blueprint of the kind of peace that ought to be concluded. 'He means business this week,' wrote Frances Stevenson, 'and will sweep all before him. He will stand no more nonsense either from French or Americans. He is taking the long view about the Peace, and insists that it should be one that will not leave bitterness for years to come, and probably lead to another war.'

Historians have made much of this document, known as the Fontainebleau memorandum; and to judge by appearances, in eloquence and breadth of vision, it indeed echoed the noblest aspirations of Wilsonism. It spoke the language and breathed the spirit of statesmanship. It called for a peace built on durable foundations, the conciliation, not the humiliation, of Germany, and the avoidance above all of fresh sources of conflict – of new Alsace-Lorraines, as the Prime Minister put it. Specifically, it required the abandonment of French demands for the detachment of the Rhineland and Saar valley, and advocated the inclusion within the new Poland of as few Germans as possible. It is not to impugn Lloyd George's motives to point out, as Clemenceau did a few days later, that while the general sentiments of the memorandum were unexceptionable, its particular recommendations invariably prejudiced the vital interests of France. British ambitions, he observed, had, within weeks of the Armistice, been satisfied – some might say amply satisfied – with the internment of Germany's battle fleet, the surrender of her submarines, the confiscation of her merchantmen and the appropriation of most of her overseas possessions: with the destruction, that is, of Germany as a naval and colonial rival. But what of France? Where were her guarantees of security? It was true that Lloyd George was offering a promise of Anglo-American assistance in the event of a future German invasion. Clemenceau was grateful for this; but he felt bound to insist on guarantees of a more concrete kind – *des garantis d'ordre physique* – in addition to, not in substitution for, paper pledges which might, who knows, be disowned before they could be redeemed, especially if the British public was indeed as weary of continental commitments as Lloyd George implied. No: if the British felt such a compelling urge to appease Germany, he replied, in effect, *que messieurs les anglais tirent les premiers.*

Significantly, the Fontainebleau memorandum did not recommend any abatement of the claim for full reparation. The secret subcommittee had completed its deliberations, and on 20 March, submitted its report to the Big Three, recommending payment by Germany of six billion pounds. Privately, all three members of the subcommittee were more or less in agreement with Keynes' figure of two billion; but they accepted, as Montagu put it, that this sum 'would have to be supplemented for public consumption', artificially inflated by what the Americans called 'phoney' money. They therefore suggested the figure of three billion pounds in gold as a politically acceptable sum for immediate payment, with a notional three billion in German currency payable later, and a strong hint at radical scaling down once public tempers had cooled. Clemenceau pronounced himself willing to accept the figure. Lloyd George too was willing: Lloyd George was willing to accept anything. 'He needed the sum', noted House, 'purely to quiet his constituents; and he was quite willing to permit the Germans to default on it.'

There was one proviso. Whatever the figure might be, it must have the backing of Hughes, Cunliffe and Sumner. Because they were associated in the public mind with the policy of maximum exaction, their approval would solve the whole domestic problem and release Lloyd George from his dilemma. It was the key to his survival. He needed it, he told the Americans, 'for his own protection and justification'. He would be 'crucified at home if his original experts were not also brought down to reasonable figures'.

Such approval was not forthcoming. Three days later, his official delegates presented their own report to Lloyd George. It called for payment by Germany of 21 billion pounds, three and a half times the figure recommended by the subcommittee. Their fear, they informed him, was of setting too low rather than too high a total, lest Germany should pay off her debt too quickly, like France after 1871, thus 'palpably escaping the just consequences of her aggression', as Sumner put it. As for the question of obtaining German consent, that was easily settled:

> 'The pressure of a state of war . . . to say nothing of the blockade, will eventually bring them to sign.'

On reading this, Lloyd George informed Wilson and Clemenceau that he could not, after all, accept the six billion pound figure.

Between 25 and 28 March, there was a last, desperate struggle for agreement; but while the Americans reluctantly consented to an upper limit of eight billion, Hughes, Cunliffe and Sumner – having conceded, ungraciously and against their better judgment, an absolute final minimum of twelve – dug their heels in. Smoulderingly, Sumner pointed out that Germany ought rightly to be 'liable not only for her own acts but for all the acts of all her allies'. In the case of the bankrupt Ottoman Empire, for example, 'we should lose the costs of Gallipoli, Palestine, Mesopotamia and probably Salonika, if Germany does not back the whole bill'. There was no shifting the implacable trio. As Davis reported, they simply 'put their heads together, went off the deep end, and refused to compromise at all'. In the face of such massive, such monumental intransigence, the whole question was referred back once more to the Big Three.

What was to be done? Everything depended on Lloyd George. Smuts, Wilson and the Americans urged him to take his courage in both hands, to ignore his delegates, to disband the Reparations Commission, to make a direct appeal to Parliament over the heads of Hughes, Cunliffe and Sumner, to 'go back to England and address the House of Commons as he alone could, pointing out boldly that his pre-election estimates as to Germany's capacity to pay were wrong'. This would mean, as Smuts wrote, 'swallowing all his statements on the subject of the general election'. 'I advised him for the sake of his own future and the future of the world to stand by the great human democratic things, even if it meant temporary defeat and eclipse. He agrees with me.'

For a moment, indeed, Lloyd George toyed with the idea. Sparks of his old radicalism re-emerged. It was not 'the English workman', he told Wilson and Clemenceau, who sought 'to overwhelm the German people with excessive demands. It is rather in the upper classes that an unbridled hatred of the Germans will be found.' Could he take on their hard-faced representatives? It would be no easy task 'to disperse the illusions which reign in the public mind on the subject of reparations. Four hundred members of the British Parliament have sworn to extract the last farthing from Germany of what is owing to us. I will have to face up to them. But our duty is to act in the best interests of our countries'. This show of resolution prompted Wilson to express his 'admiration for the spirit which manifests itself in Mr Lloyd George's words. There is nothing more admirable than to be driven from power because one was right.' Lloyd George, noted Smuts, 'appears even prepared to face the situation boldly and go under if necessary.'

But no sooner was it conjured up, than the fleeting vision faded. To be driven from power, whether right or wrong, was not a proposition to be seriously entertained by Lloyd George. The mood of the Commons, as he knew from regular, despondent reports from Bonar Law, was hostile and suspicious as never before. To mount a frontal assault on the serried ranks and entrenched positions of the 400, to go over the top against such redoubtable foes as Brigadier-General Page-Croft, Colonel Gretton, Colonel Lowther and Horatio Bottomley, seemed a prospect no less futile than the bloody offensives which he had so often deprecated in Haig.

Moreover, the parliamentarians had a potent ally on the very outskirts of Paris. Northcliffe had neither forgiven nor forgotten the Prime Minister's stinging rebuff to his ambitions; and the personal vendetta which he now indulged reveals the measure both of his malice and of his power. If he were not to be an official plenipotentiary at the Conference, he would influence it in his own way. He had no policy as such: only the desire, and the ability to injure Lloyd George. He had taken a villa at Fontainebleau; and here he now lurked, a sinister presence on the edge of things, coordinating tactics with his editors, spying out the to-ings and fro-ings in Paris, and turning all his guns on the Prime Minister. 'Northcliffe is probably the most hated man in England,' an observer noted, 'and he is also pretty thoroughly despised for his want of courage and love of shooting from behind walls.' The point at which Lloyd George was most vulnerable, and the principal target at which Northcliffe levelled his sights, was the indemnity question. The campaign of criticism in the Commons was accompanied by a barrage of banner headlines in the Northcliffe press, which accused the Prime Minister of breaking his election pledges, sacrificing British interests to Wilson's caprices, and going 'soft' on Germany.

Rumours from Paris were rife at Westminster – 'sinister rumours', Colonel Lowther informed the Commons. Their appearance was not coincidental. Instrumental in spreading them was one Kennedy Jones, formerly editor of the *Daily Mail*, now Conservative member for Hornsey, but still in league with his old employer, who supplied him with inspired leaks from Paris. Jones's task as Northcliffe's parliamentary linkman was to coordinate tactics between Paris and London, increase pressure on the Government in the House, with a view to tabling a motion of censure and perhaps even over-throwing the Prime Minister. Lowther concocted, and he and Jones circulated, a preposterous memorandum purporting to demonstrate Germany's ability to pay full war-costs. Whether they believed this inherently absurd document is of minor importance, since its real purpose was as a slogan around which to rally demands for a full debate on indemnities. The memorandum, signed by over 100 M.P.s, was handed to Bonar Law on 24 March and published next morning in *The Times*.

A week later, Parliament's attention was drawn to an article in the Liberal *Westminster Gazette*. It purported to express the 'authentic view' of a 'high British authority', and called for a 'sane peace' in which 'there must be no *casus belli* left to Germany'. The key passage concerned reparations: 'Certainly, the question of indemnities, in the sense of going beyond the mere repairing of material damage, is not even posed.' The open secret, winkled out by Northcliffe and bruited forth by the press, quickly burst upon the Commons: the 'high authority', Kennedy Jones told the House, was none other than the Prime Minister.

What was the purpose of the article? Like the Fontainebleau memorandum, of which indeed it was an abridged version designed for domestic consumption, it was a plea for good sense and moderation in the making of peace, with the significant additional warning that the public must abandon all hope of the promised indemnity. It spoke the authentic language of Liberal idealism. It invoked aspirations which, when spirits flagged during the war, the Prime Minister had held out as worthy and enduring goals. It echoed the solemn pledges which he had made to the Germans before the Armistice and which he had made to his Liberal followers before the election. Had Lloyd George, then, finally nailed his true colours to the mast? Was he ready, after all, as Smuts urged, 'to stand by the great human democratic things?'

He was not. It was, as the American, Stannard Baker, wrote in his diary, 'a struggle between Northcliffe and Wilson for the soul of Lloyd George – who has no soul.' It was not a banner he had unfurled, it was only a kite to test the velocity of parliamentary opposition, and to see whether, even now, there might not exist sufficient measure of support in the Commons to enable him to outflank Hughes, Cunliffe, Sumner and the backbenchers.

When the Prime Minister's latest *démarche* became known, parliamentary uproar redoubled. It was agreed that a debate on the indemnity question would be held on 2 April. Bonar Law would again hold the fort. As it was clear that the outcome would be akin to a vote of confidence, Lloyd George was careful to brief Bonar Law on the line to take. While he should 'throw cold water on the idea that a big amount can be obtained from Germany', he should at the same time stress that 'the British Government has never recognised that there is a logical distinction between reparation and indemnity, including cost of war'. He should strenuously deny, in other words, that the Government was breaking its word, while hinting at the same time that it might not be possible to carry it out.

Such equivocation was unlikely to pacify the backbenchers, and the debate, in a crowded House, was a stormy one. It culminated in an onslaught on the Government by Colonel Lowther and a forthright threat by Commander Sir Edward Nicholl that 'if this country does not get that indemnity, my constituents will want to know the reason why. The life of the Government', he warned, 'will be a very short one'. Bonar Law braved the tempest as best he could, in a somewhat rambling reply, but he failed utterly to quell it. 'I had a bad time about indemnities last night,' he wrote to Lloyd George the next day. 'I do not think I convinced anyone, and probably nine out of ten of the Unionist members at least were very disgusted.' Bonar Law's vapid attempts at reassurance served to infuriate rather than appease. The House sensed that he was prevaricating, and the atmosphere remained sulphurous. Within a few days, the Government faced open rebellion.

On 8 April, a telegram, containing the signature of some 200 dissatisfied Coalition members, was sent *en clair* to the Prime Minister in Paris, and published in *The Times* the next morning. It spoke of 'the greatest anxiety' at the 'persistent rumours from Paris' and asked Lloyd George, 'as you repeatedly stated in your election speeches, [to] present the bill in full, make Germany acknowledge the debt, and then discuss ways and means of obtaining payment'. The author of the telegram was Kennedy Jones, its inspiration – Northcliffe. The missive was described, deprecatingly but felicitously, by Asquith, as 'a minatory round robin'. From his exile in the political wilderness, Asquith, for all his classical restraint and lack of rancour, was only human in savouring a certain sense of poetic justice in the spectacle of Lloyd George at bay. There he was, his erstwhile colleague, rich in Liberal antecedents, Liberal credentials and Liberal professions, threatened with parliamentary demise at the hands of his Unionist followers. *Que diable*, it may be wondered, *allait-il faire dans cette galère?* The answer was simple. He was in the same boat as the Conservatives because at the time of the election it had seemed the most seaworthy, and because after the election, having burned his Liberal boats, it was the only vessel available. The Coupon Election, reflected Asquith, the pact with the Unionists, had all been 'a clever piece of electioneering legerdemain' on the part of the Prime Minister. But his days as captain of the Coalition seemed to be numbered, with a mutinous crew threatening to make him walk the plank. And yet – would the Welsh wizard sink, or would he swim? That, after all, was the ancient test of witchcraft.

Chapter 3

Draftsmanship

When the extraordinary man is faced by a novel and difficult situation, he extricates himself by adopting a plan which is at once daring and unexpected. That is the mark of genius in a man of action.

> Lloyd George, in conversation with Riddell, 3 April 1919 (Riddell, *Diary of the Peace Conference*)

In abruptum tractus – audax, callidus, promptus, et, prout animum intendisset, pravus aut industrius, eadem vi. (Faced with a crisis, he was bold, cunning, quick and, depending on whichever he had set his mind on, equally ripe for mischief or for constructive action.)

> Tacitus, *Historiae, i.48*

gain, the Prime Minister found himself threatened with impalement on the horns of the same basic dilemma. Unable to negotiate a fixed sum high enough to satisfy Hughes, the Twins, Northcliffe and the House of Commons on the one hand, and foiled on the other by Wilson's veto on indemnities, he cast about energetically for some alternative method of inflating Britain's share of the spoils. All he had secured so far was 20 per cent of an undetermined total. There was, as far as he was concerned, no question of returning to London with such meagre pickings. Parliament, as he told Colonel House, would 'crucify' him.

His lawyer's eye once more scoured the Lansing note for a loophole. Could not some further head of damage be squeezed out of it, to Britain's advantage? At the time of the election, there had been talk of making Germany pay for British disability pensions and allowances for dependants of the dead and injured. Clearly, these belonged to the forbidden category of war-costs; but if, somehow, he could engineer their inclusion, Britain's share of the spoils would be doubled. He had discussed the matter generally with House in Wilson's absence, and the Colonel did not seem averse to some sort of accommodation. But how was the President to be squared? That was the question. A further memorandum by Lord Sumner was produced for the President's perusal. This contended that pensions might legitimately be construed as part of 'civilian damage', because a soldier was, after all, 'simply a civilian called to arms . . . his uniform makes no difference', an argument which Wilson found 'very legalistic' and rejected, we are told, 'almost with contempt'. A further memorandum to the same effect from the Attorney-General and Solicitor-General, specially summoned from London by Lloyd George, had no better success.

Lloyd George tried a more personal, rhetorical approach. Were the Germans to pay damages for a broken chimney-pot on a French cottage, he asked Wilson, but not for the dependants of a British soldier killed defending it? On its own merits, the argument was not without force; but it plainly flouted the unequivocal limitation of the Lansing note. The claims on Germany, Dulles declared passionately to Sumner, must stand up 'in good conscience before God and the future'.

Wilson, prompted by Dulles, refused to countenance it. The question of pensions, he observed, was 'a point that the Germans may dispute and concerning which the jurists may well have a different opinion'. 'Let this be well understood,' rejoined Lloyd George angrily in a sudden, illuminating flash of *Realpolitik*, 'we cannot leave the interpretation of such a clause to the lawyers.' There was deadlock. Reporting to Bonar Law on 31 March, Lloyd George wrote: 'Wilson does not like damage to combatants being included in cost of reparation. I told him that unless this were included, I might as well go home, as I had no authority to sign unless this were admitted. That is where the matter was left last night.'

Dulles was an able young man and a conscientious lawyer, quick to spur the President to defend the right. But his stalwart logic and New England rectitude were no match for the practised wiles and lightning ingenuity of Lloyd George. The Prime Minister was well known as a psychologist of almost uncanny penetration. He had studied Wilson face to face, and he saw behind that somewhat forbidding exterior. Those who regarded Wilson as cold and remote, mistook the man. He was, on the contrary, though reserved – affable, generous and responsive. He yearned for friendship with almost feminine sensibility.

No man was closer to him than Colonel House, as Mrs Wilson observed, not without a twinge of jealousy. But even House, while there could be no doubt of his devotion to the spirit of Wilsonism, sometimes showed a distressing lack of commitment to its letter, and, particularly while the President was in America, a too great readiness to compromise. 'House has given away everything I had won before we left,' Wilson complained to his wife. Wilson also sensed, and the First Lady was not slow to suggest, that during their absence the Colonel had courted, or at least enjoyed, a popularity which eluded his master. The friendship was momentarily clouded.

Wilson appeared stand-offish, but craved affection. By contrast, Clemenceau and Lloyd George, behind an ebullient sociability, were remarkable for their inner independence. Clemenceau in particular thrived on attack. His whole career was a succession of violent offensives – against his political adversaries, against the enemies of the Republic, against the Germans: from first to last against them. To his countrymen, in the adversity of war, he came to embody in his own dauntless person the courage and defiance of France. 'What is my policy?' he said in the Chamber of Deputies. 'Victory.' Such was his credo in peace as in war. Like the image of the Tiger, popularly associated with his looks and character, the main impression he produced was one of fierce tenacity. Even his Cabinet colleagues, whom he treated like acolytes, feared his temper. He renounced, and was renounced by, his family. One thing only he cherished – the destiny of France – in contrast to his powerful disbelief in mankind generally and Frenchmen in particular. In the almost Plutarchian pride of his spiritual isolation, he spurned the comforts of friendship, as of religion or idealism, with massive contempt.

Lloyd George too discouraged real intimacy. On the surface, he was all fun, chaff, joviality – but his enormous, magnetic charm veiled an inner reserve. 'There is no friendship at the top,' he used to say. 'He neither likes nor dislikes you,' noted Beatrice Webb. 'You are a mere instrument, one among many.' He was on first-name terms with few. He often treated his colleagues as subordinates. He could snub Curzon with extraordinary disrespect and publicly administered a stinging rebuke to Milner. But Lloyd George discerned the President's particular vulnerability. He lighted with shrewd alacrity on the instrument to bring him down and win him to his own purposes. From his capacious bag of tricks, with an insight amounting to genius, he pulled out – General Smuts.

Smuts, like Wilson, was an intellectual, a scholar, a Christian and an idealist. Yet his ideas were not, as Wilson's sometimes seemed, bookish or cerebral. It was in him, rather than in Wilson, that one might more aptly discern the lineaments of the philosopher-king. As a soldier, general, statesman and farmer, he brought to the stuffy, overheated conference-rooms a breath of the sanity and freshness of the Veldt, free from all intrigue and artifice. Smuts was venerated by the younger liberals in the British delegation. 'A splendid, wide-horizoned man,' wrote Nicolson. 'His sense of values takes one away from Paris and this greedy turmoil.' By the elder statesmen too he was respected as a rare moderate. He had consistently urged caution on Lloyd George, particularly over reparations. Only a few days earlier, he wrote again, urging the Premier to 'look at the matter from a large point of view and not ask the impossible'. The President thought especially highly of Smuts, and valued his opinion, House told him, 'more highly than that of any other person on the British delegation'. This, not only because Smuts had all along firmly supported his own stand against indemnity, but, more important, because of his passionate, burning commitment to the League of Nations. This commitment predated that of Wilson himself: the President's drafts for the Covenant were essentially based on the ideas of Smuts.

Lloyd George had enlisted Smuts once already to smooth over a similar crisis. When Wilson set his face firmly against the outright annexation of the German colonies, as imperialism at its worst, Hughes, who made no secret of his contempt for Wilsonism, insisted volubly that Australia, for one, would have her pound of flesh. Tempers ran high. When Wilson loftily demanded whether Australia were really 'prepared to defy the appeal of the whole civilised world', Hughes, cheerfully adjusting his hearing-aid, replied: 'That's about the size of it, Mr. President!' It was Smuts, at Lloyd George's prompting, who succeeded in bringing the President around to the more palatable solution of the mandate-system. 'I could agree to this,' Wilson said then, 'if the interpretation were to come in practice from General Smuts. My difficulty is with the demands of men like Hughes.' Lloyd George took note, and, in the present difficulty, applied the same remedy. On the night of 30 March, Smuts found himself busily penning a legal opinion, 'a thing I had not done for more than twelve years'.

For some reason, Smuts supported Lloyd George on the question of pensions. How he came to do so remains one of the unsolved mysteries of the Conference. All that is known is that on 29 March, he opposed the Prime Minister's view; on 31 March, he was for it. Whether, in the meantime, as one suggestion has it, Lloyd George hinted to him that the securing of a purely notional head of damages, adding nothing to Germany's actual burden, would enable him to make territorial concessions to Germany; or whether Smuts, himself a former distinguished law graduate, genuinely persuaded himself that pensions were a legitimate aspect of 'civilian damage', or, at any rate, that the demand for them was not inherently unjust, remain matters of speculation. Doubtless the Prime Minister, in converse with Smuts, selected from his formidable gamut of charms the *vox humana*. 'He feels acutely', noted Smuts, 'that liberals have everywhere forsaken him and that he has to cope alone with the great opposing forces.' 'He is at present leaning on, or to, me.' At all events, the Prime Minister's persuasions and the General's lucubrations produced the desired memorandum. 'The Prime Minister wanted my opinion to show Wilson,' wrote Smuts, 'as he says Wilson will not listen to the English lawyer, but will pay attention to what I say. It is a farcical world.'

Smuts's case was essentially indistinguishable from Sumner's: a soldier discharged as unfit through enemy action became, *ipso facto*, a civilian, and his injury could therefore fairly be constructed as 'civilian damage'. But, as Lloyd George so shrewdly foresaw, what Wilson rejected in Sumner as mere sophistry he accepted with enthusiasm from Smuts. To the utter consternation of his advisers, the President pronounced himself 'very much impressed', and announced his intention of complying with the demands of Lloyd George.

The horrified, incredulous Dulles and his colleagues pressed him to reconsider, protesting that to include pensions under 'civilian damage' was not logical. 'Logic! Logic!' exclaimed the President, 'I don't give a damn for logic. I am going to include pensions.' He did not, he explained, regard the question 'as a matter for decision in accordance with strict legal principles.' He was 'continuously finding new meanings and the necessity of broad application of principles previously enunciated'.

For the tragedy of the Peace Conference to be understood, it must be taken as axiomatic that Wilson's make-up contained no tincture of cynicism. Whatever might be imputed to him on the score of naïveté or self-deception, he was a man utterly without guile. Yet somehow it happened that the Fourteen Points, which from the sequestered calm of the White House cast so sure and illuminating a beam upon the

My dear Robin - this is The Peace, makes as he really is - tie and all
Taken direct from the official portrait painted by Sir William
Orpen KBE, RA. RI. Otherwise Known as bloody old Bill

PARIS.
16ᵗʰ June 1919

2. Woodrow Wilson (William Orpen, 1919): 'I feel the terrible
responsibility of this whole business.'

problems of Europe, seemed in the heated conference-rooms of Paris only to bring out their bewildering complexity; to amplify in heightened relief the tangled, tenacious, intractable roots of history, geography and race, and to proliferate the difficulties which they were intended to resolve. The President had not come blinkered to the Conference. He had foreseen, in general terms, the immensity of the task awaiting him. Yet in a characteristically American fashion, he had expected faith to move mountains. He had lent to principle, to goodwill and to steadfastness of purpose, qualities of efficacy which they did not and could not of themselves possess, unless geared to absolute system and precision. 'It will now be our fortunate duty' he had announced at the end of the war, 'to assist, by example, by sober, friendly counsel and by material aid, in the establishment of just democracy throughout the world.' But the guiding lights of principle, instead of yielding the hoped-for result in the form of definite, clear-cut solutions, too often, like prisms, refracted blurred, ambiguous penumbras of light and shade; or, like flickering will-o'-the-wisps, led on and on through matted undergrowth into impenetrable thickets and unfathomable morasses. Should a linguistic frontier be severed in order to accommodate an existing rail-link? Or a mining area, vital to the economies of contiguous nationalities, be divided and dislocated? What of the innumerable parts of Central and Eastern Europe where the races were so inextricably intermingled, that no conceivable rearrangement of frontiers could do justice to all? Was there not on occasion something to be said for not tampering with prescriptive, historic rights, and even for making allowances for considerations of strategic defence? To such questions there could be no simple or single answer, save that the new states must be made, as the French put it, 'viable'; and that the doctrine of self-determination if rigidly applied, would prove not a panacea but a Pandora's box. Somewhere, lines must be drawn. But where? Frequently the President, stumbling through murky and treacherous labyrinths, bogged down in a mass of detail, harassed by conflicting interests, found himself resorting for guidance to his own inner sense of right.

Unfortunately, the inner light can prove a fallible guide in determining, not between right and wrong, but between varying degrees of right. Sometimes, as he floundered in a quagmire of doubt and indecision, the President was haunted by something approaching despair. Colonel House was quick to point the way out. 'It was sometimes necessary to compromise in order to get things through,' he reminded 'the Governor'; 'not a compromise of principle, but a compromise of detail.' It was true, beyond peradventure; and yet how, precisely, in that Cimmerian gloom, could one distinguish the crucial borderline between a compromise of detail and a compromise of principle, and avoid crossing that shadowy threshold? *Facilis descensus Averni.* In such extremities of mental perplexity and spiritual demoralization, who knows what fancies of the unconscious, what siren voices, calling from the unknown, can turn the scale and release the springs of action? Certainly Lloyd George, in introducing General Smuts onto the scene at precisely that moment, had touched on an operative reflex in Wilson's psyche.

In holding the question of pensions to lie beyond the ambit of 'strict legal principles', in 'finding new meanings and the necessity of broad applications of principles', there was in Wilson's mind, we must repeat, no thought of sophistry. As a jurist and a scholar, no less than as a statesman, he meant only to breath new life into the familiar and venerable maxim of equity, that where simple justice demands, the letter of the law must bend to the dictates of right and conscience. Was not this the plain meaning of the first of his own four Principles, of his insistence that 'each part of the final settlement must be based upon the essential justice of that particular case?' General Smuts had pointed out the broad, the just, the obvious human stand. It was clearly right, in the widest sense and without being distracted by narrow categories and pettifogging distinctions, that Germany should compensate in full the victims of her aggression – and whom should these include, if not the cripple, the widow and the orphan?

But among his entourage, and beyond, a palpable unease began to stir and spread. 'Tell me what's right, and I'll fight for it,' he had urged them aboard the *George Washington*. Was this, they asked themselves, how he kept faith? Was this the pattern of the American crusade? To the disciples of Wilsonism, the President's acquiescence was scarcely less shocking than it would have been for the Apostles, if Jesus, instead of chasing the money-lenders from the temple, had sat down to bargain with them, and had been short-changed. What was shocking, demoralizing beyond measure, was not that the President had been duped, if he *had* been duped, but that he had ever condescended to do business. The phenomenon which now emerged, to swell in ever-widening ripples, has been dubbed 'the slump in idealism'.

Lloyd George might well smile, when the Big Three reassembled on April Fool's Day. He had pulled off a stupendous *coup*. It was true that Wilson still appeared to waver. What were they to say if the

Germans baulked at pensions? he asked. Lloyd George pushed home his advantage with bluff vigour. In that case, they would tell the Germans that 'we shall resume our unlimited right to compensation for all damages suffered'. If the Germans objected to pensions, they would be threatened with war-costs. Wilson made no reply. The point was taken.

In what form should Germany's liability appear in the Treaty? Wilson favoured simply repeating the stipulation of the Lansing note. This was agreed, and in its final version, appeared in article 232, whereby Germany undertook to 'make compensation for all damage done to the civilian population of the Allied and Associated Powers and to their property'. Even with the contentious inclusion of pensions, article 232 bore at least an ostensible resemblance to the liability agreed at the Armistice. Had the Big Three left it at that, German objections to the reparation clauses would have been confined to interpretation of detail, rather than to principle.

This, however, was nowhere near enough for Lloyd George. 'May I stress the importance,' he had warned Wilson, 'from the point of view of British internal policy, of not abandoning our claims covering the total expenses of the war.' Now Wilson, no less than Colonel House, was far from blind to the political problems of Lloyd George and Clemenceau; he was, as a matter of fact, more sensitive to theirs than to his own. While continuing to resist any assertion of liability for war-costs, he came up with a sensible compromise: 'Why not simply say,' he suggested, 'that the losses are so stupendous that Germany cannot pay them all?' Lloyd George was insistent that nothing less would do than an unequivocal statement of Germany's total liability. 'It is important to state,' explained Clemenceau, 'that our right to compensation is unlimited; that it is we ourselves who have set a limit, after taking the possibilities into account.' Lloyd George chimed in: 'From the political point of view, it is very important to mention that our right is unlimited.'

Wilson was deeply disturbed. Reparations were far from being his only problem. In addition to two gruelling sessions each day with Clemenceau and Lloyd George, he was chairing evening meetings for the drafting of the League of Nations Covenant. In what remained of his time, he felt duty bound to give a patient hearing to whatever might relate to the individual application of his principles. His apartment was besieged daily by emissaries from innumerable nationalities, pleading volubly for the inalienable rights of Greeks, Albanians, Egyptians, Lithuanians, Armenians, Poles, Jews and

Irishmen. Had he realized that so many nations existed, he said, perhaps only half in jest, he might have had second thoughts about the principle of self-determination. He was beset by issues of daunting importance and complexity, each requiring thought, each demanding decision, each going to the very heart of the Fourteen Points. The French were demanding not only the Rhineland, in flagrant contradiction to the Points, but also the Saar, of which, as Wilson protested to Clemenceau, no question had been heard until after the Armistice. 'How did you get on?' House asked Clemenceau after a stormy session with Wilson. 'Splendidly,' replied Clemenceau; 'we disagreed about everything.' A few days later, Clemenceau called Wilson a pro-German and stalked out of the room. The Italians clamoured for Fiume, and Wilson's resistance was shortly to drive Orlando from the Conference. Makino of Japan and Hughes of Australia clung to their spoils in the Pacific, the one with oriental politeness, the other with his customary abrasiveness. The ambitions of the Great Powers were mirrored or exceeded by the distressing rapacity of the lesser states. Paderewski insisted on Danzig, as the pledge of Poland's promised 'free and secure access to the sea'; Wilson, as author of the pledge, felt bound to redeem it, even though, complained Smuts, Poland had no more right to Danzig than Czechoslovakia to Hamburg. Even little Belgium was grasping out at Luxemburg, and proposing a territorial 'accommodation' with Holland at the expense of Germany.

On all sides and at every turn, the points, principles and particulars, jointly and severally, were under vigorous sustained assault. It could not go on, Wilson told his advisers: 'We've got to make peace on the principles laid down and accepted, or not make it at all.' But to continue standing firm threatened the future of the Conference and the peace of Europe. 'He is at a loss to know what to do if the impasse continues,' wrote one of his delegates. 'I really pitied him.'

Wilson also suffered as the butt of the French press – which was, if that were possible, more irresponsible even than the Northcliffe press. At first, it had lauded Wilson to the skies as France's friend and ally. But on perceiving that his aims were not totally subservient to those of the Quai d'Orsay, it turned on him with malice and with a mockery that was wholly Gallic. The President, though he could face martyrdom with equanimity, was for a politician unusually sensitive to ridicule. Jibes that glanced off the broad shoulders and thick skins of Clemenceau and Lloyd George, caused Wilson the most exquisite and evident agony; and the more acute and obvious his torment, the faster and gayer flew the lampoons. When, in addition, he received from the owner of his Parisian residence a notice to quit, he might well feel that he had drained to the dregs the cup of humiliation. House appealed discreetly to Clemenceau. Clemenceau at once issued a communiqué to the effect that on all issues between France and the United States there existed the most complete understanding; and, we may suspect, not without a twinkle, privately urged the press to subdue its mirth. When Wilson, after long and strenuous resistance, finally consented to French control of the Saar, and the Paris headlines resumed their former adulation, there were smiles and nods among the wiseacres.

It was, in truth, no laughing matter. Physically and psychologically, Wilson was at the end of his tether. Weeks of unremitting argument and discord took their toll on an organism not inherently robust. His voice grew hoarse. A nervous facial tic, apparent some years before, recurred. His hair, Mrs Wilson noted with concern, seemed to whiten by the day. In the privacy of his apartments, he fretted and raged against Clemenceau and Lloyd George – 'madmen', he called them. He began to suffer severe headaches. One particularly blinding attack of migraine he attributed to 'bottled-up wrath at Lloyd George'. On 3 April, he fell ill with a high temperature and sickness. His physician diagnosed influenza, but the indisposition may well have been more serious. It was, perhaps, a mild stroke, a forerunner of the attack that was to fell him in the autumn. At all events, he was obliged to take to his bed. His place at the meetings of the Big Three was taken once again by Colonel House.

The role of Colonel House was a remarkable one. The State Department was in effect unrepresented at Paris. Lansing's attendance was merely *pro forma*: he sat, a shadowy presence in the conference-room, silent and functionless, drawing odd little caricatures and 'hobgoblins' on American Delegation notepaper while the President expatiated. It was House who from time to time exerted the real power – not that he craved the limelight: the Colonel was the most tactful and self-effacing of men. His ambition, rather, was of the kind which finds satisfaction in supervising the smooth progress of the drama, as it were from offstage and in prompting from the wings. A word in the President's ear, a scribbled note passed discreetly beneath his elbow, a query satisfied, a qualm assuaged, a point taken – and the thing was done. The Colonel took pleasure in the consciousness of such important, though half-hidden contrivances.

The day before Wilson's collapse, the two men pored over the vexed problem of the Saar. 'The President tried to get me to admit', recorded House, that the proposed solution 'was inconsistent with the Fourteen Points. I replied that there were many who thought otherwise.' The President acquiesced. Two days later, on the very evening of Wilson's illness, Stannard Baker called on House in his suite at the Hôtel Crillon, and found him 'quite serenely dictating his diary'. The impression imparted was one, so to speak, of a diplomatic connoisseur, mulling over the events of the day in the tranquillity of slippered fireside retrospection, savouring with modest complacency the effectiveness of his various interventions. 'He gains experiences to put in his diary,' noted Baker, 'makes great acquaintances, plays at getting important men together for the sheer joy of making them agree. He is a matchless conciliator, but with the faults of his virtue, for he conciliates over the border of minor disagreements into the solid flesh of principle.'

The Colonel's effectiveness was not lost on the other participants at the Conference. During Wilson's absence in America, the Colonel's apartment was frequented by a constant succession of important petitioners. Their numbers did not appear to diminish on the President's return, as Mrs Wilson observed. The Conference, it was felt – the Colonel felt so himself – proceeded more expeditiously and smoothly, certainly more rapidly, when the affairs of the United States were represented by the dapper little Texan – 'a good American,' chaffed Clemenceau; 'very nearly as good as a Frenchman.' And now, once again, quite unexpectedly, they were.

Wilson's collapse was meat and drink to Clemenceau and Lloyd George. For long weeks they had sat confined with him in close and unnatural proximity. Even without the formidable and constant differences that divided them, it was inevitable that their personalities clashed with his. They were of the earth earthy, and his spirituality got on their nerves. He amused, bored and exasperated them, this Presbyterian from Virginia, with his black, parsonical Sunday suit and his prim, missionary manner; his thoughts for the day methodically typed out on his own machine; his pulpit approach – 'My dear friends!'– thus, to their intense irritation, he would apostrophize them in what Clemenceau termed his '*sermonettes*'; his solemn invocations of 'the worrrld', mimicked behind his back by Lloyd George; his unvarying, unruffled, evangelical affability; his repertoire of genteel little jokes; the nervous half-laugh, suggestive perhaps of reproof, perhaps of self-doubt, which, as Lansing noted, 'frequently interrupted his flow of language'. Above all, the cumbersome impedimenta of Points, Principles and Particulars, which he dragged

along to every meeting like a collection of large Victorian portman-
teaux – 'his wretched, hypocritical Fourteen Points', complained
Hankey – his incessant and highly inconvenient qualms, the troublesome, prickly Puritan conscience that he seemed, half-apologetically,
half-provokingly, to sport, almost like a crown of thorns. Dealing
with Wilson, grumbled Clemenceau, was like dealing with Jesus
Christ.

Dealing with House was altogether different. 'One can do business
with you,' Clemenceau told him. House was inclined to agree. He too
had been growing increasingly impatient with 'the Governor' as days
and weeks passed without a settlement and the President communed
interminably with his conscience. House was keen to cut the cackle.
'If he had it to do,' he complained, 'he could make peace in an hour.'
Now he had it to do. 'In my opinion,' he told Clemenceau and Lloyd
George on 4 April, 'it was more important to bring about peace
quickly than to haggle over details. I would rather see an immediate
peace and the world brought to order than I would see a better peace
and delay. . . . 'I jestingly remarked,' he noted, 'that by tomorrow
night we ought to be able to settle all subjects necessary for a peace.'

House was almost as good as his word. Clemenceau bubbled over
with delight at this gift of fortune. He was 'very pleased at Wilson's
absence', noted Frances Stevenson on 5 April, 'and could not conceal
his joy. "He is *worse* today", Clemenceau said to Lloyd George, and
doubled up with laughter.' Lloyd George had equal cause for
jubilation, following the morning session. A draft formula, submitted by the experts for discussion, read as follows: 'the Allied and
Associated Governments affirm the responsibility of the enemy states
for causing all the loss and damage to which the Allied and Associated
Governments and their nationals have been subjected as a consequence of the war imposed upon them by the aggression of the enemy
states.'

Clemenceau and Lloyd George at once pressed home their advantage. This was not enough, they objected. There must be a German
acknowledgement of liability, not merely an Allied assertion, which,
Lloyd George emphasized, would be 'hardly adequate to meet the
political situation, either British or French'. He drew attention to the
Lowther debate of three days earlier. 'The British House of Commons', he explained, 'has not been satisfied with the declarations
made the other day by Mr Bonar Law. British public opinion
demands that Germany pay all the loss that they have caused.' He
repeated to House the argument which Wilson had consistently

rejected. 'We must say that the Allies assert their claim and that Germany recognises her obligation for all the costs of the war.' House, like Wilson, at once warned against flouting the Lansing note; at the same time, he pointed to a solution: 'The text must be drafted so as not to constitute a violation of our engagements.'

This was the critical breakthrough. For House, the problem was one not of principle, but of technique. The answer lay in one of those adroit compromises of detail in which the Colonel excelled, and which he was constantly urging upon the President. It was simply a question of drawing up an acceptable formula. Clemenceau concurred. 'It is a question of drafting,' he said, 'I think we can reach agreement.' The deal was clinched. The fateful words were inserted: *'and Germany accepts'*. The war-guilt clause was born. The statesmen were content. Lloyd George, wrote Miss Stevenson, 'came back from the morning meeting very pleased.' *'We are making headway'*, he told her, *'which means that I am getting my own way!'*

After lunch, he crowned one success with another. Not only would Germany acknowledge full liability, but the extent of that liability would remain undetermined. The Allies being quite unable to agree on a total, no sum at all would be specified. Instead, a decision would be deferred for two years, when a special Inter-Allied Commission would produce its report. By that time, the dust would have settled and many changes would have taken place; a clearer idea would be available of Germany's true capacity; the French would be in a position to assess the full extent of their war damage; the British public would have had time to come to its senses; Hughes would be out of harm's way in Australia, and the Twins – who knows where the Twins might be? It was true, as the Americans complained, and as Lord Robert Cecil at once wrote to Lloyd George to point out, that as far as resuscitating the European economy was concerned, 'the latest proposals for "settling" the reparation question' were no settlement at all; that they combined 'the maximum of financial disturbance with the minimum of actual result' and cast 'a heavy cloud on all financial transactions'. But as a political device to tide the Prime Minister over the immediate crisis, they seemed foolproof. By the simple expedient of postponement, Lloyd George, a modern Fabius Cunctator, would be able to save the day – or at any rate, his political skin. 'Now I understand why you are Prime Minister,' an American told him after the meeting. 'You are far and away ahead of the whole lot.' It was overlooked, in the euphoria of agreement, that the Germans might not care to put their signature to a blank cheque, still less to accept responsibility, entire and indivisible, for the World War.

The President was still confined to his rooms. The next day, a Sunday, he summoned his principal delegates to his bedside. Such meetings had been so rare during the Conference that the holding of this one, at this late stage, suggests on Wilson's part some unusual perturbation of spirit. The President was indeed profoundly troubled by what had taken place in his absence. It was not that he doubted the Colonel's good faith, or that House had acted in any way surreptitiously or out of turn. The crucial meeting had taken place in Wilson's own apartments, in a room adjacent to his own bedroom. House had been in constant communication, had kept the President fully informed of the proceedings. The problem was not that House had been false to the President, as Mrs Wilson believed, but that he had been true to himself and his own conviction of the rightness and the inevitability of compromise. But the President, having slept on it, and slept most uneasily, saw that it could not, must not be. He would leave the Conference, he told House, 'unless peace was made according to their promises, which were to conform to the principles of the Fourteen Points'.

In her *Memoirs*, Mrs Wilson recalls her husband's remarks from his sickbed the next morning. 'I can never sign a treaty made on these lines,' he declared, pale and hollow-eyed, 'and if all the rest of the delegates have determined on this, I will not be a party to it. If I have lost my fight, he continued, 'which I would not have done had I been on my feet, I will retire in good order; so we will go home.' He summoned his physician, and when he came, said: 'I want the *George Washington* put in shape at once for my return home as soon as you think it is safe for me to make the trip.' Was it a piece of kite-flying, a dramatic attempt to break the deadlock and force Clemenceau and Lloyd George to come to heel? Clemenceau likened him to a disgruntled housekeeper packing her bags. It is inherently unlikely that Wilson had any such ploy in mind. Such a tactic would have been out of character: both beneath his dignity and beyond his capacity. In a war of nerves, particularly in his distraught condition, his would have been the first to crack. The summoning of the *George Washington* was more probably an admission of despair, a cry for help, than a diplomatic ruse. What destroyed him was not stratagem, but scruple.

The President faced appalling alternatives. If he stood by his principles, as he had already shown himself ready and able to do, he seemed likely to precipitate the disintegration of the Conference, perhaps even of the Alliance. Clemenceau and Lloyd George insisted that failure on their part to bring home an acceptable formula over reparations would result in their overthrow; and, for all that the President knew, they may have been right. Lloyd George warned that his place at the Conference might be taken by Northcliffe or Bottomley; Clemenceau – with greater plausibility – that he risked falling victim to the rumbling pressures of the National Assembly or the machinations of Marshal Foch and President Poincaré. Would Wilson find it any easier to deal with men pledged not to fulfil, however imperfectly, the Fourteen Points, but to ignore or even to repudiate them?

The President was also haunted by the spectre of Bolshevism. The malevolent, grinning masks of Lenin and Trotsky, like Lansing's 'hobgoblins', were ever-present at the Conference table. They, it was plain, had no interest in making the world safe for democracy – 'bourgeois' democracy, as they called it – only in spreading their specious and sinister doctrines by terror and subversion. The example of Russia had already spawned revolutionary regimes in Hungary and Bavaria. Spartacism had been bloodily put down in Berlin. Even in Britain, troops had been ordered to the Clydeside, where rioting workers seemed on the brink of insurrection. The President understood well the attraction of Bolshevism to hungry and desperate multitudes, just as he grasped that its proliferation must poison the life, and perhaps extinguish the freedom, of Europe. Was it wise, was it right, however impeccable one's motives, to court by further delay the risks of general, perhaps uncontrollable conflagration? Was he in danger of temptation by the sin of pride and the political error of making the best the enemy of the good, or at least, of the possible? '*Mais voyons, donc!*' Clemenceau would exclaim, as each issue was individually dissected by the President, held up for illumination to the fast-fading light of the Fourteen Points, and weighed in the now wavering balance of the President's conscience – '*mais voyons, donc! Il faut aboutir!*' House too fumed at Wilson's legalistic scrutiny of the small print: was this not fiddling while Rome burned? 'If the world were not in such a fluid state,' he wrote in his diary, 'I should not object to matters going as deliberately as they have been going; but under present conditions we are gambling each day with the situation.'

By a strange but unconscious irony, a few years before, the President had adumbrated the very dilemma in which he now stood. In an elegant essay, entitled 'When a man comes to himself', he describes in his own compelling style the evolution of great statesmen;

how, from ardent visionaries, with 'such strong, unhesitating, drastic opinions', they become practical men of action:

> They are at last, at close quarters with the world. Men of every interest and variety crowd about them; new impressions throng them; in the midst of affairs, the former special objects of their zeal fall into new environments, a better and truer perspective; seem no longer so susceptible to separate and radical change. The real nature of the complex stuff of life they were seeking to work in is revealed to them – its intricate and delicate fibre, and the subtle, secret, inter-relationship of its parts – and they work circumspectly, lest they should mar more than they mend.

Here indeed, were new impressions, new environments, and perspectives, which, whether better and truer, were certainly very different from those which inspired the writing of the Fourteen Points.

Meanwhile, Wilson had just brought off what he saw as his greatest triumph. The Covenant of the League, 'the cornerstone of the peace', as he called it, was finally accepted as an integral part of the Treaty. For Wilson, the League lay at the very heart of peacemaking, the focus of his energies and aspirations. To call his attitude towards it an obsession would be too much; but in his eyes the League did possess a simplifying, purifying element, an element almost of grace, which overreached and subsumed all other aspects of peacemaking. 'We have got to keep our eyes fixed on the main objective,' he insisted. Once the Covenant was firmly 'intertwined' with the Treaty, the dead wood encumbering the latter would be replaced by healthy new shoots. To that all-encompassing end, much might, and perhaps should, be sacrificed. 'If that objective can be safely reached,' Wilson declared, 'we can afford to allow a number of decisions to be made touching the reconstruction of Europe which might neither meet with my approval nor correspond with what a strictly impartial judge would consider proper. It will be the business of the League to set such matters right.'

Clemenceau's attitude to the League was one of impatience, tempered by melancholy. His large, limpid eyes, which reflected the ineffable sadness of things, would also flash with impatience at the suggestion that things could ever be other. He was wearily sceptical of the President's idealism. He, for one, entertained no hopes of a brave new world of peace and brotherhood. 'Do you really believe it,' he exclaimed on one occasion; 'a peaceful world founded on violence?' When Wilson, to impress upon him the ultimate, inevitable triumph

THE TIGER.

Paris 12ᵗʰ June 1919.

3. Clemenceau (William Orpen, 1919): 'Always as straight as a die'
– Col. Hankey.

of right over might, pointed out that Napoleon himself admitted on his deathbed that force solves nothing, Clemenceau acidly observed that the confession came somewhat late in the Emperor's career. He saw no change of heart in mankind, not at any rate of the German heart.

What difference, Clemenceau asked, had the war made to the eternal combativeness of nations in the European jungle? None – but its effect on the Balance of Power was catastrophic: France weakened by the loss of 1,500,000 men, half her fighting manhood under 30 dead, and deprived of her great ally and counter-weight in the east, Russia. A league of victors, armed, alert and resolute to check any new German aggression, he was all for that; but the moment he suggested ways of putting teeth into the League – an international army, a general staff, Wilson shied nervously away and spoke of the Monroe Doctrine. The world, he explained, was to be governed by 'the organised moral force of mankind'. Clemenceau's bushy eyebrows rose incredulously. He shrugged his stocky shoulders. A milk-and-water league of arm-chair philosophers and good intentions, of paper resolutions and covenants without swords, could excite only his bitterest contempt. However, Wilson had set his heart on this chimera; and that being so, the League of Nations, while it could do little good in the real world, was an invaluable bargaining-counter at the Conference. Clemenceau was perfectly willing to indulge the President's unaccountable sentimentality in return for solid gains for France. He therefore held out until the time was ripe, and in return for the League, secured Wilson's adherence to the British undertaking to come immediately to the aid of France in the event of a fresh German invasion.

Wilson obtained his league of Nations – Clemenceau and Lloyd George their war-guilt clause. To see the process in terms of a crude *quid pro quo*, however, would be a distortion. It was rather that the absolute necessity of all-round compromise, as it impinged itself upon the peacemakers, produced its inevitable outcome in a variety of mutual concessions. 'There has, unfortunately, to be a great deal of give and take,' admitted the President. Some, however, gave, and some took, more than others. For a person of normal sensitivity, it is disagreeable always to be digging in one's heels. The President was a man of exquisite sensitivity. He sympathized with his colleagues. He understood, even if he did not approve, their predicaments; and he longed to oblige. He would not, of course, yield on matters of principle; but where principle appeared not to be directly at stake, he was more than willing, even without House's promptings, to compromise if he respectably could. Clemenceau, in the grim last months of war, had always said that the winning side would be the side which held out a quarter of an hour longer. So now at the Conference, it was Clemenceau and Lloyd George, those shrewd and seasoned poker-players, who played out the waiting game; and Wilson, unable to withstand the *mauvais quart d'heure*, who gave in first and most damagingly.

The President had, in a sense, and as he put it, 'come to himself'. But in so doing, he had in another, truer sense, lost himself. There was still a dimension in which he really was, as he believed, a trustee for the conscience of mankind. Nothwithstanding the storms of mass hysteria and folly, necessarily consequent on a war of peoples, the President's obvious sincerity won him involuntary respect. His 'programme' for 'the final triumph of justice and fair dealing' might bring a smile to the lips of practised statesmen and diplomatists, to Clemenceau, say, or to Sir Henry Wilson or Colonel Hankey. But thousands, perhaps millions of ordinary people shared, or at least admired, his faith. Even to the democratic leaders themselves, amid the scramble for security and spoils at Paris, even to the very multitudes who urged them on to yet greater feats of 'sacred egoism', the President remained a man apart, a symbol and reminder of other things. He stood, in his own words, upon 'an elevation from which we can see the things for which the heart of mankind has longed'.

By coming 'at last, at close quarters with the world', he shed, unwittingly, his one indubitable quality of greatness - his radiant vision of things above and beyond the orbit of knowing politicians – and his ability to communicate that vision and endow it with form and beauty. There, in the compelling grandeur of his vision and the intensity of his inspirational fervour, lay Wilson's strength – and his salvation. From those lofty heights he was unassailable: the light of his Gospel shone forth resplendent, thrilling, noble and ennobling. Once he descended from that solitary eminence and began to deal, or to appear to deal, with Lloyd George and Clemenceau on their level, he was done for. His prophetic mantle, as he rubbed shoulders with them, became sullied with their dross. His moral, and therefore his political, authority was fatally impaired. To witness that descent was painful; it was painful to watch him, step by faltering step, coming to terms with Mammon: to see him not only fallen as it were among thieves, but giving his apostolic blessing to their division of the spoils. With each successive downward step, Orlando's hand – for he was back in the fray – might be seen to steal discreetly across his lips, a faint, almost imperceptible tremor to play about Clemenceau's eyelid, and a puckish grin to crease the face of Lloyd George.

Of the disastrous impression he was creating, the cruel and mocking imputations to which he laid himself open, the President was not wholly insensitive. 'He knew', he said, 'that he would be accused of violating his own principles.' But he believed, or professed to believe, that he had 'only learned discretion'. He spoke justifyingly, proudly almost, though with a slightly puzzled smile, of reconciling idealism with *Realpolitik*. To those who observed, with growing dismay or contempt, his lack of system, the clumsy, flustered interventions and tergiversations, the desperate and undignified scrambles from one untenable position to another, to which his descent from the mountain had reduced him, his claims were wildly, derisively inapposite. But discretion, even had he possessed it, was not the way to impose Wilsonism upon the world. Boldness, fortitude, unflinching, rocklike integrity – these alone, at that fluid and pregnant time, might have saved the peace – or at any rate the President. It was too late. From the moment he made his own peace with Clemenceau and Lloyd George and cancelled his order for the recall of the *George Washington*, he lost all credibility as a statesman. 'We ceased', records Nicolson, 'to believe that President Wilson was the Prophet whom we had followed. . . . We saw in him no more than a presbyterian dominie.'

Some protested at the obvious violation of the Lansing note. But most acquiesced. The war-guilt clause, though objectionable in principle, seemed to those like Keynes and Dulles, who helped to draft it, harmless enough in practice. It added nothing to Germany's real burden. It promised to ease Lloyd George and Clemenceau through their domestic difficulties. It seemed a reasonable compromise, as compromises go. It was not as if this were Wilson's first or most serious deviation from the Fourteen Points. At almost every turn, he appeared to be throwing them to the winds. The award to Italy of the South Tyrol, of the Saar mines to France and the Sudetenland to Czechoslovakia, of Hungarian Transylvania to Roumania; the partitioning of Asia Minor into 'spheres of influence': the broken pledges swirled around like leaves in Vallombrosa. 'Peoples and provinces', he had declared in the second of the four Principles, 'are not to be bartered about from sovereignty to sovereignty, as if they were mere chattels or pawns in a game.' And now here he was, sowing the continent with new irredenta, scattering 'peoples and provinces' right and left, displaying, as far as the doctrine of self-determination was concerned, all the apparent insouciance of the Old Diplomacy. 'President Wilson has a very elastic mind,' sneered Hankey.

Consciousness among the President's followers of this undeniable elasticity led inevitably to demoralization. It had been Wilson's strength that, however impossible-sounding his aims, he manifestly meant what he said. To his jaundiced advisers, seldom permitted to advise, it now seemed not only that he no longer meant what he said, but that all too often he did not know what he was talking about. His experts kicked their heels in the Hôtel Crillon, while the President, so terribly conscious of his responsibility, consulted his conscience and Colonel House and pronounced *ex cathedra*. He was ignorant, when he promised Italy the South Tyrol, that its population was Austrian. When he approved the boundaries of Czechoslovakia, he had no idea that they contained three million Germans. When he assented to the incorporation of Transylvania within Roumania, he was unaware of sanctioning an act of annexation. When some of these fearful and irreparable errors were brought to his notice, he looked pained, and spoke of the remedial powers of the League. In the bar of the Hôtel Crillon, they shrugged their shoulders and downed their drinks. Were they to be more Wilsonian than Wilson? His very confidence in the League was distressing. He seemed to envisage it as a kind of international pharmacopoeia, with a patent remedy for every problem. He alone seemed indifferent to the inescapable evidence of hostility in the United States. Was he sure of the Senate, Smuts asked anxiously, could he guarantee ratification of the League? 'I absolutely can,' replied the President. His advisers were abashed at the falsity of his position and their own. How could they demand of the Allies sacrifices in the name of an idealism which America herself might renounce?

Il faut aboutir. Clemenceau was expressing a general impatience. For three months, the real work of the Conference had been virtually suspended, while the President deliberated on the good, the true and the democratic. With his capitulation, idealism fled from the Conference like air from a balloon. The points, principles and particulars having been abandoned, like so many crumpled drafts in the waste-paper basket, the delays of the early months were succeeded by an intensive, frank and most unholy rush for 'deals', a universal *sauve qui peut*. The President himself sat silent and sardonic, as Lloyd George and Clemenceau squabbled like fishwives over Syria. True, he was making a determined stand for Fiume: but was not this, as the Italians asked bitterly, simply a belated attempt to regain his lost innocence, *'se refaire une virginité* at the expense of Italy'?

For Lloyd George, it was victory, total and unalloyed. Wilson had raised the stakes immeasurably by his threat to leave the Conference – but Wilson, not he, had capitulated. Nor was the war-guilt clause the Prime Minister's only trophy. After prolonged wrangling, he also secured Wilson's reluctant consent to the trial of the Kaiser. He thus brought off, simultaneously, the two tricks that mattered most to him. He had promised to 'Make Germany pay'; he had promised to 'Hang the Kaiser'; he could now claim, with some real semblance of probability, to be redeeming these important pledges.

With the war-guilt clause safe in his pocket, Lloyd George felt himself in an impregnable position to face the House of Commons. He had followed to the letter the demands in the backbenchers' telegram: he had drawn up the full bill of war-costs for presentation to Germany, together with a clear acknowledgment of the debt for her signature. The function of article 231, in the succinct description of an American historian, was 'to enable Allied statesmen to fulfil, *at least in words*, the expectations of their constituents'. For Lloyd George, as for Clemenceau, the war-guilt clause was an escape-clause, a safety-net, the magic formula, the conjurer's rabbit, which he would if necessary pull out of his hat at the last minute, to confound his critics, amaze his supporters and save the day.

On 8 April, Bonar Law flew over from London with an alarming report on the rumblings and clamourings at Westminster. He was the 'ultra-pessimist', noted Henry Wilson. Lloyd George, by contrast, was at the top of his form. The gloomier he found Bonar Law, the more merrily he beamed and chuckled. The next day, when the backbenchers' telegram appeared in *The Times*, Lloyd George cabled back a confident, even defiant reply, agreeing to submit his conduct to Parliament, 'and, if necessary, to the country'. The threat of another general election was a shrewd piece of bluff, since the Conservatives had been shaken by a succession of sensational by-election gains by the Asquithians. 'I think my reply was on the right lines,' he observed to Bonar Law. Bonar Law agreed, but with the groans and catcalls of his own backbenchers still ringing in his ears, was worried about the phenomenal, virtually unanimous Tory support for the cable. He noted too that it was 'signed by four excellent men, in addition to Kennedy Jones.' 'He then went over the names,' noted Riddell, adding that Bonar Law clearly 'attached grave importance to the message . . . [and urged] Lloyd George to return to England for a few days.'

Before leaving, however, Lloyd George attempted to settle with Hughes. Throughout the Conference, Hughes had proved almost as great a bugbear to him as Wilson. Would he now lend his support, so that Lloyd George could face Parliament with the backing of a united delegation? Would he at least keep his dissent to himself? Or would he, as at the time of the Armistice, make a nuisance of himself behind the Government's back, stirring up hostile publicity, perhaps even making common cause with Kennedy Jones and Colonel Lowther? To the end, Hughes – 'the ineffable Hughes', as Cecil called him – remained wholly intractable. Like an old, deaf and obstinate mongrel, he bit and worried at the dry bone of indemnity, and growled at his colleagues when they pointed out that there was no meat on it. At a meeting of the Empire Delegation on 11 April, he barked and whimpered by turns. Where was the promised indemnity? Why was Germany being let off the hook? The Dominions were being cheated. The Empire itself might not survive this.

The Twins themselves tried vainly to soothe him. Sumner wearily complained that thanks to the Americans, the indemnity cause was 'hopeless'. No one, agreed Cunliffe, would accuse him, the ex-Governor of the Bank, of being pro-German. 'He would stake his reputation that these were the best terms that we could hope to get.' Hughes continued to whine and snap. Hankey argued vainly with him for 'an hour or two after the meeting, trying for an accommodation, but could get nothing from Hughes that Lloyd George could take'. On the contrary, Hughes pursued the Prime Minister with a letter of complaint: 'I feel I ought not to be asked to assent to the proposal,' he grumbled. 'Its acceptance does not depend on my assent.' Safe in the crucial support of the Twins, as he left Paris on 14 April, Lloyd George could indulge the luxury of a parting kick at the troublesome, yapping Australian. 'I quite understand your attitude,' he wrote back; 'it is a very well known one. It is generally called "heads I win, tails you lose".'

It was the equivalent of the 'Go to hell!' with which he had dismissed Northcliffe half a year earlier. That spirited malediction had returned with a vengeance to haunt the Prime Minister throughout the Conference. Northcliffe was the master hand behind the ceaseless campaign against him in press and Parliament; and now, with the springing of the 'round robin', the trap appeared to be set, so Northcliffe must have thought; he had forced Lloyd George onto the gridiron for a final roasting by the Commons. A *Times* editorial on 11 April, entitled 'The Indemnity', stated that 'he has aroused in the popular mind hopes which he has not fulfilled'. No Prime Minister could be faced with a more mischievous challenge. It was characteristic of Lloyd George's pluck and daring boldly to take up the gauntlet. Having cocked a farewell snook at Hughes, Lloyd George, in resilient, swashbuckling mood, determined at last to strike back. He 'left for London in excellent spirits', wrote Frances Stevenson. 'He has made up his mind to attack Northcliffe and declare war to the knife.'

The Prime Minister prepared his speech with care. The counter-stroke that he launched on 16 April was a *tour de force* of pugnacious virtuosity that took friend and foe by storm. It was Lloyd George at his best – and his worst. He told a House crowded to overflowing:

> So far from my coming here to ask for reconsideration, to ask release from any pledge or promise which I have given, I am here to say that every pledge we have given with regard to what we pressed for insertion in the peace terms is incorporated in the demands which have been put forward by the Allies.

This was greeted by loud cheers. He continued:

> There are some who suggest that at the last election, I and my colleagues were rushed into declarations of which we are now rather ashamed, and wish to get out of. I do not wish to get out of them in the least. . . . [if] I had arrived at the conclusion that I had gone too far, and pledged the Government and the country to something that I could not carry out, I should have come down here and said so, because it would have been folly, even for an electioneering pledge, to imperil the people of Europe. [Further cheers.] Then the House of Commons, of course, would have been free to take its own action.

What hubris, what wanton spirit of contrariness induced him to open wide for himself such a perfect escape-hatch, only to slam it shut? Was it the breath-taking thrill of careering close to the verge? The conscious, calculated bravado of the tight-rope walker? Or was it the sheer devilry of a stupendous bluff, the matchless joy of the unanswerable lie? He ridiculed Northcliffe's political ambitions. 'When a man has deluded himself that he is the only man who can win the war, and he is waiting for the clamour of the multitude that is going to demand his presence there to direct the destinies of the world, and there is not a whisper, not a sound, it is rather disappointing.' Tapping his brow, he denounced the 'diseased vanity' of Northcliffe and the Northcliffe press. 'In France,' he said, 'they still

4. Lloyd George (Bert Thomas, 1919): 'A wonderful performance'
    – Thomas Jones.

believe that the *Times* is a serious organ. They do not know that it is merely a threepenny edition of the *Daily Mail*.'

This masterly show of parliamentary candour – one of the most successful defences of policy ever made by a Prime Minister in the House – he rounded off with a devastatingly witty peroration, in which Northcliffe, whom he made the scapegoat of the attempt to topple him, was utterly trounced. Northcliffe had been described as a 'reliable source' of the rumours leading up to the debate. Lloyd George rolled the phrase lingeringly on his tongue. 'Reliable! That is the last adjective I would use. It is here today, jumping there tomorrow, and there the next day. I would as soon rely on a grasshopper.' The House roared its delight.

Under weight of this brilliant cascade of rhetoric, of intoxicating banter alternating with seeming earnestness, the opposition, as Hankey noted from the gallery, 'collapsed utterly'. 'I am going back,' Lloyd George announced, adding with a bold flourish: 'if the House wants me to – unless it prefers some other choice.' There were cries of 'No, no!' 'There are many eligible offers,' the Prime Minister interjected amid laughter. He had the die-hards eating out of his hand. Colonel Lowther himself rose to assure him that the telegram had been sent with the best possible motives, in order to strengthen the Premier's hand during negotiations. Lloyd George affably replied that he had never doubted the good faith of the signatories, before sweeping magnificently out of the Chamber. The House was 'counted-out' and dispersed happily for the Easter recess.

One cannot deny Lloyd George his hour of triumph. It was a famous victory, splendidly carried off – 'Lloyd George's oratorical Austerlitz,' wrote Garvin in the *Observer*. With the backbenchers baying for his blood and Northcliffe bellowing View Halloo, the Prime Minister had most cunningly thrown his pursuers off the track by rounding on his chief assailant. He gained, as Frances Stevenson noted, 'complete mastery of the House, while telling them absolutely nothing about the peace conference'. Well might he return to Paris next day, the eve of Good Friday, 'in the highest of spirits and very pleased with himself'. The glittering Maundy money he had thrown to the Commons was counterfeit; but for the moment it passed for sterling. The whole thing, as Thomas Jones, the Cabinet Secretary, told Miss Stevenson over the line from London, was 'a wonderful performance – one of his very best'. 'Performance' was the word.

Chapter 4

Versailles

Behold the tears of such as were oppressed, and they had no comforter; and on the side of their oppressors there was power; but they had no comforter.

Ecclesiastes, 4, i

The Treaty will in any case emerge as a rotten thing, of which we shall all be heartily ashamed in due course.

Smuts to Keynes, June 1919

At the end of April, a special train from Berlin pulled into the little station of Vaucresson, near Versailles. From it descended the German delegates, summoned to receive the terms of peace. During the journey across northern France, the train had slowed down almost to walking pace, to allow the emissaries, indeed to compel them, to see the devastation of the war-zone. The sight, wrote Dr Simons, Commissioner-General of the delegation, was 'overwhelming'. They looked 'until we had seen all we could endure'. At Versailles, wooden palisades topped with barbed wire were thrown up in the streets, behind which, it was explained, they might pass and repass from their various hotels to the headquarters assigned to them, without danger of molestation by the citizens. They were informed that the peace terms would be communicated to them on 7 May, that no oral discussions would take place and that written representations must be submitted within a fortnight. From sundry leaks and semi-official communiqués, the Germans had a general idea of what awaited them, and, in particular, that the terms would be based on the assumption of German war-guilt. Until they had seen them, however, there was little they could do. They wandered disconsolately in the gardens of Marie-Antoinette, gaped at through the railings by American dough-boys and Parisian weekenders, out to enjoy the spring sunshine and *pour voir les Boches*.

It had not originally been decided to treat the German delegates as pariahs. 'It was the force of circumstances,' recalled Philip Kerr, rather than any deliberate decision, which determined the matter.' The Foreign Office, the Quai d'Orsay and the State Department had all assumed that peace negotiations would be commenced within days, or at any rate within weeks of the Armistice; that military terms would be laid down by the Allies, but that the permanent political settlement would be worked out, in accordance with normal diplomatic practice, in face-to-face negotiations between plenipotentiaries of the former belligerents. But the summoning of an immediate conference had been prevented by the British general election, with its harvest of recrudescent anti-Germanism. This was a passion which Clemenceau already shared to the full and from which Wilson himself was not wholly immune. Lloyd George, whatever his own inner feelings may have been, felt he could not afford to seem to show undue tenderness to German susceptibilities.

To this may be added the holding of the Conference in Paris. Which other city might have been selected is difficult to say. The obvious and desirable choice of The Hague was ruled out by the proximity of the Kaiser and the refusal of the Dutch to hand him over. Switzerland, at the moment when the question fell for decision, was feared by Wilson to be on the verge of revolution. But the designation of Paris, that febrile and shell-shocked metropolis, with its cynical, volatile, mischievous and frankly venal press, was singularly unpropitious to calmness of thought and emotion, particularly when combined, for the ceremonial aspects of peacemaking, with Versailles – Versailles, with its ominous echoes of 1871, and the shade of Bismarck stalking the corridors and parterres.

There also loomed in the minds of the Big Three the earlier precedent of the Congress of Vienna; of how Talleyrand, by an astute and subtle diplomacy, succeeded not only in absolving his government from the errors of Napoleonic rule, but in dividing the victors one from another, turning the peace greatly to France's advantage and largely delivering her from the consequences of defeat. No such opportunity, it was tacitly agreed, should be vouchsafed to the present enemy.

But the overriding reason for the veto on direct discussion with the Germans was the fact that the terms themselves were no longer negotiable. They represented the hard-earned fruit of endless argument, bitter heart-searching and painful compromise, an elaborate and intricate framework of interlocking agreements, none of which could be substantially altered, still less removed, without upsetting the delicate balance between the three constituent elements and toppling the whole fragile structure. Of this structure, the war-guilt clause was, for Clemenceau and Lloyd George, perhaps the keystone.

As a compromise of divergent political interests, the terms might be regarded as a triumph of diplomacy; as a treaty of peace, they were a disaster. Yet until 6 May, they had not even been collated in a single document; so that not only the Allied delegations but even the Big Three themselves were unable to discuss them as a whole, or barely even to scan them through before their presentation to the Germans. All that the British Empire delegation knew of them emerged from a summary of extracts read aloud by Lloyd George at a hastily convened meeting. Copies of the full text were available only on the eve of presentation. 'I don't think in all history this can be matched,' commented Sir Henry Wilson, to whom the Prime Minister admitted that he had not yet received a copy himself. 'And Lloyd George sees nothing odd in this,' Wilson exclaimed, 'although we are to present the terms to the Boches at 3 p.m. tomorrow!'

To most of the British and American delegates, the Treaty, once copies had been secured, came as an appalling shock. Judged individually and on their own merits, as they had been in the innumerable subcommittees of the Conference, most provisions could be justified, at least as maximum demands open to subsequent modification. Viewed collectively, as a more or less final settlement, they presented a terrible, an impossible aggregate. The sum was greater than the parts, said some delegates. Others spoke of 'peace with a vengeance', of laying the foundations of 'a just and lasting war'. The draftsmen stood aghast at their own creation.

Their instant misgivings were forcefully summarized in a memorandum by Keynes. Even leaving aside the territorial losses which Germany was to suffer, the terms, to him, were unthinkable. The disarmament and demilitarization clauses alone, he wrote, 'go beyond what any self-respecting country could submit to'. The occupation of the Rhineland 'would appear to lend itself to the most terrible abuse'. Even the internationalizing of Germany's rivers was 'humiliating and interfering'. As for the reparations scheme, he doubted whether it could 'possibly persist as a solution of the problem, showing as it does a high degree of unwisdom in almost every direction'. Was such a document to be taken seriously by anybody, let alone by the Germans? 'That they will sign the treaty in the form in which it now stands,' he concluded, 'I cannot for one moment believe. Why should they? What worse fate have we in store for them in the event of refusal?'

Three men arose, sleepless, in the small hours of 7 May, and walked the deserted boulevards, pensive and downcast. One was the American, Herbert Hoover, Director-General of Allied Relief, a man who had constantly urged the lifting of the blockade. 'Within a few blocks,' he recalls, 'I met General Smuts and John Maynard Keynes . . . We seemed to have come together by some sort of telepathy. It flashed into all our minds why each was walking about at that time of morning.' 'The Conference', reflected Keynes, 'has led us into a bog which it will take more statesmanship to lead us out of than it has taken adroitness to lead us in.'

Representatives of 27 nations were assembled in the dining-room of the Trianon Palace Hotel, at Versailles, the former Allied headquarters, and rose to their feet when, on the stroke of three, the German delegation was ushered in. Count Ulrich von Brockdorff-Rantzau, Foreign Minister and chief of the delegation, pale, drawn and chain-smoking, showed obvious signs of strain as he took his seat. Facing him, at the centre of a semi-circular row of tables enclosing the Germans on two sides, sat Clemenceau; on his right, Wilson and Lansing; on his left, Lloyd George and Bonar Law. Clemenceau wasted little time on diplomatic niceties. Rising to his feet, he opened the proceedings with an icy brevity and, from the French point of view, a certain classic sense of occasion. 'This is neither the time nor the place for superfluous words,' he told the Germans. 'You see before you the accredited representatives of the Allied and Associated Powers, both small and great, which have waged without respite for more than four years the pitiless war that was imposed on them. The time has come for a heavy reckoning of accounts. You have asked for peace. We are ready to grant it to you.' 'I must of necessity add,' he continued, 'that this second Peace of Versailles which is now to be the subject of our discussions, has been too dearly bought by the peoples represented here, for us not to be unanimously resolved to use all the means in our power to obtain every lawful satisfaction that is due to us.' 'There will,' he reminded them, 'be no verbal discussion, and observations must be submitted in writing. The plenipotentiaries of Germany will be given fifteen days in which to submit their written observations on the entire treaty.' The large white folio volume, containing the conditions of peace, was formally presented to Brockdorff-Rantzau, who, says Riddell, 'received it with a stiff little bow', and requested permission to take the floor.

The company fell silent and all eyes were fixed upon him. How would he respond, the representative of the new Germany, in this first direct overture by a German statesman since before the war? Count Brockdorff-Rantzau was a diplomat and an aristocrat; but at this all-important encounter, where appearances were of the essence, appearances were against him, for he displayed none of the ease or suavity of his calling, and all the unbending hauteur of his caste. His very name suggested to English ears the villain of a novel by Anthony Hope. 'Brockdorff-Rantzau', noted Hankey, 'is a most sinister-looking person, an incarnation of the whole Junker system. I can imagine no more typical exponent.' As for appeasing that assemblage of victors, Talleyrand himself might have quailed at the task. The situation required every ounce of delicacy and tact, the one occasion on which he would be permitted to address the Big Three. Whether delicacy and tact would have been of any avail, is a matter of speculation: Wilson and Lloyd George at least were apparently willing to lend an impartial ear. Brockdorff-Rantzau had prepared two alternative speeches, the one mollifying and co-operative, the other a dignified but unequivocal protest. Taking his cue from Clemenceau, he chose the latter. The decision did more credit to his patriotism than his diplomacy. He ignored Talleyrand's most elementary counsel: *Surtout jamais trop de zèle.* 'At the start,' wrote Philip Kerr, 'everybody felt a little sympathy with the Hun, but by the time Brockdorff-Rantzau had finished, most people were almost anxious to recommence the war.' It was hardly an exaggeration.

'We are under no illusions,' Brockdorff-Rantzau began, 'as to the extent of our defeat and the degree of our powerlessness. We know that the strength of German arms is broken. We know the intensity of the hatred which meets us, and we have heard the victor's passionate demand that as the vanquished, we shall be made to pay, and as the guilty, we shall be punished.' He went straight to the question of war-guilt. 'We are required to admit', he said, 'that we alone are to blame for the war: such an admission on my lips would be a lie.' He was, he assured the Allies, 'far from seeking to absolve Germany from all responsibility for this World War, and for its having been waged as it has.' Nevertheless, 'we emphatically deny that Germany, whose people were convinced that they were waging a war of defence, should be burdened with sole responsibility.'

The origins of the war, he pointed out, could not be confined to the immediate events of July 1914, but were rooted in the imperialist rivalries of the previous half-century. Crimes had indeed been

5. Count Brockdorff-Rantzau (George Grosz, 1921): 'Insolent beyond description' – Lloyd George.

committed. But 'Germany was not the only one who erred'. He recalled 'the hundreds of thousands of non-combatants who have perished since November 11th because of the blockade. . . . Remember that, when you speak of guilt and atonement'. He proposed the setting-up of a neutral commission to investigate, in objective and scholarly fashion, the whole question of responsibility for the war. He reminded his listeners that peace had been promised on the basis of the Fourteen Points and the Lansing note, 'principles binding on you as well as on us'. Germany confirmed her full liability for civilian damage in Belgium and occupied France: 'We solemnly accepted the obligation, and are determined to carry it out.' Germany would fulfil its obligations, 'if the agreed bases of the peace remain unshaken'.

Not only was the content of Brockdorff-Rantzau's speech inopportune. His manner of delivery also lost him whatever sympathy he might otherwise have evoked. The Count spoke in German. His tone was curt and rasping. The phrase 'would be a lie' – *wäre eine Lüge'* – was pronounced with an air of bitter defiance. This was unfortunate enough. Worse still was his notorious failure to stand up. This gave rise to considerable and kindly speculation about his state of nerves. In fact, his extraordinary discourtesy was the result of a deliberate decision to remain seated. He refused, as he saw it, to be placed in the invidious position of the prisoner-in-the-dock, so powerfully suggested by the seating arrangements and by the general style of the proceedings. He too had his public, as well as his dignity, to consider.

The effect, however, was calamitous. As for the speech itself, there was something in it to offend everyone. As it was being translated, the Big Three conferred together in angry whispers. Clemenceau and even Bonar Law were visibly flushed. Lloyd George shifted uneasily in his chair. An ivory paper-knife with which he was toying in his irritation, snapped and broke. In the middle of the proceedings, Hughes stalked over to Lloyd George and said: 'Is Clemenceau going to allow this fellow to go on like this?' That evening, Lloyd George told Frances Stevenson that 'he felt he could get up and hit' Brockdorff-Rantzau. 'He says it has made him more angry than any incident of the war . . . For the first time, he has felt the same hatred for them that the French feel.' 'Insolent beyond description,' he told Headlam-Morley the same evening, 'not so much merely in what they said, but the manner in which they said it.'

Wilson too erupted in exasperation. 'The Germans are really a stupid people,' he said on the way out. 'They always did the wrong thing during the war, and that is why I am here. They don't understand human nature. This is the most tactless speech I have ever heard.' Marshal Foch stroked his moustache, and looked knowing, as if to say 'I told you these Germans are incorrigible.' Clemenceau's sense of personal outrage was tempered by the reflection that German stupidity had amply served his purpose, and that Brockdorff-Rantzau's clumsy exhibition, far from driving a wedge between the Big Three, had served to unite them and even to inflame their hostility. Of all the many errors of German policy, the appointment of Brockdorff-Rantzau was, from the German point of view, perhaps the most grievous since the sinking of the *Leinster*. As Talleyrand remarked on another occasion, it was worse than a crime: it was a blunder.

But if there was folly in the manner of the German presentation of their case, there was none in the matter. Few of the terms escaped their trenchant and usually well-justified criticism. But from first to last, from their earliest written comments two days later, until their final pleas for mitigation a week before the signing of the Treaty, their most heartfelt and indignant protests were levelled at the war-guilt clause. The rest, they were prepared to consider – so, at least, they said. But the abandonment of the Pre-Armistice Agreement, the Lansing note rendered illusory, the acknowledgement of collective guilt before the bar of history – that, in honour and conscience, they could never accept.

The Big Three, for their part, were indignant to see their own honour impugned, to be told that they had violated their agreements and broken their promises. On the contrary, they insisted in their formal, written replies, they had been 'constantly prompted' by the Fourteen Points and the Pre-Armistice Agreement, and on this they informed the Germans that they could allow no further discussion. The Germans must confine their remarks to practical suggestions for implementation. Still less were they prepared to discuss the question of war-guilt.

In Britain, however, the tide of anti-Germanism had begun to turn. Even at the time of the Armistice, there had always been a patrician minority – Asquith, Haldane, Milner, the Warden of All Souls, the Archbishop of Canterbury, Lord Buckmaster, Lord Bryce, Lord Lansdowne, Lord Esher, Lord Stamfordham and the King, who privately deplored the hysteria of the election, and vainly attempted to assuage the hurricane of popular passion. In the Upper House, Lord Buckmaster had warned in February against any violation of the Pre-Armistice Agreement. 'I cannot understand any public man,' he declared, 'who desired to show his face in public and state that he was prepared to attempt to extract from an enemy who had laid down their arms on certain conditions, something which the conditions did not justify.' The Liberal press, the *Manchester Guardian*, the *Observer*, the *Daily News*, the *Daily Chronicle* and the *Westminster Gazette*, argued consistently for moderation.

These were voices in the wilderness. Haldane and Milner were denounced as pro-German by *The Times*. Asquith was hooted down. Buckmaster's admonitions in the Lords went unheeded amid the baying for indemnities by the backwoodsmen in the Commons. But the Lower House was out of touch with the changing mood of the country. In the spring, the Government suffered a quick succession of by-election defeats. Most spectacular was the loss of Central Hull, a Tory stronghold for 30 years, where on 11 April a Coalition majority of 10,000 was wiped out by the Asquithian Liberal, Commander Kenworthy. Kenworthy's platform was a pledge to lift the blockade and to secure 'a good, an early and non-revengeful peace.' This was taken by all sides as a warning that the 'hard faced men' were no longer so representative of national feeling. The voters, said the *New Statesman*, had recovered from the post-Armistice 'fit of light-headed aberration' and were flocking back to a traditional 'faith in a broad, progressive Liberalism'. The *Spectator* concurred that the country, 'which is always "Left Centre" in its ideas, agrees with Mr Lloyd George, in so far as it believes him to have been labouring for a peace which shall not sow the seeds of future wars'. The *Observer* struck the true note of sober idealism. 'This country is a country with a conscience,' it declared. 'This country wants, above all things, the clean, the just, the sane peace, the reconciling and enduring peace.'

True, even before the premiminary terms were published, Bottomley was busy mischief-making in the Commons. On 7 May, he asked, 'when the Prime Minister will be here to receive the congratulations of the House on having fulfilled, as he told us he intended to fulfil, his election pledges'. On the publication of the terms, which provoked a fresh eruption of criticism in the Northcliffe press and in Parliament, Bottomley gave notice that he would raise the matter of indemnities at question time. Bonar Law tried privately to dissuade him, on the grounds that it would prejudice negotiations with the Germans. His real concern was the embarrassment it would cause the Government and the line he would have to take in the House. 'In my reply', he wrote to Lloyd George 'I must, of course, justify us on the ground that we have kept our pledges and that the amount is the most Germany could pay.' As he added, however, 'anything of that kind said by a member of the Government must be bad'. But both Bottomley and Bonar Law were out of touch with feeling outside the lobbies.

Publication of the terms in the British press caused general shock and dismay in liberal circles. 'A hard and brutal peace,' wrote Beatrice Webb. This was not what people had been led to expect by the Prime Minister's great speech of 16 April. 'The fundamental question', wrote C.P. Scott in the *Manchester Guardian*, 'is whether we desire a peace of appeasement or a peace of violence'. The *Daily Mail* continued to seethe about reparations; but not even Bottomley wanted more war, and it was clear to the most hardened Germanophobes that, if Germany refused to sign, the Allies would have to march again to impose terms by force. The public, already clamouring for faster demobilization and an end to conscription, was no more reconciled to fresh hostilities against Germany than for the crusade against the Bolsheviks urged by Churchill.

The public was also touched and stirred by reports of civilian famine in the enemy states. Among the first was the Archbishop of Canterbury. Randall Davidson, while free from any taint of vindictiveness, and absolute in condemning the tactics of the Coupon Election, had been critical of what he saw as 'a mawkish spirit which ignores the facts of the last few years'. 'It is to me amazing to find how many good Christian people emasculate Christianity into a sort of sentimental good nature', he complained. A visit to the devastated areas of France and Belgium and the occupied zone of Germany produced sights and impressions which Davidson admitted finding 'solemnising, saddening and suggestive'. The torn fields and shattered cities of Flanders, now silent and strewn with the dismal wreckage of war and the poignant symbols of death – 'whole hillsides of cemeteries, the thousands of small crosses'; the enemy himself in defeat – 'I could not help remembering how depressed-looking had been the German prisoners'; the blockade and its meaning – 'the children do, many of them, look very pinched and white'; the native, unquenchable generosity of the British soldier – 'the children everywhere revelling in our Tommies' kindness and gifts. . . . They *give* food away.' 'All this', the Primate pensively concluded, 'gives, and has given, food for quite new thoughts about international life and human progress, and, in the very largest sense, the duty of man to man.'

At a crowded meeting in the Albert Hall to launch the Save the Children Fund, the audience was shocked by first-hand accounts of starvation in Vienna. In Parliament, Bottomley might discount the sufferings of 'Hun' children as a regrettable necessity; but such cold-blooded cynicism was regarded as bad form, particularly among army officers on duty in the occupied zone and naval officers maintaining the blockade six months after the war had ended. Commander Kenworthy was 'furious with indignation', and the plight of the innocent had a sobering effect generally on those who six months before had joined in the anti-German rampage. The brutality of war had shaken but not shifted the deep roots of English decency. The feeling was well put by a friend of Smuts, Alice Clark, a former suffragette involved in Quaker relief work during the war. 'The English people', she wrote to Smuts, 'are not filled with a passion for vengeance. They do not find it interesting to trample on a beaten enemy. Be very sure that Lloyd George's action is the result of his own weakness, if he goes wrong. He is not helpless before the blind passion of the multitude.' Apart from Northcliffe and Bottomley – 'that little gang . . . noisy froth' – there was no party in England 'who want to starve the Germans or to demoralize them'. The peace, declared Asquith, should be 'a peace of security, a peace of finality'. And this time he was not shouted down.

Even at the time it was possible to see that the die-hards, whom Lloyd George continued to hold in such awe, were for the most part paper tigers – 'an alliance', said Sir Eyre Crowe, 'between scamps, lunatics and ignorant boobies'. Even then it was clear that Colonel Lowther was unbalanced and absurd, that Kennedy Jones was insignificant, that Bottomley was a rogue and Northcliffe an egomaniac; that even Hughes and the Twins were no more than a nuisance, albeit a serious nuisance; and that the pandemonium of the Coupon Election, of which these men were the mouthpiece, was a spent force. 'There is no force in this country worth considering,' wrote Alice Clark, 'which is pushing George from a right settlement. . . . People are not really interested in the terms of peace. They do not understand the details, and will accept whatever Lloyd George tells them is right and fair. Therefore he has no excuse.' The view of a Quaker pacifist is supported by no lesser authorities than Churchill and Walter Long. 'The newspapers', as Churchill told Bonar Law, 'misrepresented the country, and so did the wild men in the House. . . . The country would be quite satisfied.' Walter Long, fiery and irascible, staunchly patriotic and no friend of Germany, was English to the backbone in his honest bluntness. Always a reliable barometer of feeling in the Conservative Party, he had from the first had his doubts about German capacity. Now he wrote to assure Lloyd George that although 'as regards indemnities, no doubt there will be some disappointment', the state of public opinion was 'eminently satisfactory . . . you can confidently rely upon the support of your countrymen.'

Walter Long had reason to vent his spleen on the Germans. His son's death in the war had almost broken him. But neither Long, nor Barnes, nor Bonar Law – whose naturally melancholic spirits were fearfully cast down by the loss of two sons – nor Fisher, with two brothers dead, nor any member of the Government, ever gave way, or would have thought of giving way, to base hatreds. They left that to the Bottomleys and the Northcliffes. In their lack of rancour, their unspoken stoicism, these men were, in their way, fitting representatives of an imperial race; though the very idea would have reduced Walter Long to spluttering incoherence, and the well-known bandana handkerchief would have mopped the familiar rubicund brow.

The great body of the nation, solid, phlegmatic, unimaginative, with no more sympathy for pacificism than for Prussianism, felt in its bones an instinctive disquiet. Cecil was invited to Lambeth Palace. 'The Archbishop wanted to consult me about the Treaty, as to which he is very uncomfortable.' The Primate wished, indeed, to make a public statement at the General Assembly of the Church, but was dissuaded from this as a step which might serve to delay still further the conclusion of peace. With Cecil's approval, however, he unburdened himself in a letter to the Prime Minister: 'I am anxious to deliver my soul, because of the number of communications which are reaching me from really weighty and trustworthy people, . . . people who to a large degree eschew ordinary politics, . . . a great central body which is ordinarily silent and which has no adequate representation in the ordinary channels of the Press.' (In this, the Anglican establishment was at one with the *New Statesman*: 'Seldom', declared the latter, 'have we known public opinion so unanimous, little as it may find utterance in the Press.') The effect of the present peace terms, continued Davidson, was

> to ask impossibilities . . . This view is entertained with almost trembling earnestness by a great many people who have no sort of wish to minimise German wrongdoing. . . . We trust you and your colleagues to succeed in securing a Peace which shall correspond with our purposes in entering the War, which shall be such that we can ask God's blessing upon it.

The Conservative *Spectator*, no friend to Lloyd George, itself defended him against Lowther and the backbenchers, pointed out that there was no need for subterfuge and advised him that on this occasion, honesty really was the best policy. 'Mr Lloyd George's position', it declared, 'is quite strong enough for him to take the perfectly simple course. The vast majority of people recognise that, clear though our right is to demand every penny from Germany, we shall not, as a matter of fact, ever be able to get all that is owed to us.'

At Paris, too, the liberals were making a desperate struggle for the Prime Minister's soul. Smuts, most deeply unhappy, took the lead in canvassing support, buttonholing Botha, Milner, Cecil, Barnes, Balfour and Lloyd George himself. A succession of impassioned memoranda fluttered onto the Prime Minister's desk. 'The terms', complained Barnes, 'seem to be out of character with the aims of the mass of our people.' 'I doubt if English opinion will support the reimposition of the Blockade,' wrote Cecil, 'unless it is very clear that our quarrel with the Germans is thoroughly just. . . . I should feel myself considerable hesitation in starving their children to force them to accept terms, which, as you know, I am by no means sure about myself.' Smuts added his particular and prophetic anxiety that the Germans 'should not merely be made to sign at the point of the bayonet, so to speak. The Treaty should not be capable of moral repudiation by the German people hereafter.' Cecil wrote again, pointing out 'the growing conviction that the Treaty is out of harmony with the professed war aims [of the Allies]. . . . We were said to be "fighting for peace," engaged in a "war to end war," anxious to "make the world safe for democracy" and so on. . . . I cannot help feeling', he concluded, 'that in these negotiations our moral prestige has greatly suffered.' Churchill lent his voice to conciliation: 'Agree with thine adversary whilst thou art in the way with him,' he advised. 'It seems to me quite natural that they should put forward a series of counter-propositions and we ought to take these up *seriatim* with patience and goodwill and endeavour to split the outstanding differences. In this way we shall get a genuine German acceptance.' Sir Henry Wilson concurred.

The German counter-proposals, a voluminous sheaf of 443 pages submitted on 29 May, Ascension Day, made a formidable impression even on those least disposed to sympathy. 'The document is a very able one,' wrote Bonar Law to Lloyd George, 'and in many particulars is very difficult to answer.' 'A good case, and in several particulars an unanswerable case,' echoed Henry Wilson, who observed that the Germans had not only 'driven a coach and four through our terms', but, in their own, had produced a 'much more coherent . . . set of their own, based on the Fourteen Points'. A most powerful statement of the German case,' Smuts wrote to Lloyd George. 'They raise the point to the very forefront which I have always considered vital, viz., that we are bound by the correspondence of last October and November to make a Wilson peace, that is, one within the four corners of the Wilson points and speeches. This was a solemn international engagement which we must keep. It would be dreadful if, while the war began with a "scrap of paper", it were also to end with another "scrap of paper", and the Allies' breach of their own undertaking.' He had decided not to sign the Treaty 'unless important alterations are made in it'.

Once alive to the resurgence of moderate feeling and the extent of support which it commanded, Lloyd George was in a fever of anxiety to accommodate it. If the terms were too harsh, the Germans would not sign, or might even throw in their lot with the Bolsheviks. If the Germans did not sign, the Allies would have to march again. Lloyd George wished to avoid that at all costs: just as public opinion would not countenance Churchill's crusade against Russia, no more would it look kindly on a resumption of the war against Germany that he had come to Paris to terminate. 'Bring the boys home!' roared Northcliffe. For once he spoke for the nation.

In order to sound the collective opinion of his Cabinet, Lloyd George had summoned from London every member of the Government who could be spared. Smuts, Cecil, Churchill, Birkenhead, Chamberlain, Milner, Montagu, Barnes and Fisher all favoured concession. Travelling out with Chamberlain and Fisher, Montagu noted: 'We were all in agreement that the Germans had made out a case requiring considerable modification of the Treaty.'

On the evening of 31 May, the Cabinet dined with Lloyd George in his apartment. Churchill led the talk, and 'the whole drift of the conversation', recorded Montagu, 'was unanimous'. 'It was amazing', Henry Wilson agreed, 'what unanimity there was in criticizing *all* the terms.' The German counter-proposals, argued Fisher, 'were in themselves the most brilliant treaty that victors had ever imposed upon conquered'. Discussion lasted until midnight and resumed at breakfast next morning, concession again being urged by Churchill, Birkenhead and Montagu. The Prime Minister, according to Montagu, was 'very much impressed'.

Later that morning, the full Empire delegation convened in Lloyd George's flat. 'The strangest thing about the proceeding,' wrote Montagu, 'which was the best discussion I ever remember between so large a body, was the unanimity.' Smuts began with a root-and-branch attack on the terms, reiterating the arguments he had so often urged in private. 'The draft treaty was an impossible document. . . . To sign it would be a real disaster, . . . comparable in magnitude to that of the war itself.' The Allies were bound to make 'a Wilson peace. . . . Let them keep to their agreement.' 'The treaty bristled' with provisions that were both outside and 'inconsistent with the Fourteen Points'. He instanced the occupation of the Rhineland as 'indefensible', the Polish settlement as 'thoroughly bad'. He pressed for a fixed sum on reparations and Germany's admission to the League of Nations 'as soon as the Treaty was signed'. Churchill, for his part, 'implored the Delegation' to give the Prime Minister 'the greatest possible liberty' to conclude what he called a 'split-the-difference peace'. Chamberlain, Birkenhead, Milner and Barnes all spoke for concession.

Lloyd George summed up. The Cabinet wanted concessions on the Polish frontier and the occupation of the Rhineland, Germany's immediate admission to the League, and concessions on reparations. He would expect the fiercest resistance from Clemenceau: 'The French would give up nothing unless they were forced.' He asked for the Cabinet's authority to state that, unless concessions were made, Britain would decline to lend her army for further hostilities or her navy to continue the blockade. There was unanimous agreement.

Lloyd George was now the most powerful Prime Minister in our annals, invested with greater authority for the disposition of European affairs than has ever fallen to the lot of a British statesman. Even allowing for concessions, as Churchill told him, 'already it was the greatest triumph in the history of the world'. His authority freshly renewed by the Cabinet grant of absolute discretion, Lloyd George was empowered to speak and act from a position of unparalleled strength, at a moment when the effect of his words and deeds must be decisive and historic. It was, Botha reminded him, 'exactly seventeen years on that very day that peace was signed in South Africa. On that occasion it was moderation which had saved South Africa for the British Empire: and he hoped on this occasion that it would be moderation which would save the world'.

Thus charged and briefed, the Prime Minister presented Wilson and Clemenceau with his volte-face. 'Public opinion in England', he told them, 'wanted peace, and did not care so very much about the details.' Britain would not renew the war 'without very substantial reasons'. British opinion was much impressed with the German counter-proposals; and of his own delegates, Barnes and Smuts were actually 'refusing to sign'.

On the occupation of the Rhineland, on the Saar, on the Polish frontiers, on Germany's admission to the League, Lloyd George was all for compromise. He even professed himself ready to concede over colonies, provided that France did likewise. On reparations, however, as Cecil noted with surprise, he was 'curiously reluctant to make any changes'. 'He would not', he told Wilson and Clemenceau, 'cut out a single one from the categories of reparation. . . . The German counter-offer was inadequate.' Why, having been given full authority from the Cabinet and the Empire delegation to secure a fixed sum, did Lloyd George disregard his mandate? His brief was clear and unequivocal. Smuts's insistence on a fixed sum had been powerfully supported by Chamberlain, Birkenhead, Barnes and Milner. Chamberlain declared himself 'very strongly of the opinion of General Smuts'. Birkenhead described the naming of a fixed sum as 'obviously both expedient and just', while Milner pointed to its absence as 'the weakest of the many weak points of the Treaty'. Sir George Foster, in what Montagu called 'a very impressive oration', urged Lloyd George to 'make the sum as moderate as possible'. Only two delegates were against change. The first, naturally, was Hughes, though even he went no further than saying that 'he thought it would be most unwise to agree to any alteration', and in Montagu's opinion, 'behaved very well'. The second was Massey of New Zealand, who with what Montagu called 'all his honourable wooden-headedness', spoke out for a hard line; even he, 'at the end, however, said that he would give up a good deal to get a signature'.

There was nothing mysterious in the Prime Minister's 'curious reluctance' to obey the Cabinet's injunctions. The explanation lay in his constant preoccupation with Parliament. 'We shall not be influenced by public clamour', he assured the Archbishop of Canterbury in answer to the Primate's plea, 'if we think that we ought to make concessions to meet the German point of view'. But public clamour, at least that public clamour which emanated from Parliament, was precisely what was foremost in his mind. The House of Commons showed no great interest in the territorial settlement. The new succession-states, with their unpronounceable names and curious shapes, were doubtless worthy things. Self-determination seemed a sensible formula for the avoidance of future strife: even Hughes agreed that it was 'monstrous to put Germans under Polish rule'. On reparations, however, the House had Lloyd George over a barrel. He had promised them indemnity many times over; he must deliver the goods, or at any rate the invoice. Here, therefore, he took his cue from Cunliffe and Sumner.

The Twins remained implacable. The German proposals, Sumner informed him, were 'arrogant' and 'unacceptable'. They 'afford no room for concession or negotiation'. 'No defeated belligerent', he insisted, 'has ever been treated more fairly . . . *No concessions should be made on the Reparation clauses.*' Cunliffe chimed in. The proposals, he wrote, 'should not be entertained'. The German offer of five billion pounds in gold marks 'must certainly not be even considered.' 'The demands of the Allies', he concluded, 'have fallen far short of the German capacity to pay, and I am more than ever convinced that Germany can and will pay the whole of what is demanded, and that without nearly as much interference in her economic life as she so richly merits.'

Against the Twins' verdict, no further appeals, whether from Botha, Cecil, Barnes, Montagu or even Bonar Law, had any effect on Lloyd George. Brooding disconsolately with Keynes, Smuts wryly recalled the Kaffir prayer that God himself should come down to earth instead of sending his son, as it was no time for children. To Lloyd George he wrote one last time, 'to make it quite clear that I cannot agree to anything less than the very drastic course I proposed.' He begged the Prime Minister to 'cut the Gordian knot'.

> I feel deeply that this is no time to mince matters. When you are up against a position so terrible in its possibilities for good and evil, you can only do one thing, even if you fail utterly. And that is the right thing, the thing you can justify to your conscience and that of all other reasonable, fair-minded people. This Treaty breathes a poisonous spirit of revenge, which may yet scorch the fair face – not of a corner of France, but of Europe.

But the next day, Sumner again warned Lloyd George against unravelling the Treaty: 'Any serious alteration of the clauses as they stand reopens the whole of an agreed settlement.' There was no possibility of agreeing a fixed sum 'except at a cost of strife and delay, and then, in the long run, only at the cost of concessions by Great Britain'. 'There is no prospect,' he concluded, 'of agreeing any sum which the Powers could accept, without giving away a great part of what they claim and most of all they have said.' 'The Treaty', he informed the Prime Minister two days later, 'must be signed.'

Sumner's message was reinforced by Northcliffe. Continuously, since April, on Northcliffe's instructions, the *Daily Mail* bore emblazoned across its front page the slogan: 'They will cheat you yet, those Junkers.' On 6 June, a *Times* editorial, headed 'An amazing rumour', spoke of 'the rumours from Paris that the Prime Minister is weakening over the Allied demands in the face of the German counter-proposals. Nothing could be more disgraceful to a British statesman than such weakening; nothing could more fatally impair his credit in this country.'

Thus Lloyd George finally came down on the side of the Twins and against a fixed sum. 'Any figure that would not frighten them [the Germans]', he told Wilson, 'would be below the figure with which he and M. Clemenceau could face their peoples in the present state of public opinion.' It would be 'like asking a man in the maelstrom of Niagara to fix the price of a horse'. Since he was well aware of the view of his Cabinet, and of those representatives of public opinion whom the Archbishop of Canterbury had described as 'really weighty and trustworthy people', by 'public opinion' Lloyd George can only have meant the Twins, Northcliffe, Bottomley and the House of Commons. Smuts wrote:

> The last battle of the war is being fought out in Paris, and we look like losing that battle and with it the whole war. . . . Hankey came this morning to say the Prime Minister *really* agrees with me and is doing his best; why am I so hard on him? etc. etc! You get, however, to a stage where nothing matters except doing the right thing. There is no longer any time for dodges and subterfuges.

A man who does not know his own mind is commonly worsted by one who does; and Lloyd George's last-minute change of tack was implacably opposed by Clemenceau, who had never shifted his basic position. Concession was not the way to make the Germans sign, he argued. Revision of parts of the Treaty would only encourage further demands; a firm refusal would bring speedy compliance. Clemenceau had already gone to the very limit of concession in the cause of Allied unity; for this he was under heavy fire in France. He did not complain of this, but he could go no further without risking the loss of all political credibility with his people, with whom, in any case, he was essentially at one. It was not, he said, a matter of obstinacy or personal ambition: he was an old man; public honours meant nothing to him – but of satisfying France's deepseated and desperate need for security: 'I do not want to do anything to break the spirit of our people.'

Lloyd George found his path blocked not only by Clemenceau – that was to be expected – but also by Wilson. This was an unlooked-for and unwelcome turn of events. But the President, having convinced himself of the essential justice of the terms, was not to be talked out of them by arguments of expediency. If the terms were unjust, they should be modified; but let them not be tampered with because the British were 'afraid the Germans won't sign, and their fear is based upon things that they insisted upon at the time of the writing of the treaty; that makes me very sick'. In the privacy of the Hôtel Crillon he poured forth to the American delegation his contempt for the British Cabinet: 'unanimous, if you please, in their funk.' Wilson had every right to feel irritated, but the plain fact was that Lloyd George, albeit out of pure expediency, was now embattled in defence of Wilsonism – while Wilson, in setting his face against concession, was objectively defending a settlement that bore all the hallmarks of Lloyd Georgeism, a 'peace of shreds and patches', of compromises and 'deals', of those 'arrangements' which Wilson professed to, and indeed did, abominate. Arguing fiercely against a tight-lipped President in favour of a plebiscite in Upper Silesia, to enable the local population to determine for themselves whether they should live under German or Polish rule, Lloyd George protested with every justification, 'I am doing nothing other than abiding by your Fourteen Points'. 'Cannot understand Wilson,' wrote Nicolson. 'Here is a chance of improving the thing and he won't take it.'

Why this strange and seemingly perverse reversal of attitude by the President? Three considerations, it seems, jostled for priority in his mind, each on the side of standing firm. The first was the cohesion of the alliance. The collapse of a united front still seemed to him an eventuality worse even than an unsatisfactory peace. Besides, he respected Clemenceau's reservations, since they were reservations of principle. He was ready to allow concessions, if Clemenceau would agree to them, but he would do nothing to undermine Clemenceau's position. Conversely, the antics of Lloyd George aroused his frank disgust. As a man of principle, he was provoked beyond measure by these unconcealed last-minute shifts of expediency, still unredeemed by any willingness to accept the fixed-sum solution for reparations – indeed, accompanied not only by mutterings about Britain's right to recoup trading losses from Germany but even by the proposal, prompted by Keynes, that the United States should underwrite the payment of reparations. As Lloyd George, with an air almost of truculence, announced his latest, and, as it must have seemed, most

impudent volte-face, the President heard him out with contemptuous stare and set jaw, one foot tapping ominously on the floor. 'Mr
Prime Minister,' he said, after a short silence, when Lloyd George had
finished, 'you make me sick!'

The third inhibiting factor also stemmed from the President's
moral essence. His motive force at Paris was not, as Mr Howard
Elcock argues, some deep-seated hatred of Germany, akin in its
intensity to Clemenceau's, but irrational and inexplicable in its origin.
He was not well disposed to the Germans, certainly – they had seen to
that – but the truth, more complex and more tragic, lay precisely in
his determination to rise above prejudice, to remain, despite everything, in charity with all mankind, showing goodwill towards all and
malice towards none:

> He only in general honest thought
> And common good to all made one of them.

Both the strength and the weakness of Woodrow Wilson derived from
his passionate sense of justice. 'Justice and only justice', he declared
in his first presidential address, 'shall always be our motto.' First of
his five 'Particulars' for peace was 'impartial justice' for all and
'even-handed and dispassionate justice for Germany', 'a justice that
plays no favourites'. 'I am just as anxious', he assured Smuts, 'to be
just to the Germans as to be just to anyone else.' That last weekend, in
what many considered the most memorable of his orations, delivered
at the American war-cemetery at Suresnes, he reaffirmed his fundamental credo, his pledge to keep faith with the living and the dead.
The only questions to be asked, he declared, the only considerations
to be weighed, were 'Is it right? Is it just?'.

But in his mind, more susceptible to wishful thinking than is
common even among the best of idealists, desire and fulfilment
merged indistinguishably in a burning vision of right. He believed in
justice; he had come to Paris to do justice; therefore the Treaty,
steeled and tempered in the fire of his conscience, was just too. 'His
judgments were always right in his own mind,' Lansing reflected
acidly, 'because he knew that they were right. How did he know they
were right? Why, he *knew* it, and that was the best reason in the
world.' His critics, and they were now legion, scorned the syllogism
and derided him as a hypocrite. They were wrong: he was utterly
sincere. There was no trace of disingenuousness in what Clemenceau,
half-mockingly, called the 'noble candour' of his nature. If hypocrisy
came into it at all, it was by that largely subconscious process of

self-deception which Orlando sardonically diagnosed as 'spontaneous hypocrisy'. He took his stand on the justice of the Treaty, and from this stand he was not to be moved. 'If the Germans', he said, 'had had the good sense to say to us: "We are in your hands, but we were not the only ones to blame,"' he might have been inclined to magnanimity. But when they pointed out the inconsistencies between the draft treaty and the Fourteen Points; when, quoting chapter and verse from the Wilsonian gospel, they proved, with shocking directness, that the President had betrayed his principles, they touched him on the raw. Their passionate denials of war-guilt served only to convince him of their incorrigible impenitence and put them beyond the pale. 'Justice', he pronounced 'had shown itself overwhelmingly against Germany.'

The more they disputed their war-guilt, the more they exasperated and alienated him. Of this Brockdorff-Rantzau was clearly unconscious. With vain and pathetic optimism he submitted an elaborate memoir on the diplomatic origins of the war, drawn up with meticulous care by a distinguished team of German scholars. The Big Three waxed indignant: were they to be drawn into an academic disquisition with German professors on a question so eminently self-evident? Was the President of the United States to be addressed as if he were still merely the President of Princeton? It was, did the Germans but know it – and it seems that the German Government did, since it now expressly forbade the presentation of the memoir – another well-meaning blunder, another psychological gaffe. Brockdoff-Rantzau's earlier experience might have taught him that this was not the moment to raise the hackles of the Big Three again. But then, as Wilson had already observed, the Germans always did the wrong thing.

In the inter-war years, historians of distinction were at pains to demonstrate that, in drafting the war-guilt clause, the Big Three intended only to denote Germany's financial liability. The clause was a bill of costs, not a moral indictment. The argument, as has been seen, is partly true: this was indeed the original design of the Big Three. The thesis overlooks one fact, however – a fact not immediately foreseen at the time – namely that whatever construction the Allies might wish it to bear, the Germans would inevitably take it as a statement of their moral culpability at the bar of history. To the Germans – perhaps, too, partly as a result of ambiguities in translation – the financial and the moral elements were both implicit from the start; and now the Big Three themselves did not deny it, but slipped imperceptibly from the narrow construction to the broad. A catalyst in this metamorphosis of meaning was the submission of final reports to the Big Three regarding the trial of war criminals and the indictment of the Kaiser. Coming on top of these, German protestations seemed unpardonably gross. The moral imputation arose, as it were accidentally, through the inadvertence and the immediate preoccupations of the Big Three; but once it impinged itself in their consciousness, they did not disclaim it.

On the contrary, the proclamation of German guilt became a necessity. For Wilson, it was essential to the preservation of his self-esteem. It was the banner which he held aloft as the standard-bearer of justice. It showed the world, and it showed Wilson, that whatever tactical concessions he had been forced to make, he had, after all, remained true to his first and fundamental principle. 'I feel the terrible responsibility of this whole business,' he wrote to Smuts, 'but inevitably my mind goes back to the very great offence against civilisation which the German state committed, and the necessity for making it evident, once for all, that such things can lead only to the most severe punishment.'

For Lloyd George, it was a flag of convenience to wave in the face of his critics: to convince the liberals that the Treaty was fundamentally just, and the reactionaries that it was fundamentally harsh. 'The terms', as he declared, presenting the Treaty to the House of Commons, 'are in many respects terrible terms to impose upon a country. Terrible were the deeds which it requites.' Thus the Prime Minister, while performing his sudden about-turn and pleading for radical modifications in many areas, continued to maintain the same unbending intransigence over war-guilt.

To Clemenceau, the issue was simply another example, predictable and characteristic, of German shamelessness. Only Prussian insolence could ignore the glaring evidence of the war-zone. Invasion, occupation, devastation – these were proof enough for France. As for replying to the German dissertation, he was indifferent. The names of Dr Mendelssohn-Bartholdy, of Count Montgelas, of Professors Max Weber and Hans Delbrück were nothing to him. 'As far as French opinion is concerned,' he said, there is no point, as we are entirely convinced of her guilt.'

Wilson agreed. They could simply reply that 'we do not believe a word of what the German Government says'. Nevertheless it was thought proper that the Allies should have the last word. The final Allied reply to the German counter-proposals, on 16 June, was therefore accompanied by an extensive covering-note, drafted by Philip Kerr. This was glowingly approved by the Big Three as an apologia of the entire work of the Conference, a vindication of the Treaty as the instrument of right. It spoke of Germany's conduct as 'almost unexampled in human history', of 'the terrible responsibility which lies at her door', of Germany's 'gratifying her lust for tyranny by resort to war', of the 'greatest crime, ever consciously committed' by 'any nation, calling itself civilised'.

To the Germans these were terrible words, more searing even than the war-guilt clause itself. To Clemenceau they spelled out truths that the enemy, with characteristic arrogance, presumed to question. To Wilson, they were the emblem of the Treaty as the shield of Justice. To Lloyd George, they might also be turned to other purposes, since, if the Germans refused to sign and the Allied armies had to march once more: 'it might be necessary to stir up public opinion again to a certain extent.'

From this necessity the Big Three were relieved by a dramatic and convenient development, with the scuttling of the German High Seas Fleet at Scapa Flow. This last gesture of suicidal defiance did not lack a certain dignity, a certain Wagnerian grandeur; but like Brockdorff-Rantzau's earlier protests, it served only to harden hostility still further and to hasten the final dénouement. The Big Three saw it, or chose to see it, as the culminating proof, if proof were needed, of German arrogance and perfidy. When, the following day, the German Government announced its readiness to sign the Treaty, with the single exception of the war-guilt clause and the articles providing for the surrender of the Kaiser and his fellow 'war criminals', the Big Three refused outright, Wilson, most adamant of all, demanding 'an unequivocal decision . . . to sign or not to sign'.

A political crisis at once supervened in Germany. The first Government of the Weimar Republic resigned; and Brockdorff-Rantzau and Dr Simons quitted Versailles, to the hisses and stone-throwings of the populace. A request by the new government for a 48-hour delay was unanimously rejected by the Big Three. Two hours before the expiry of the final Armistice, the Allied armies awaiting the word to advance, President Ebert announced Germany's decision to sign under protest – 'yielding to overwhelming force, but without on that account abandoning its view in regard to the unheard-of injustice of the conditions of peace.'

Everyone knows the final set-piece at Versailles. The glittering symbolism of the Hall of Mirrors. The Big Three together for the last time. Wilson. Tall, earnest, professorial. The top hat, the prim pince-nez. The lantern-jaws, still champing on some universal truth. The distant gaze. The wide but worried smile. Was it a peace of justice? It must be, he says later that day, because no one is happy with it. Clemenceau. Short, thickset, dynamic in triumphant repose. The fierce moustache. The sceptical brow. The Mongol eyes, now dull and inscrutable, now blazingly eloquent. The sleek, gloved hand, emphasizing some more earthy reality. *'C'est une belle journée,'* he says, and the eyes fill with tears. *'En êtes-vous sûr?'* mutters Nicolson under his breath. Lloyd George. The little man. Goat-footed, agile, fertile in resource. The large head. The white, bardic locks. The plump, cajoling hands and cadenced, hypnotic rhetoric. The smile – winsome, roguish.

The clock strikes three. Clemenceau: *Faîtes entrer les Allemands.* The German signatories enter, two drab, frock-coated civilians, flanked, in an unusual reversal of stereotypes, by sword-bearing Allied officers, splendidly bemedalled. They tread impassively the parquet floor, their shoes clack-clacking between the rows of silent, staring spectators. Dr Müller and Dr Bell. Tweedledum and Tweedledee. Crop-headed, monocled, expressionless. 'They do not appear as representatives of a brutal militarism,' notes Nicolson. A stiff bow to Clemenceau before signing. And so they play their part. Next Wilson and the Americans. Then the British. Lloyd George, looking, we are told, 'brisk and cheerful'; Bonar Law – 'dour', Balfour, 'smiling almost to the point of hilarity', Milner, 'impassive', and Barnes 'benign'. Then the Empire delegates, including, after all, the reluctant Smuts. Whirring cameras record a general chaos of bustling officials, handshakings, autograph-hunters and jostling, excited crowds. From the grounds, a boom of artillery announces the Treaty of Versailles. Afterwards the Big Three skylark on the terrace amid the bronze and marble deities, the writhing, majestic tritons and mischievous, dimpled cupids. The fountains also play.

Chapter 5

The Peacemakers

We have to enquire how it came about that men who throughout intended and believed that they were acting with strict regard to honour became entangled in a position in which it could be plausibly represented that they were guilty of the grossest violation of every dictate of honourable conduct.

> J.W. Headlam-Morley, *Reparation. A Chapter of a History of the Peace Conference.* Confidential Foreign Office memorandum, 27 June 1922 (Headlam-Morley Papers)

Perhaps what happened at Paris was inevitable, the personalities being what they were.

> Keynes to Bonar Law, 8 December 1919 (Keynes Papers)

In his recent study of the Conference, *Portrait of a decision,* Mr Howard Elcock rightly stresses the impact on peacemaking of personality. The absence of any one of the Big Three must have left its mark on the Treaty of Versailles. If the assassin's bullet that wounded Clemenceau in February had grazed his heart rather than his lung; if Wilson had remained in Washington, as he was so strongly advised, leaving the business of negotiation to House or Lansing; if Lloyd George had been toppled by the backbench revolt; or, to take the characters of second rank, if Germany had been represented by a Balfour, say, instead of a Brockdorff-Rantzau – a different treaty must surely have emerged. Colonel House, it is true, held otherwise. For him, looking back, the day after the signing, Versailles could not have been other than it was. He ranged himself on the side of the disappointed liberals, with Smuts, Cecil and Montagu; but he prided himself above all on his realism. 'While I should have preferred a different peace,' he wrote, 'I doubt whether it could have been made.' It was 'too much to expect of men come together at such a time and for such a purpose'.

6. The Big Three and Balfour (William Orpen, 1919): 'Perhaps what
happened at Paris was inevitable, the personalities being what they were'
– John Maynard Keynes.

This view is not lightly to be dismissed. The Colonel, as has been seen, was not only a close and shrewd observer, but a leading participant in the events which he describes. Not merely was his the guiding hand behind much that went into the Treaty, drawing together with consummate skill and patience the threads of settlement – it is not too much to assert that without his adroit and harmonizing supervision, the Treaty could not have emerged as it did. Here indeed lies the basic objection to the Colonel's view of Versailles. It is significant that *his* objection to revising the Treaty during the final days of negotiation was that, once the terms began to be unravelled, it would be impossible to predict where the process might end. It is difficult not to discern in such reservations not only the Colonel's characteristic and healthy pragmatism, but also a justifiable pride in his own achievement and a reluctance to see his handiwork undone. Colonel House himself provided the living proof that for better or worse, Versaille was indelibly stamped with the different characters of its various authors.

The British Prime Minister was compared by Northcliffe to 'a dishevelled conjurer' and by Orlando to 'a slippery prestidigitator'. The likeness is apt. The war-guilt clause, though politically astute, was after all no more than a confidence-trick, designed, as Nicolson observed, 'solely to please the House of Commons'. Like all conjuring tricks, what the 'Welsh wizard' had performed was based on illusion. The Germans would be hard put to pay what they had agreed to pay, let alone the costs of the war – and Lloyd George knew it. He knew that the war-guilt clause was worthless, a blank cheque signed under duress by a bankrupt, a dud cheque that would never be met. No matter: at first glance it looked like a cheque, and for Lloyd George, living politically from hand to mouth, that was enough. His concern, as Keynes put it, was to 'bring home something which would pass muster for a week'. A week, as has been said by an admiring successor to Lloyd George, is a long time in politics.

As Nicolson noted, article 231 was 'senseless' as well as 'immoral'. Lloyd George clung to it as a fig-leaf to conceal the fact that, in the matter of war costs, he was returning naked from the Conference. Yet to anyone who bothered to take a closer look, the fig-leaf was transparent. Its true purport, as Bottomley complained when the Prime Minister presented the Treaty to the Commons, was the exact opposite of its literal meaning: whatever else Germany might pay, it would not include war-costs. This was explicit in article 232, which recognizing 'that the resources of Germany are not adequate

. . . to make complete reparation for all such loss and damage', confined Germany's liability to 'compensation for all damage done to the civilian population'.

Ostensibly at least, article 232 conformed with what was stipulated in the Lansing note. By adding the war-guilt clause, making the origin of reparations appear tortious or punitive rather than arising from contractual agreement, and introducing the wholly spurious connection between reparations and war-guilt, the Big Three gave Germany the chance to argue that if she could prove she was not responsible for the war, she could not be held liable for reparations either. Lloyd George himself later insisted: 'German responsibility for the war is fundamental. It is the basis upon which the structure of the Treaty has been erected, and if that acknowledgement is repudiated or abandoned, the Treaty is destroyed.' This was precisely the German argument. The war-guilt clause gave a powerful additional boost to German revisionism: it was no coincidence that one of the first acts of the Weimar Republic was to set up a permanent commission of historical inquiry – the 'War-Guilt Department'.

Responsibility lies as much with Clemenceau as with Lloyd George. Clemenceau was no less committed to making Germany pay; indeed he was more so. The French Government, unlike the British, had, during the war itself, promised an indemnity to match that which Bismarck had extorted in 1871. Under pressure of the *revanchisme* of President Poincaré, on the one hand, and on the other of the Chamber of Deputies, from where, throughout the Conference, the cry went forth repeatedly: '*Que l'Allemagne paie d'abord*', Clemenceau authorized the same reassuring and definite reply: '*L'Allemagne payera.*'

But to give Clemenceau his due, he at least never claimed to be a convert to Wilsonism. 'Fourteen points!' he growled. 'God himself only had ten!' For Clemenceau, the objection to Wilsonism was that it defied experience and flew in the face of history. Power, not principle, ruled the world; and the past was ignored at the world's peril. His memories, deeply etched, went back to the Franco-Prussian war. With his own eyes he had seen the smoke curl up from the burning palace of Saint-Cloud. The tramp of jackboots along the Champs-Elysées still echoed in his mind. Clemenceau believed in a Carthaginian peace with every fibre of his being, believed in making Germany pay, even if it killed her – especially if it killed her. That was his policy, the fruit of his experience and the expression of his conviction. For all his laconic scepticism, there was no halfheartedness in his fiercely possessive love of France, at once protective and despairing. Here his integrity burned as bright as Wilson's. Direct, emphatic, he hid nothing – 'always as straight as a die,' noted Hankey. 'I never caught him seeking self-advantage,' wrote House. 'It was France, always his beloved France.' In his weary but clear-sighted and implacable logic, there was no place for magnanimity. Generosity towards a fallen adversary? Sentimental folly. Justice? Justice did not come into it. 'You want to do justice to the Germans,' he told Wilson. 'Do not imagine that they will ever forgive us: they will seek only the chance to obtain revenge.' In the age-old, eternal struggle for supremacy between Gaul and Teuton, there were only winners and losers; and no one knew better than Père la Victoire how close France had come to defeat and at what price she had purchased victory. The democratic trappings of the Weimar Republic, its top-hatted politicians and ideal constitution left him unmoved. He saw only a Germany untouched by invasion, her industries unimpaired, 70 million Germans facing 40 million French. Victory under such odds must be hollow, precarious and short-lived unless rendered sure and solid by impregnable guarantees. If the French frontier were not to be on the Rhine, at least the Rhineland should be demilitarized, at least Germany should be disarmed, at least she should not gain from the war by union with Austria; and at least France would have her reparation. These views stemmed not from rapacity or aggressiveness, as was so often believed in England, but from a profound war-weariness and a sense of insecurity and foreboding all too well founded. The Tiger's roar masked an underlying pessimism. It was the voice, not of Harpagon, but of le Misanthrope: and it was muted in comparison with those of Poincaré, Foch, the Chamber of Deputies and the Paris press.

What of Wilson? Wilson, whatever his failings, put up a stout fight. He took a firm and successful stand against Lloyd George's initial struggle for war-costs, with his forthright telegram from the *George Washington*. At the end of March, however, his resistance crumbled. Deadlock over reparations and other issues of the first consequence threatened to break up the Conference and suggested the inevitability of compromise. The unquiet condition of Europe added the element of desperate urgency. It was a race, as Wilson himself acknowledged, between peace and anarchy.

It was not just that he faced insoluble dilemmas demanding instant solution; not just that his political ideals and his political authority were under fire in the United States; not just that he was almost overwhelmed by the sense of his responsibilities, physically exhausted, and hounded by the French press. He was utterly demoralized, worn down in mind and spirit. If it was personally disagreeable for this polite, even affable Princetonian, to be obliged day after day to oppose his European colleagues, to counter their practical demands with his lofty principles, how deadly was the cumulative effect on his slower, more ponderous academic mind, peppered by the rapid and incessant fire of their intellect. He had looked forward to the Conference, he told House, as 'an intellectual treat'. How appallingly different was the reality. From the safety of the New World, he might, perhaps, have vindicated his principles. Away from the pressures of Clemenceau and Lloyd George, he might, in tranquillity, have tested their arguments against his own, and through the medium of the cablegraph and the instrumentality of Colonel House, have continued to exert his will from the White House as effectively as he had from the *George Washington*. As President of the United States he might have proved invincible. As head of the American delegation in Paris, he was the Innocent Abroad. When, as Colonel House records, 'he stepped from his lofty pedestal and wrangled with representatives of other states upon equal terms, he became as common clay'.

It is unnecessary to postulate, in the manner of Wilson's apologist, Stannard Baker, the notion of conspiracy between Clemenceau and Lloyd George to undermine the President. Wilson's undoing was, in truth, his decision to go to Paris. The moment he set foot in the same room with them, he was doomed, overborne by their infinitely nimbler wits, their irresistibly stronger wills. 'No two people can be half an hour together,' says Dr Johnson, 'but one shall acquire an evident superiority over the other.' Wilson was closeted, day after day, for weeks on end, not with one but with two of the most determined and resourceful politicians in history. Inevitably his morale was destroyed. The wonder is not that he collapsed, but that he held out so long.

When at last he succumbed, with Clemenceau and Lloyd George cawing and cackling like a pair of vultures, it was Colonel House who agreed to the incorporation of the war-guilt clause. But just as the hypothesis of a plot against Wilson by Clemenceau and Lloyd George is redundant, so too Mrs Wilson's image of Colonel House as the betrayer of Wilsonism, the President lying sick and helpless in the next room, is a distortion. House desired compromise and urged it on Wilson. But Wilson, ill though he was, was still his own man. His ratification of House's decision was conscious and deliberate. It was part of the price he felt he must pay for the safe delivery of the League of Nations: God helping, he could do no other. Seldom was the vanity of human wishes to be more cruelly exposed than in Wilson's return to America as a prophet without honour in his own land. In sacrificing the Treaty for the League, he gave up the substance for the shadow. 'A living thing is born,' he announced; but following its rejection by the Senate, the League was stillborn. It was the Treaty, ugly and misshapen, that survived.

'*Il n'y a que le premier pas qui coûte.*' Wilson took the first step when he yielded, at Smuts's persuasion, to the inclusion of pensions in the burden to be charged to Germany. The second step, the sanctioning of the war-guilt clause, though less convoluted in its casuistry, was no less indefensible, and far more disastrous in its ultimate consequences. The President committed grave errors of judgment, the consequences of lack of system and method, never of stratagem or guile – but errors nonetheless.

He then withdrew into an impenetrable spiritual fastness. Once fallen irredeemably from grace, he could not, in his pride of being, admit it, least of all to himself. He would not allow that there was any real inconsistency between the Treaty and the Fourteen Points: none, at least, that could not be smoothed out by the League. He could not descend from his own inner hideout, without acknowledging himself to be a fraud. Secure only in the consciousness of his own rectitude, he pulled up the drawbridge. 'No more changes in the Treaty will be considered,' he declared. 'Here I am. Here I have dug in.' No one, not even Smuts, could tempt him forth. Impervious to further argument, he became as obdurate for the Treaty as it stood as he had previously been adamant in standing by the Fourteen Points.

At the last minute, Lloyd George struggled tenaciously for the President's soul – 'like a Welsh terrier,' said Nicolson. But if his efforts were now unavailing against a Wilson unmoved and immovable, beyond the reach of reason or emotion, who had driven him to this extremity of distraction, had harried and worried him, like a mongrel at a sheep – if not Lloyd George?

In principle, Lloyd George was as fervent a liberal as Smuts. His Fontainebleau memorandum reads like a model of statesmanship. Even his notorious Commons speech of 16 April contains a memorable and moving passage in which he stated the resolve of the peacemakers 'not to soil this triumph of right by indulging in the angry passions of the moment, but to consecrate the sacrifices of millions to the permanent redemption of the human race from the scourge and agony of war'. There is no reason to doubt his sincerity. 'With all his faults,' observed House, 'he is by birth, instinct and upbringing, a liberal.' He fought for a better peace; he even secured some marginal improvements; and doubtless he would gladly have jettisoned the war-guilt clause too, if only he felt he could. Unfortunately, he could not bring himself to throw away what he saw as the lifeline to his political survival.

The immediate obstacle to a reasonable settlement by Lloyd George was the attitude of Hughes, Cunliffe and Sumner. Their stony insistence on the astronomical sums which they had conjured up out of nowhere deterred the Prime Minister from giving official sanction to the more realistic figures recommended by Keynes and Montagu: figures supported by the rest of the British and the entire American delegation, figures with which Lloyd George privately agreed, and which Clemenceau and the Germans themselves were willing to endorse. It was, Lloyd George asserted many times, 'the most baffling problem in the Peace Treaty'. His inability to shift his reparations delegates forced his hand. He dared not ignore them, as he told House, for fear of being 'crucified' in England. Writing to Keynes, later in the year, to congratulate him on the success of his *Economic Consequences of the Peace*, Austen Chamberlain observed: 'You ignore in your book the part played by Lord Cunliffe and Lord Sumner. . . . How could Lloyd George, or anyone else, definitely reject advice tendered on such high authority?'

Certainly, the Prime Minister's task was made no easier by the presence of Hughes, Cunliffe and Sumner, hovering and screeching at his back and breathing down his neck like three voracious harpies. Their attitude throughout the Conference was one of flint-like obduracy. Hughes's opinion had long been public knowledge. Well before the Armistice, he was the clamorous instigator of the campaign to make Germany pay, voicing his dissatisfaction with the Lansing note and warning that Australia would not be bound by it. It is not to depreciate Australia's contribution to the war-effort to note the disproportionate influence exerted by Hughes in the Imperial War Cabinet and on the Prime Minister himself, a 'poisonous influence', observed Thomas Jones. Yet this was the man whom Lloyd George made chairman of the Committee on Indemnity, whose report he later described as 'a wild and fantastic chimera'. Sumner, for his part, made little pretence to the standards of impartiality that might have been expected of a distinguished judge. He made no secret of his outspoken anti-Germanism. Warned by Lloyd George that too much severity might push Germany into Bolshevism, Sumner, according to Lloyd George, replied: 'In that case the Germans will cut each other's throats, and I couldn't ask for anything better.' As Lloyd George not unreasonably observed to Wilson and Clemenceau: 'A discussion with a person in that state of mind is not much use.'

On the other hand, it is evident that Sumner saw his role not as a judicial one, but as that of an advocate for British interests. The British representatives, he wrote, 'are delegates, not judges. . . . They must be prepared to give full weight to considerations of policy. . . . It is not their business to temper justice with mercy.' Sumner fulfilled his brief out of genuine, though narrow, patriotism. Cunliffe was another strange choice. He had proved so autocratic as Governor of the Bank of England during the war, that Bonar Law had actually forced his resignation. His hectoring manner at Paris concealed an occasional willingness to see reason. From this tendency, however, he was propelled back into extremism by his seething hatred of Germany and his reliance on Sumner, from whom he was inseparable. 'Did you know Cunliffe?' Cecil said later to Thomas Jones. 'He had courage and tenacity, but no intellect; and as for Sumner, have you not observed that some very able lawyers can be very cruel men?'

Why, then, did Lloyd George appoint such men in the first place? Why did he not take with him to Paris, instead of Sumner, a lawyer of the standing and broad outlook of Buckmaster, Haldane, Edward Grey, or, as the King urged, Asquith? Had any of these been on the Reparations Commission, it may be doubted whether the chicane that produced the war-guilt clause would have been tolerated for one moment, and questioned whether the Treaty itself might not have been an instrument of a very different order. 'It is a thousand pities', wrote Fisher, 'that Asquith was not among them.' Why, if the Prime Minister felt that he could not enlist these Liberals, did he not invoke the moderating authority of his own Lord Chancellor, Birkenhead, and ask the 'Keeper of the Public Conscience' to prevail upon the refractory Sumner? Or why did he not appoint Keynes to the Commission, at least as the equal of the economically illiterate triumvirate? 'I do not believe', writes Keynes's biographer, 'that the upshot would have been quite the same had Keynes been on the Commission, representing the Chancellor of the Exchequer. Had he been a co-equal member with Sumner, speaking with the authority of the Chancellor, Sumner would have had to give close attention to his views. Sumner may have been a bigot, but he was also a judge, and thereby trained to listen to arguments.'

Lloyd George's choice was political. Hughes was an outspoken imperialist and protectionist, popular with the Conservatives. The Prime Minister appointed him to the Committee on Indemnity in order to stem his embarrassing public outpourings and to divert them into the private channels of an advisory board. Cunliffe, wrote Keynes, 'was not brought in as an expert: for who that knows him could suppose that his opinion as to Germany's capacity to pay was of the slightest value? He was brought in for electioneering and parliamentary purposes; and for parliamentary and press purposes he and Lord Sumner were retained. The Prime Minister was never under the slightest illusion as to the value of their advice'. Keynes's verdict, which might otherwise seem jaded, is confirmed by the account of Cunliffe himself, who admitted all along that his original and crucial estimate of German capacity had been 'little more than a shot in the dark, as he had been pressed to arrive at it between a Saturday and a Monday'. Such was the trio which Lloyd George presented to Parliament and the public as 'a very strong committee' and 'singularly able men'.

Lloyd George's strategy was to hedge his bets. He backed Hughes and Cunliffe during the election in order to ease himself back into power on the cry of 'make Germany pay'; and he took them and Sumner with him to Paris to keep the backbenchers happy in the belief that British interests were being jealously guarded. Meanwhile, he kept Keynes in reserve to argue for sensible figures when it came to serious negotiation. What he did not foresee was the parliamentary hurricane, whipped up by Northcliffe at the end of March, which created for Hughes and the Twins an importance wholly disproportionate to their expertise and even to their official capacity. The Committee on Indemnity, after all, was subordinate to the Imperial War Cabinet, and both were purely advisory and subject to the War Cabinet proper.

Why, then, did the Prime Minister not do as Davis recommended: 'Get rid of them by winding up the Commission,' and 'start afresh . . . with some human beings', like Keynes? It was easier said than done. Lloyd George was hoist by his own petard. How could he, as Keynes admitted, 'persuade the Commission to commit hari-kiri' or simply ignore it? Not even Lloyd George, for all his political agility, felt that he could get away with that. His skills were those of the juggler, not the acrobat. He could keep two balls in the air simultaneously, but he could not change horses in midstream, not at least in the merciless glare of Northcliffe's publicity, without coming a cropper. 'I never believed in costly frontal attacks, either in war or politics,' he wrote in his *Memoirs*, 'if there were a way round.'

Some historians stress the unbalanced, 'shell-shocked' atmosphere of Paris. Certainly, Wilson had cause to regret his choice of venue. It would have been more auspicious had the Conference been held in some neutral capital, away from the acrid, all-pervasive miasma of war and from what he called 'exaggerated feelings and exaggerated appearances'. With the nearby battlefields the scene of weekend visits by the Big Three, the ghosts of the myriad dead lowered over the capital, making German denials of war-guilt seem further proof of mocking recalcitrance. It may be doubted, however, whether fixing the Conference at Geneva, Lucerne or some other tranquil littoral, would have made any real difference to the policy of Lloyd George. The atmosphere to which he was most keenly alive was the atmosphere of Westminster.

Others stress the unhealthy state of public opinion and blame parliamentary pressure. Observers like Nicolson present Lloyd George as 'a British liberal at the mercy of a jingo Commons and a jingo press'. The political crisis at the end of March made it impossible, it is said, for Lloyd George to bring home the sort of peace he would have liked, or indeed to conclude peace at all, without some sacrifice. Nicolson questions 'whether any British statesman then alive could, given the state of public opinion at home, have achieved, or rather have avoided, so much'.

According to this view, which commends itself to the weight of historical opinion, Lloyd George was a victim of the *Zeitgeist*, of the spirit of what Nicolson calls 'that year of anguish 1919', carried away against his will by the prevailing and irresistible current of vengefulness. Lloyd George himself argued as much to Colonel House. He had not, he said, 'purposely misled the English people', but 'somehow, during the recent elections, there was a perfect groundswell for the Germans to pay for the cost of the war, and while he knew it was an impossibility to realise such expectations, he followed, and was one of the most vociferous of the lot, in demanding that the cost of the war should be paid by Germany.'

The historians lament, in effect, that the time was out of joint, that judgment had fled to brutish beasts and men had lost their reason. But Lloyd George was not 'shell-shocked'; he did not lose his head when all around were losing theirs. He was not carried away, but carried up and along by the groundswell. To a recent American historian, 'his real error was perhaps in underrating his own prestige and power in the hour of victory. Instead of bending with popular passion and seeking to evade its impact, he might have elevated British public opinion to an ethical level compatible with his own genuine moderation'. He might indeed: and it is inherently unlikely that such a master of the arts of persuasion was in genuine doubt about his ability to sway opinion.

Nor, if Lloyd George declined to come clean, is there any question of lack of courage. Whatever his faults, his whole career suggests that faint-heartedness was not one of them. In the black days of the Ludendorff Offensive, he had rallied the nation's spirits with dauntless and cheerful buoyancy. It was not that he did not dare: he did not choose. His suppression of the truth was deliberate. He had no intention of jeopardizing his career at the moment of his greatest triumph. In his appearance before the Commons on 16 April, he had the golden opportunity to disengage himself from his election pledges, to pass them off as platform oratory, to cast the blame on his advisers, or to take responsibility on himself, in one of those displays of apologetic frankness which, whether candid or calculated, seldom fail to move the House. He chose on the contrary to pledge himself again, irrevocably and up to the hilt.

The arguments of his apologists would be more convincing had the ineluctable tide of extremism of which they complain not been summoned up for his own purposes by Lloyd George himself. He pleaded in retrospect the futility of playing the role of Canute. Was he then the Sorcerer's Apprentice, who, having conjured up the flood which swept him back into power, was impotent to stem it? The truth is otherwise: he was not the Sorcerer's Apprentice, he was the Sorcerer. He could by a word have broken the spell; he chose not to, for fear of provoking another tempest that might sweep him out again. It came ill from Lloyd George to deprecate the 'too fierce ardour of an expectant public', since no one had fanned the flames more energetically than he himself.

Nor, in the last resort, was that public opinion, which is held to justify so much shabby duplicity, quite the Pandora's box it is made out to be. The election campaign indeed was rank and fetid; but the election itself, far from being a Walpurgisnight, was particularly quiet, and the poll was the lowest on record. The Bottomleys and the Northcliffes maintained themselves in a lather of frenzy throughout the Conference but, as spring passed to summer, the popular storm soon blew itself out: people at large turned to other concerns and seemed to want only to have done with the Conference and enjoy the peace.

The Conservative backbenchers may have been extreme, hard-faced, ignorant or puerile – a 'pack of ninnies', as Sir Eyre Crowe complained. They were, at any rate, honest, in that they genuinely believed in Britain's right to make Germany pay. Colonel Lowther, after all, had not been privy to the formulation of the Lansing note; Colonel Guinness had not scrutinised the meaning of 'civilian damage'. They took the Government's word for it. If the Commons believed in making Germany pay, who had led them to think so? 'What authority had we for giving those pledges?' asked Lieutenant-Commander Astbury. 'We had the authority of the Prime Minister.' If when, by a word, he could have disabused them, he chose not to, it was hardly for him to complain that he was a victim of their extremism. Nor were the backbenchers the agents of some irresistible wave of capitalist reaction. Brigadier-General Page-Croft, of the minuscule right-wing 'National Party', and Colonel Lowther, for all that he was founder of the Anti-Socialist League, were no capitalists: their ideas of reparation were crude to the point of fantasy, ridiculed both by Keynes and Bonar Law. They harboured the wildest suspicions of the City and of international finance, and resented Cunliffe only slightly less than they did Wilson. Lowther was simply the *reductio ad absurdum* of that native, xenophobic and thoroughly honest toryism, prevalent far beyond the confines of the City, which felt in common justice that Germany should pay for her misdeeds and be rendered harmless to repeat them.

The Congress of Vienna was held out to the British delegation as a horrendous example of secret diplomacy, dictated at the arbitrary fiat of aristocrats, who determined the destinies of Europe on their own authority and according to their own reactionary prejudices, indifferent to the wishes of the peoples of whose future they so cavalierly disposed. But there were advantages in that Old World diplomacy denied to an age of universal suffrage. In the days of Castlereagh, Metternich and Talleyrand, it was possible for statesmen to agree on far-reaching decisions without the continual need to lend an ear to public murmurings or the cavils and importunities of the press; and in their virtually unfettered discretion, to produce settlements which reconciled the practical exigencies of national self-interest with the more enlightened principles of European concord.

For the Big Three, it was otherwise. They wielded supreme

executive power, but throughout the Conference they remained at the beck and call of popular assemblies capable at any moment of engineering their downfall. The Paris Peace Conference, in Churchill's words, was 'a turbulent collision of embarrassed demagogues', periodically obliged to descend from the summits of the Supreme Council into the market-place, and to have recourse to those devices of cajolery or persuasion in which the art of politics principally consists. Indeed, it was Wilson's disdain for this vital political element that led in the end to his own undoing. Instead of conciliating his Republican opponents and making friendly overtures to Senator Borah or Senator Lodge; instead of undercutting them, by inviting Senator Taft or Senator Root to serve, as they might well have done, on the American delegation; instead of meeting some of their objections, as Colonel House implored, in order to wrest at least half a loaf from Congress – the President gathered around his shoulders his protective mantle of self-righteousness, taking refuge from criticism in the unassailable conviction of his own integrity, of the self-evident justice of his cause, of the transcendent loyalty of the American people and of the ultimate sanction of that Democracy for which the world had been made safe. 'America has taken much from me,' he said of the League of Nations; 'this too she will take.' But he was wrong. The Senate's refusal to ratify the Treaty came in large part because Wilson was 'too proud to fight'. The stricken President died, as he lived, a martyr to the doctrine of justification by faith.

Can it be altogether wondered that Lloyd George, at least, ever conscious of the basic precariousness of his own position, lacked the serenity and detachment conducive to a more lasting settlement? 'I am doubtful', he told the House of Commons, 'whether any body of men with a difficult task have worked under greater difficulties – stones clattering on the roof, and crashing through the windows, and sometimes wild men screaming through the keyholes.' Time and again, when urged by Wilson to take a broad, a generous line, he pointed to the watchful, suspicious eyes of his backbenchers, and appealed, not in vain, to the President's understanding.

Lloyd George's sense of vulnerability was underscored by his very real isolation: his isolation from the organized support, material and moral, of a permanent party machine. His breach with the Asquithians was deep and seemingly mortal. His arrangement with the Conservatives, at least as far as the majority of backbenchers were concerned, was little more than a marriage of convenience. He was sensitive, oversensitive indeed, to the risk of offending them. Ironically, for a man who aspired to a role of national leadership, above party or faction, he was more alert to party pressures than conventional politicians, knowing himself to be, in essence, performing on dangerously thin ice.

Democracy, certainly, and the constraints of the party system, hardly provide an ideal seed-bed for the nurture of a wise diplomacy. Yet the image of Lloyd George as the helpless myrmidon of the House of Commons surely contains a fallacy. According at least to our most respected constitutional authorities, the politician is the people's representative, not its delegate – the servant, not the slave, of the electors. Certainly, he is answerable for his trusteeship, and Parliament can repudiate his actions and demand his resignation. What he may not do, in a matter of principle, is to plead the ignorance or prejudice of his supporters against his own better judgment.

To Lloyd George, such nice scruples were the merest sentiment. 'If you want to succeed in politics,' he chuckled to Riddell, 'you must keep your conscience well under control.' For him, the first rule of politics was at all costs to maintain himself at the top of the greasy pole. The politician, he explained, 'has got to keep afloat in order to give effect to his principles'. But what *were*Lloyd George's principles? What were the ends, towards which he alternated such serpentine deviousness with such audacious brio?

To penetrate the character of Lloyd George – 'our mercurial, tricky Prime Minister', as Smuts called him – baffled contemporaries. To Northcliffe, who aptly described him as a 'chameleon', he was 'oblique, evasive and Welsh. . . . You never know what he is up to'. The kaleidoscopic array of attitudes assumed by Lloyd George in 1919 leaves the historian no less bemused. A succession of masks, whipped on and off: the statesman of vision and forbearance who penned the Fontainebleau memorandum; the stern advocate of retribution, who justified the Treaty's severity like the Ancient of Days – 'terrible were the deeds which it requites' – the friend of Wilsonism and the League of Nations; the jingo patriot, who vowed to search German pockets 'to the uttermost farthing'; the radical, siding with the working classes against the plutocrats who sought Germany's ruin. Which, if any, was the real Lloyd George?

Was he, as Baldwin believed, that 'very terrible thing' – 'a dynamic force' – an elemental, self-justifying phenomenon of nature, an iridescent shooting-star of words, a fathomless ocean of guile, now blue, as Fisher noted, now green? To Keynes, the secret of Lloyd George was indeed that there was no secret: 'Lloyd George is rooted in nothing; he is void and without content.' To Smuts, too, he was 'unstable, without any clear guiding principle. . . . One never knows the orbits of minds like his'.

Was he a natural cork afloat on the ocean of events, 'swayed by his surroundings', as C.P. Scott put it, a sphinx without a riddle? Or, as Philip Kerr suggested, a deep practitioner of *Realpolitik*, donning from his immense repertoire a role for every occasion and every taste; Machiavelli's complete politician, devious in method, unswerving in purpose; the deft manipulator, the illusionist, to whom other men are as instruments, to be variously won over according to their weaknesses; 'a past master in craft', as Frances Stevenson told him to his grinning face?

Certainly, his lack of principle, instinctive perhaps rather than systematic, was one clue to his peculiar success. The statesman, according to La Bruyère, 'is never the dupe of his own phrases'. Words to him are but the common coin of politics. 'To Lloyd George,' wrote Beaverbrook, 'no policy was permanent, no pledge final.' 'It always amuses me', wrote Colonel House, 'to have Lloyd George say [that] he has done this or that or the other for political effect, but that he really knows better. He does not seem to have any ingrown sense of right or wrong, but only looks at things from the standpoint of expediency.' Shakespeare's ideal princes are men, 'who moving others, are themselves as stone'. 'He could charm the birds off a branch,' wrote Thomas Jones, 'but was himself always unmoved.'

Was the Lansing note itself, perhaps, part of a Machiavellian ploy? The suspicion remains only a hypothesis, but one which deserves consideration. When, at the Allied Conference of 3 November, 1918, Lloyd George advised the Belgian Prime Minister against including an indemnity in the armistice agreement, his words were: 'I think it will be a mistake to put into the armistice terms anything that will lead Germany to suppose that we want a war indemnity.' Is it not possible that his meaning was, not that it would be wrong to demand an indemnity, but that it would be imprudent to indicate before an armistice was concluded, that an indemnity might subsequently be demanded?

The conjecture gains in plausibility with his advice as to the meaning of the all-important phrase 'damage done to the civilian population'. 'When you get the armistice and the bridgeheads on the Rhine,' said Lloyd George, 'you can interpret this as you like.' Was the Lansing note, then, in Lloyd George's eyes no more than a *ruse de guerre*? The possibility of fraudulent intentions towards the Germans is paralleled, though not necessarily confirmed, by the web of disingenuousness with which, in the view of Dr Trevor Wilson, Lloyd George was simultaneously deluding his Liberal supporters at home. The contrast between the ideals proclaimed to the pre-election gathering of Liberals the day after the Armistice and the pledges held out to the electorate at the hustings a fortnight later, reflects, according to Dr Wilson, not some sudden change of heart or switch of policy, but on the contrary the fulfilment of a policy, a policy of premeditated guile. Whether his actions are to be attributed to such deep-laid schemes, or to the more innocent and widely held explanation that Lloyd George's left hand commonly ignored the doings of his right, there indubitably hovered around his words a peculiar and characteristic ambivalence, equally convenient to the casual opportunist or to the long-term strategist.

The image of Lloyd George as the pupil of Machiavelli, however, is only one side of the picture. It contains all the attraction of logic; it omits the vital element of paradox, inconsistency and emotion. Lloyd George was every inch the political animal, frisking to the thrill of the game. His ruling passion was a passion for brilliant improvisation. It was not simply that the ends justified the means: the means justified themselves. He enjoyed playing Machiavelli far too much to be a genuine Machiavellian. The mark of the political genius, he told Riddell, is that 'faced by a novel and difficult situation, he extricates himself by adopting a plan which is at once daring and unexpected'. He was out to win, of course; but as much as the victory, he relished the challenge of the game for its own sake, not least the dazzling contrivances and vertiginous contortions that made him a political Houdini, 'a greased marble spinning on a glass table-top', as an American noted. He looked back on the Conference as the happiest period of his life. 'It has been a wonderful time,' he said to Riddell, as their train steamed homeward out of Paris. He had, after all, played upon the world stage. 'He was giving the law to Europe,' recalls Beaverbrook, 'fixing the boundaries of all the nations, giving out encouragement to some countries and severely reprimanding others. He was the arbiter of all Europe.'

It was the greatest show on earth, a world Eisteddfod, and Lloyd George – 'the little Welsh conjurer', Beatrice Webb called him – was, as she noted, not merely a conjurer, but an 'actor-conjurer' of protean versatility. His powers of mimicry were thought uncanny by those privy to his imitations of Mr Asquith drunk or President Wilson sober. He was also playwright and spectator: he was Shakespeare,

Falstaff, Iago and the groundlings in one, revelling in his delectable, self-generating cunning and agility. 'Figaro here, Figaro there,' muttered Clemenceau during a performance of *The Barber of Seville*, 'he's a kind of Lloyd George.' Carried away by the exuberance of his own virtuosity, he could not always resist the temptation to improvise: he played to the stalls and to the gallery. He was, noted Cecil, 'always scoring'. Inevitably, his improvisations led him some distance from the script. He was not, wrote Amery, 'deliberately inconsistent or untruthful. But living entirely in response to the immediate stimulus, he had no clear memory either of past events or of his own former motives'. His élan, his flair, his extraordinary range of eloquence and invective made him easily the master of the Commons. His speech of 16 April remains a *tour de force* of parliamentary oratory: it leaps from the pages of Hansard with scintillating verve. But superb though it was as a political triumph, it was not, of course, an explanation, but an obfuscation of his policy, a tissue of deceit, a stupendous bluff, another inspired improvisation, another stunt. Compared with Wilson's prophetic vision of the world as it might be, or with Clemenceau's tragic vision of *le monde comme il va*, the brilliant 'cleverness' of Lloyd George – *splendide mendax* – falls surely below the level of events. As for his own level, did he fall below that, or did he find it? It was more than just a question of tactics. The impish outsider, taking his bow in the full flush of victory and the self-attracting magnetism of his Welsh *hwyl*, could not resist outdoing Bottomley in deceit and Northcliffe in enormity. Did he perhaps revel in the thought of making fools of the Conservatives? Was it fun for this Celtic Till Eulenspiegel to hoodwink those solid, unsuspecting Englishmen, whom he both admired and despised? 'One catches in his company', wrote Keynes, 'that flavour of final purposelessness, inner irresponsibility.'

It was not Bottomley, but Lloyd George, who more closely resembled the character of Mr Toad. 'The driver's seat', wrote Beaverbrook of the Prime Minister, 'was, as he believed, his rightful place. He clung to the wheel.' Was there not a side of Lloyd George curiously suggestive of the jaunty, feckless, road-hogging Toad, in whom, writes Kenneth Grahame, 'as if in a dream, all sense of right and wrong, all fear of obvious consequences, seemed temporarily suspended'?

Thirty-eight years before, when the unknown stripling from Llanystumdwy first clapped eyes on the House of Commons, he confided to his diary a burgeoning ambition. 'I will not say', he wrote, 'but that I eyed the assembly in a spirit similar to that in which William the Conqueror eyed England on his visit to Edward the Confessor – as the region of his future domain. Oh vanity!' Now, as Prime Minister, returning in triumph to London after the signing of the Treaty, he was met by the King-Emperor at Victoria Station, and rode with him in the royal carriage to Buckingham Palace, an unprecedented mark of favour. Someone in the cheering crowds tossed a wreath of bay leaves into the carriage. 'This is for you,' said the King. When Lloyd George rose in the Commons to present the Treaty, the members leaped to their feet to acclaim him, shouting and waving their order-papers in a personal ovation, the like and length of which the Mother of Parliaments had never beheld.

Just as House and Lansing foresaw that Wilson would inevitably fail at Paris, so Foreign Office professionals, like Hardinge, feared that Lloyd George would succeed only too well. If war, as Clemenceau said, was too serious a business to leave to the generals, to entrust peacemaking to a politician like Lloyd George seemed to them like playing with fire. It was not his ignorance of Europe that mattered, for with the virtual transfer of the Foreign Office to Paris, he did not want for expert advice. Indeed, there was an abundance of information at his disposal; so that though, as he admitted, he had never heard of the Duchy of Teschen, and did not know that Luxemburg was a duchy, he was quick to master his brief – and besides, his better instincts told him unerringly where Europe's long-term interests lay. No professional could have penned a wiser prognosis than the Fontainebleau memorandum. It was not his judgment, but his character that was fundamentally unsuited to the business of peace.

What controls, what restraining influences were exerted on the Prime Minister by his Cabinet colleagues? They knew his faults and his temptations. It must be remembered that Lloyd George in 1919 was at the height of his power and prestige: his energy and sparkle still poured forth inexhaustibly, and his war-time ascendancy continued to exert its momentum over the Imperial War Cabinet. Thus Balfour's policy of 'a free hand for the Little Man' enabled Lloyd George to run the peace as he had run the war.

The Foreign Secretary was no cipher, and his contributions to peacemaking, particularly during Lloyd George's absence in London, were not slight. His drooping exterior masked an intellect which, when he found a topic on which to whet it, was taut and incisive. But these interventions were rare and capricious. More often, it was his peculiar whimsy to light on some random issue, and to weave around it a complex dialectical tracery. *'Pour ou contre?'* smiled Clemenceau after one such gossamer disquisition. It was seldom on a question of principle, however, that he chose to rouse himself from his more customary torpor. He had rightly predicted that the Conference would be 'a rough-and-tumble affair'; and Balfour was not the man to plunge into the mêlée. Spruce, sleek and somnolent, he looked on, from the comfort of a sofa, with the bland, unruffled curiosity of a Siamese cat.

His attitude is recalled by his bitter enemy, Curzon, who noted that though he was living in the same building as Lloyd George, 'he did not know, was not told, and was as a rule too careless to inquire, what was going on'. He was not invited to Fontainebleau: he was not privy to the drafting of the famous memorandum or even of the Anglo-French treaty of guarantee, of whose existence he learned only later. 'Balfour freely admitted it,' continued Curzon, 'and in his half-cynical, half-nonchalant way, expressed his astonishment and his ignorance of what the Little Man was doing.' Curzon's partisan account is corroborated by the charitable Smuts, who dined with Balfour on 20 May. 'I stated to him some of my principal objections to the Treaty. He appeared much puzzled and asked me whether *that* was in the Treaty! Poor, innocent soul, he disclaimed all responsibility, although I reminded him that he was Foreign Secretary and really responsible in the eyes of the Constitution.' A week later, Cecil too dined with Balfour, 'and told him I was very unhappy about the Treaty. He only said that he should not defend it, but apparently thought it was all right'. At the all-important meeting of the Empire delegation to discuss the German counter-proposals, Balfour casually revealed that his knowledge of these was restricted to a published summary in *The Times*. Montagu noted his 'valiant but futile effort' to defend the Treaty, particularly the reparation clauses – an exhibition of ignorance which 'shocked some of his hearers'. 'What on earth he meant,' comments Montagu, 'where he learnt his economics, I haven't the foggiest notion. But he was greeted with a howl of derision, even from Hughes.'

As for the legal bases of Versailles, Balfour indulged in a flight of fancy so utterly remote from truth, that it can be explained, though not excused, only by that chronic absentmindedness and vagueness which his admirers saw as endearing eccentricities. He agreed, he told Smuts, 'that if the Fourteen Points were pressed from a legal point of view, it was possible to make out an awkward case, [but that] it was impossible to interpret the Fourteen Points and the supplementary speeches as if they constituted a contract between two litigants'. Yet that was precisely how he saw them at the time of the Armistice, when he agreed to them as the conditions on which the war was to be ended and by which 'we should certainly be bound'.

What, one is entitled to ask, was the Foreign Secretary doing in Paris? Golf, lawn-tennis, concerts, select little dinner-parties, formed, it appears, important items in his day. On one occasion, deliberations with his French counterpart at the Quai d'Orsay were interrupted on Balfour's plea, apologetic but firm, of an unavoidable engagement elsewhere. The suspicious French had him followed to Saint-Cloud, where he was seen, a rapt spectator at a tennis-tournament. One might have been back in the nineties, the debonair septuagenarian playing the role of an elegant, though ageing, Ernest Worthing. His detachment had its commendable aspect: he stood aside from the self-righteous cawing of the victors. It was at Balfour's suggestion, on the day of the presentation of the terms to Brockdorff-Rantzau, that as the Germans entered the room, the Allied delegations stood up, in a faint echo of the courtesies of the Old World diplomacy. Asked what he thought of Brockdorff-Rantzau's own failure to rise when delivering his speech, Balfour replied: 'I failed to notice. I make it a rule never to stare at people when they are in obvious distress.' Of this, Nicolson remarked: 'AJB makes the whole of Paris seem vulgar.' It was typical, however, of the limitations of Balfour's gentility that while he was scrupulous not to embarrass the Germans, he was oblivious of or indifferent to the fact that they were being cheated.

Good breeding and good form were not enough. Curzon was not alone in his anger at the sight of Lloyd George activating his one-man-band, while the Foreign Secretary dozed nearby, languid, ironic, insouciant, 'an amused spectator', noted Montagu – watching, recalled Vansittart, 'as if the Welshman were a dynamic insect under a microscope'. At a dinner-party at the British Embassy on 5 May, Henry Wilson spoke to Balfour 'about the terms, and he, of course, like the others, has not seen them. He was openly joking, in front of ladies, about the farce of the whole thing – and yet he has to sign'. At that time and place, such characteristics suggest something other than amiable foibles. The detachment of Balfour was the expression not so much of the philosophical sceptic, or even of the self-distancing, conscious ironist, still less the useful disinterestedness of the active critic, but rather a feckless indifference bordering on the inhuman – 'the detachment of a choir-boy at a funeral service', wrote Vansittart.

'Perhaps one should never have expected anything better,' wrote Alice Clark to Smuts, 'if the idealism of England was left to be represented by Balfour.' 'Balfour was a tragedy,' agreed Smuts, 'a mere dilettante, without force or guidance, when a strong British Foreign Minister might have saved the whole situation.' Such was Balfour – effete, spinsterish, a trifler – 'charming, tired and wholly useless,' noted Montagu. Can Clemenceau's description of him be bettered: '*Cette vieille fille*'? Only, perhaps, by Lloyd George. What place would Balfour have in history? he was asked. He replied: 'He will be just like the scent on a pocket handkerchief.'

Bonar Law enjoys a reputation for probity and sobriety. He was moderate, sensible and unambitious, without desire for the limelight, content to take a back seat in government, as long as it was a Conservative Government. More than once he attempted to exert a calming influence on Lloyd George. He cautioned, unavailingly, against 'Hanging the Kaiser'. He agreed that the Treaty was too severe. Almost from the first, he was sceptical about indemnities; but once they became, as he saw it, inevitable, he favoured a fixed sum and a businesslike 'deal'.

But his very pragmatism was a weakness. 'He lacks the force which comes from strong conviction,' wrote Riddell. 'His attitude towards life is one of negation. Nothing matters very much.' Nothing, that is, except the unity of the Conservative Party. Against the background of his constant solicitude for backbench opinion, indeed, the genesis and rationale of article 231 fall into sharpest relief. If, as he told Lloyd George, 'he had had to say to the House that he had abandoned the principle of costs of the war, the position would be hopeless.' From behind the camouflage of the war-guilt clause, however, 'he would not be afraid to face the House.' Was such advice, from the Leader of the House, to be disregarded? Was it likely to be disregarded by Lloyd George?

Bonar Law was not a man of straw, any more than Balfour, but his nerveless lassitude, his gloomy resignation and debilitating melancholy made him driftwood on the ebb and flow of parliamentary tides. He wanted a fixed indemnity, certainly – but, as Lloyd George told Wilson and Clemenceau, 'the moment any possible figure was mentioned, he began to shrink from it.' 'What will our lunatics at home say to this?' he asked. 'If it were practically possible,' he wrote to Lloyd George in the final days of decision, 'I think it would be far wiser to fix a sum, even five thousand million pounds – though that would probably cause an outcry here.' 'I have written all this,' he concluded, with characteristic despondency, 'but I feel that it is of no use to you; and I need not say that I have complete confidence in your doing the best possible.' He shook his head, and wrung his hands, and that was all. As a practical politician, as a party manager, his concern was to find a face-saving formula that would satisfy the House of Commons. The war-guilt clause did the trick; and for Bonar Law, that was enough.

Cecil had fundamental doubts about the Treaty, and put them squarely to Lloyd George. He did not, however, follow them up with any more decisive step. This seems strange, at first sight. If, of all the delegation, Balfour had the most gentlemanly manners, Cecil possessed the most gentlemanly soul, the nicest sense of punctilio. After the Armistice, he made a point of resigning from the Government over the disestablishment of the Welsh Church, which, as a devout Anglican, he disapproved on principle. Why did he not take a similar stand over the Treaty, with which he was no less unhappy? Was this not straining at a gnat and swallowing a camel? Not in Cecil's eyes. Having tried and failed to influence Lloyd George, he considered he had done his best; to do more might be counter-productive. He refused to attend the important plenary delegation meeting on 1 June. 'You do no good by jogging a man's elbow,' he wrote in his diary. 'If you can't manage a thing in the way you think right, it is better to leave someone else to do it altogether, rather than, by making pushes for this or that change, reduce the whole scheme to incoherence, without curing its injustice.' It was true, no doubt; and yet one cannot help perceiving, in Cecil, the distinction between a patently good man, and a great one. 'It is, he added, 'very disappointing, and makes me more glad than ever that I am going away.' So he too passed by on the other side.

Cecil too was mindful of the imperative need for peace. Before Wilson, even before Smuts, Cecil was the true begetter of the League of Nations, to which his thoughts and energies were passionately directed as humanity's best hope. But his own moral position, as he was uncomfortably aware, was terribly vitiated by his commanding role in the enforcement of the Blockade. He was haunted by the sufferings of which he was an accomplice. The waifs of Vienna begged for bread and milk, and Cecil offered them internationalism and the League of Nations. With the signing of the Treaty, the blockade would be lifted: could there be any doubt as to the right course?

Milner had no illusions about the Treaty. 'The Peace Conference is making a mess of things,' he noted at the end of March. 'Unless we settle something quickly, and approach Germany with terms far more moderate than those usually contemplated, we shall go to disaster.' His view never changed – 'the peace to end peace', he scoffed. But what did he do to press his opposition, apart from passing Cassandra-like observations at Cabinet meetings, and confiding contemptuous remarks on Lloyd George and his 'circus' to his private diary? Milner was a man of large, though somewhat indefinable moral authority. 'His greatest strength', noted Amery, 'lies in his knowledge and grasp of big principles, which makes him a diplomat.' His influence as Secretary of State for War had been crucial, perhaps decisive during the Ludendorff Offensive, when his swift intervention produced the vital subordination of the Allied armies under the single command of Foch. According to Hankey, 'Lloyd George relied on him more than on any other colleague, except, perhaps, Bonar Law'. But that was in 1918. The war won, Milner was no longer the man of the hour, the only type for whom Lloyd George had any time. He was not an asset during the elections, from which he stood disapprovingly aside, having published his moderate peace views shortly before the Armistice and having in consequence been pilloried by Northcliffe as a pro-German. In January 1919, he ceded the War Office for the Colonial Office; and though he was appointed to the Peace Conference, it was without expectation on his part of his ability to sway Lloyd George. 'Personal influence is such a varying thing,' he wrote at the end of May, when such influence was most needed, 'and just now I am not in the disposition to use it with the Prime Minister.'

Moreover, as Colonial Secretary, his overriding concern was with the disposal of the captured German colonies; and while he lamented the European settlement, the Imperial Proconsul appeared untroubled by any inconsistency between the Wilsonian principle of 'absolutely impartial adjustment of all colonial claims' and the appropriation to the British Empire of most of Germany's overseas territory. His imperial ambitions richly satiated, he was surely vulnerable to Clemenceau's charge, that if the British felt so strong a call to appease Germany – they might begin by disgorging some of her colonies.

Then there is Smuts. How strange, that of all men, it was the high-minded Smuts who acted as devil's advocate in abetting Lloyd George's ploy to seduce Wilson from his integrity; that he should have out-Sumnered Sumner by devising the most casuistic of all the glosses on the Lansing note and persuading Wilson that civilian damage included pensions. It was an extraordinary stroke on Lloyd George's part to have selected Smuts to do his dirty work for him. How Smuts could have been a party to it defies comprehension, except perhaps in terms of contamination by that all-pervasive miasma of equivocation that bedevilled the entire Conference. Shall a man touch pitch, and not be defiled? *'Slimme Jannie'* his Boer critics disparagingly called him – 'Clever Jan'. Smuts's memorandum on pensions, as his biographer admits, 'has done more damage to his reputation than any other document that he ever produced in his whole life'.

The reader may also share a sense of disappointment that after his fixed determination not to sign, Smuts too, in the end, capitulated; though not, let it be said, without prolonged heart-searchings. Jan Christian, like the eponymous hero of *Pilgrim's Progress*, laboured long in the slough of despond. But what, after all, was the alternative? Botha had decided that for the sake of South Africa – for whom adherence to the Treaty signified her emergence as a fully independent Dominion – he himself, as head of delegation, had no choice but to sign. Was Smuts to oppose his chief and his closest friend, whom he also knew to be a sick man, and to present himself as 'holier than thou'? Or to stand out against the entire Empire delegation? Many, perhaps most, shared his misgivings; none would join him in breaking rank against Lloyd George. No lone protest on his part would prevent the Treaty from being signed; nor would his resignation, beyond a momentary ripple, sway the course of events. Unlike Brockdorff-Rantzau, Smuts had no taste for the gratuitous gesture; like Cecil, he came to see peace at any price as better than no peace, and looked for salvation to the League. His doubts also stood suspended in uneasy equipoise with an inner confidence that all would come right in the end, and sooner rather than later – not only because of an abiding faith in the ultimate workings of an immanent providence, but also because of the Treaty's manifest inherent contradictions. 'It will and must all soon collapse anyway,' he wrote. 'Leave this Treaty to its own devices, and it will soon come to an end.'

But unimpeachable though his motives were, his final compromise, given the nature of the man, could not be altogether happy. To sign, as he did, and simultaneously to release a statement of protest against the Treaty, was to reveal a further taint of the evil spirit of the place. It was, as it happens, a solution proposed by Lloyd George, a counsel typical of Mr Worldly Wiseman, as Smuts confessed. 'I return to South Africa a defeated man,' he sighed on leaving Paris, looking back, in contrast to Lloyd George, to the darkest episode of his life. And while he departed with cleaner hands than most, he did not go empty-handed. As Lloyd George, with pointed malice, reminded him, he bore home to Cape Town the coveted prize of German South-West Africa. What shall it profit a man, he doubtless reflected, if he gain the whole world, and lose his soul?

In this unhappy catalogue, perhaps the least tainted though not the least unfortunate, was Barnes. 'He was, on the whole, I think,' recalled Frances Stevenson, 'the sanest of all David's colleagues at the time of the Peace Conference. His calm, rather slow but completely unprejudiced mind could take stock of a situation in the shrewdest way, while he had the courage to express his judgments even when they were unpopular and unpalatable. If David could have listened to him in 1919 it would have been well.' Barnes, a man of the people and a patriot, had alone of the Labour Party agreed to remain in the Cabinet after the Armistice, for the sake of national unity and in the hope of giving the aspirations of ordinary folk some voice at the Conference. Yet Barnes too, having made his point against the Treaty, did not persist in his refusal to sign. It was not only that the national interest and constitutional practice seemed to demand a unanimous signature. Barnes was naturally reluctant to pit his own untutored judgment against the collective wisdom of the Cabinet. For breaking with his fellow socialists, he was consigned to political oblivion.

Such were the human elements that shaped the Treaty. First, the final, irreducible bedrock of Wilson's faith and Clemenceau's tenacity, the doggedness of Hughes and the iron obstinacy of Cunliffe and Sumner. Against such granite projections, Lloyd George's quicksilver ingenuity could in the last resort make little impact. To these may be added such random but formative destabilizing agents as the neurotic atmosphere of Paris and the passing fury of Parliament, Northcliffe's monomania, the abrasive self-righteousness of Brockdorff-Rantzau and the accommodating pragmatism of Colonel House. But there were also influences at work that were no less effective for being negative: the graceful negligence, the airy indifference of Balfour, the innate pessimism and weary passivity of Milner and Bonar Law, Cecil's high-minded pharisaism, even Smuts's stoic providentialism and the deferential loyalty of Barnes. Add Churchill's consuming preoccupation with Russia, and the constitutional impotence of King and Primate to do more than advise, admonish or exhort – and all this left a vacuum, into which rushed the 'terrible dynamism' and the 'inner irresponsibility' of Lloyd George. Thus, wrote Montagu, was 'the wonderful chaos of Paris coaxed, driven, hurled, kicked, magnificently and with an inscrutable genius, to its appointed destiny by the Prime Minister, [notwithstanding] the collection of discontented but admiring colleagues who cling to his shirt'. Thus was victory frittered away, in the haste for shallow, specious 'deals', the sacrifices and suffering forgotten, the vision of a better world brushed aside and bespattered in the ephemeral triumph of a parliamentary ovation.

Chapter 6

The Carthaginian Peace

In England, where the sense of justice is biblical, people now
torture themselves with the thought that if the Treaty of
Versailles had been softer, a different Germany, and therefore a
different world, might have resulted.

Sarah Millin, *General Smuts* (1936)

What, will these hands ne'er be clean?

Macbeth

It was a wise precept of Machiavelli that the victor should either
conciliate his enemy or destroy him. The Treaty of Versailles did
neither. It did not pacify Germany, still less permanently weaken her,
appearances notwithstanding, but left her scourged, humiliated and
resentful. It was neither a Wilson Peace nor a Clemenceau peace, but a
witches' brew concocted of the least palatable ingredients of each,
which, though highly distasteful to Germany, were by no means fatal.
Either of the basic elements, applied alone, might have produced a
lasting settlement. In combination, they were contradictory, incompatible and ultimately ineffective: they cancelled each other out. There
was too little Wilsonism to appease, too little of Clemenceau to deter;
enough of Wilson to provoke contempt, enough of Clemenceau to
inspire hatred. In the lambent paradox of a French observer,
Versailles was 'too mild for its severity.'

That was not how it seemed to the liberals in the British delegation.
To them, in Smuts' words, it was 'this reactionary peace, the most
reactionary since Scipio Africanus dealt with Carthage'. Whatever its
faults, the Treaty of Versailles was not that. Germany lost territory to
France, Belgium, Denmark and Poland, but she was not actually
partitioned. Indeed, with the splintering of the former Austrian and
Russian empires into a chain of vulnerable succession-states, she
remained not only the dominant continental power, but potentially

132

more preponderant than in 1914. French control of the Saar would end in 15 years. Military occupation by the Allies was confined to the Rhine valley and to the same maximum term. This apart, German sovereignty suffered no substantial infringement. Disarmament and the payment of reparations would depend on German co-operation; for though Allied Commissions were to be set up to supervise the fulfilment of the relevant provisions, they could be enforced only by an army of occupation in the heart of Germany. For all the French cries of *Delenda est Germania* and hopes that the Reich might be broken up into its former constituent members, the principles of self-determination and the unitary state were on the whole fairly applied. It took another war before Berlin was actually laid waste and Germany dismembered.

Most of this was hidden from the liberals of 1919, so dark did the outlook appear to them in their despondency. For them, in Keynes's words, the Treaty was 'outrageous and impossible. . . . If I was in the Germans' place, I'd rather die than sign such a peace.' 'Not stern merely,' echoed Nicolson, 'but actually punitive. . . . There is not a single person among the younger people here who is not unhappy and disappointed at the terms. The only people who approve are the old fire-eaters.' 'The fault is that there is an old man called Lord Sumner and an old man called Lord Cunliffe, and they have worked away without consulting anyone, with the result that the Treaty is only worth the *Daily Mail* which it will be printed in.'. . .'If I were the Germans, I shouldn't sign for a moment.' Keynes resigned in protest and returned to Cambridge to write *The Economic Consequences of the Peace*. 'The battle is lost,' he wrote to Lloyd George. 'I leave the Twins to gloat over the devastation of Europe.'

As much as any physical provision of the Treaty – the military occupations, the cutting-off of East Prussia, the burden of reparations – it was the appearance, the trappings, the aura and circumstances of Versailles that left such a bad taste: the solemn tone and sanctimonious phraseology, the bad faith and blackmail of the blockade, the bad manners – the cold-shouldering of Brockdorff-Rantzau, the melancholy eyes and reproachful brow of Dr Melchior, the awful crowing in the Hall of Mirrors. 'Not a word of sympathy for them at the end,' Smuts observed sorrowfully of Dr Müller and Dr Bell, 'when one little word from Clemenceau or George or Wilson would have meant so much.'

The contrasts with the Fourteen Points, however inevitable, perhaps, at times, or even justifiable, were glaring and painful:

between the principle of open diplomacy and the refusal to negotiate; between the principle of self-determination and the prohibition on Austro-German *Anschluss*; between the promise of fair arbitration on colonial questions and the peremptory confiscation of Germany's empire overseas; between the Lansing note and what one delegate called the 'Woodrovian casuistry' whereby the war-guilt clause was evolved. 'Seldom in the history of man', wrote Nicolson, 'has such vindictiveness cloaked itself in such unctuous sophistry.' 'We are greatly to blame,' agreed Headlam-Morley. 'If we do this sort of thing, we have no right to accuse the Germans of want of good faith.'

Yet these aspects of peacemaking, odious and grotesque as they seemed – and wrongheaded and misguided as they sometimes were – were, so to speak, largely scenic and atmospheric. The Treaty, as Smuts complained 'bristled with pinpricks'; but like the captured German artillery that lined the Champs-Elysées, such pinpricks made little difference to the concrete realities of power. The trophies – including the war-guilt clause – were essentially symbolic. Germany remained Germany, but potentially stronger than in 1914 – France, France, but actually weaker than in 1914. In their collective breast-beating, their shuddering aversion from the sanctimoniousness of Versailles, the British liberals began to seem ashamed not only of the peace, 'this bloody bullying peace', as Nicolson called it, but almost of the victory. The laurels soon withered. 'I find Headlam-Morley standing miserably in the littered immensity of the *Galerie des Glaces*,' noted Nicolson. 'We say nothing to each other. It has all been horrible.' 'I suppose I've been an accomplice in all this wickedness and folly,' wrote Keynes. 'I feel I am no better than the others,' lamented Smuts, 'and that I must stand in the dock beside them. And God be merciful to us poor sinners.'

Robert Vansittart, a junior Foreign Office representative at the Peace Conference, who, in the thirties, as Permanent Under-Secretary, fought vainly against Appeasement, puts his finger on the mood of 1919. The British delegation, he recalls, was 'smitten by meaculpism'. The affliction was widespread in liberal circles. 'We are all so disgusted with the peace', wrote Beatrice Webb for the radicals, 'that we have ceased to discuss it – one tries to banish it from one's mind as an unclean thing.' Others reacted less passively. 'We propose', wrote a Liberal intellectual to Gilbert Murray in early June, 'to issue a letter or manifesto as soon as the Peace Treaty is signed, to let the world know the trend of liberal thought in England at any rate, and our intention to endeavour to get the Treaty revised.'

Here lay the deepest flaw of Versailles. Whether or not it was too hard on the Germans, it was demonstrably too hard for much of British opinion. From the outset, liberal England had no heart for it. In the years that followed, Versailles returned like a recurrent nightmare to plague its inventors. It is no use for Mr Correlli Barnett, in the *Collapse of British Power*, to castigate their lack of hard-headed realism. Such, for good and ill, is what the Protestant conscience and the public-school ethic had made them: and it would have been the mark of a true *Realpolitik* to take account of it. Given that the Treaty was not ultimately self-enforcing, what chance did it stand of durability if the victors themselves could not stomach it?

At the Hôtel Majestic, the liberals gathered at the end of May to found the Institute of International Affairs. Its very purpose, the scholarly investigation of the origins of the war, implicitly cast doubt on the official version enshrined in the Treaty and laid the foundation-stone of revisionism. 'There is no single person in this room', declared Cecil from the chair, 'who is not disappointed with the terms we have drafted. . . . Our disappointment is an excellent symptom: let us perpetuate it.'

Revisionism was explicit in the Treaty itself. Beneath its ebony surface, the worm of Appeasement lay dormant. Even Kerr's reply to the German counter-proposals, while making few immediate conces-sions of substance, pointed to 'that process of appeasement which all desire', and to the League of Nations as the instrument of concilia-tion, 'whereby the settlement of 1919 itself can be modified from time to time'. 'The real work of making peace', Smuts declared in his press statement after the signing, 'will only begin after this Treaty has been signed.' 'No-one supposes', wrote C.P. Scott in the *Manchester Guardian*, 'that the terms now accepted are eternal and immutable; and the day may not be far distant when they will be sensibly modified.'

No one was in heartier agreement than Lloyd George. To him the Treaty was after all no more than another convenient improvisation, a stop-gap device to bring a breathing-space and some momentary stability to Europe, 'a temporary measure of a nature to satisfy public opinion', as he later told Nicolson. Once it was safely ratified, no one strove more energetically to undo, at a series of international confer-ences, the package he had so dexterously wrapped up in Paris. No one tried harder to make the French see reason, to tone down the reparation demands, to conciliate German feeling, to bring Weimar Germany into a genuine comity of nations, and even to break the black spell of reparations in one great mutual waiver of international debts. If anyone could have undone the damage done by Lloyd George, it was Lloyd George. But it was now beyond even his powers.

It proved no easier to break down French resistance after Versailles than before. Unlike Lloyd George, Clemenceau was in earnest when he signed the Treaty; what French logic and persistence had joined together, no Welshman should put asunder. If Clemenceau had reservations about Versailles, they were not on the score of any excessive severity. He had gone to the outer limits of prudence to accommodate what he saw as Anglo-Saxon sentimentality: beyond the limits, in the eyes of his successor, Poincaré, more particularly with America's repudiation of Wilson's signature and the consequent lapse of the British guarantee to defend France from fresh attack – the supreme betrayal, in French eyes, by 'perfidious Albion'. Poincaré stood by every jot and tittle of Versailles. The Germans would not pay? Send the troops into the Ruhr. In British eyes, the French now became the villains of the piece, with their Shylock-like insistence on reparations, keeping alive old hatreds, rubbing salt in the wounds of war years after they should have healed.

In the hangover that followed the euphoria of victory, there also evaporated the rage to hang the Kaiser. That unbalanced and histrionic figure, once removed from the centre-stage of world history to the harmless domesticity of a Dutch backwater, no longer seemed either particularly wicked or even particularly interesting. 'Look at him,' as Churchill wrote; 'he is only a blunderer.' The Prime Minister, however, did not believe that the public shared this attitude of magnanimous contempt. The Commons did not seem to share it. He did not share it himself. The idea of a state trial in London, to which he had won the reluctant consent of Wilson, appealed richly to his bardic sense of drama, despite warnings from his colleagues that the solemn baroque spectacle he had in mind threatened, once in contact with reality, to spill over into farce. The King, in high dudgeon, as Stamfordham told the Archbishop, 'asked Lloyd George where the Kaiser was to be lodged. Lloyd George did not know; he thought perhaps in the Tower. The King asked "Are you going to take him backwards and forwards in a black maria, or what do you mean to do?". . . Lloyd George had no idea.' Again, he was out of touch with better popular feeling. In the Lords, Bryce and Buckmaster dismissed the idea of the trial with scorn as a legal impossibility, to which no English judge would lend himself. Even the Commons now turned instinctively from the prospect of a Roman holiday. The

British, with their congenital and saving incapacity for protracted hate, wanted, if not to forgive, then at least to forget. 'We are all sick of the Kaiser question,' complained Hardinge, who was responsible for securing his extradition. 'There never was a more hollow sham than the fictitious energy shown in demanding his surrender.' When the Dutch government rejected those demands, there was general relief.

In the last, bitter days of peacemaking, Smuts had urged Keynes 'as soon as possible to set about writing a clear, connected account of what the financial and economic clauses of the Treaty actually are and mean'. The outcome, written in the passionate relish of disillusion and published in December 1919, was the classic indictment of Versailles, *The Economic Consequences of the Peace*. It certainly reveals much about the psychological consequences of the Peace. 'The book', admitted Keynes, 'is the child of much emotion.' His triptych of the Big Three was lurid and unforgettable. The history of the Conference he depicted as the tale, the cautionary tale, of the Presbyterian bigot, 'bamboozled' by the French Chauvinist and the Welsh Siren; the conference-room as a thieves' kitchen and the result – a 'Carthaginian Peace', a huge repository of vindictiveness, masquerading as justice, 'one of the most outrageous acts of a cruel victor in civilised history', which, unless revised, must lead to the economic ruin, and the political collapse, of Europe.

His motives, on the whole, were pure. His credentials as an economist were formidable. His style was sharp, pellucid and compelling. Much of his criticism was moving and true: his revelations of the background to reparations in particular were as unanswerable as they were shaming. The cumulative impact of the book was irresistible. Yet what was moving was not always true; and what was most moving was sometimes quite untrue. Such parts were among the most damaging. 'Those who sign this Treaty', he warned, 'will sign the death-sentence of many millions of German men, women and children.' This terrible charge, itself the words of Brockdorff-Rantzau, bore heavily on English consciences. The prediction, though unrealized in the event, went home; and Brockdorff-Rantzau had his day after all.

A corollary of this was the destruction of Woodrow Wilson. A year ago he had come, embodying the hopes of millions, had proclaimed, in eloquent and moving language, principles which seemed the only proper basis for a better world; and had appeared resolute to translate them into shining realities. With what buoyant, Messianic hopes they had awaited the *George Washington*! They expected a Prometheus, the Light of the World; and when eventually they understood that he was only a college professor, with an outer carapace of personal vanity and an inner fund of self-delusion, their disenchantment was bitter. They did not see the wounded sensitivity, the lone misery behind the mask: the palpable, almost painful goodwill, the high ideals, the stubborn courage contending with forces beyond his strength, sapped by weaknesses not quite beyond his knowledge. 'What is expected of me', he said, gazing sadly across the ocean on his final journey home, 'only God could perform.' They denounced him as a false prophet, and in the same breath they complained of his inability to work miracles. They fancied that they had heard from his lips, for a moment, the music of the spheres – but the sound was gone, so they dismissed him as a sanctimonious windbag, just another peddler in words; and with the same alacrity with which they had acclaimed him, they rushed to trample on the fallen idol. It would break Wilson's heart, wrote an American delegate, as the Conference lumbered on to its bitter end, 'to know how the radicals of the world had left him, how they jeered and hooted at his name'.

With the weight of his precocious learning and the wit of his formidable pen, so much more lethal than the ephemeral squibs of the French press, Keynes egged on the jeering. Northcliffe himself, with the bludgeon of his laboured sarcasm, limped after him in vain. In the full light of day and in prose of poised and sustained malice, he immolated Wilson on the altar of the Fourteen Points. In the sardonic humour of his attack might be discerned the influence and even the techniques of his friend Lytton Strachey, whose *Eminent Victorians*, published the year before, had so changed the face of biography. A basis of truth underlay his account of the President, but the facsimile was thick with denigration. 'What, then, was his temperament?' asked Keynes. 'The clue, once found, was illuminating. The President was like a nonconformist minister.' He was old, he was slow, he was ignorant; he was not even cultivated. He combined dithering incompetence with mental rigidity and spiritual arrogance. He yielded where he should have stood firm, and when he should have bent, he was inflexible. From such a temperament, Keynes concluded, arose 'that web of sophistry and Jesuitical exegesis that was finally to clothe with insincerity the language and substance of the whole treaty'. Nor, when observation or jaded inference flagged, did Keynes disdain the arts of fiction. Just as Strachey invented short legs to complete his portrait of Dr Arnold, so Keynes obliquely ascribed the same incongruity to Wilson: 'Like Odysseus,' he wrote, 'the President looked wiser when he was seated.' In both cases, the object was the same, less that of verisimilitude than of derision, the President having been marked down as the first live victim of 'debunking'.

To the horror of Smuts, who quickly repented of his former encouragement, he 'made an Aunt Sally of the noblest figure, perhaps the only noble figure, in the history of the war'. As the President's reputation with all his imperfections, real and imputed, on his head, toppled and crashed from its pedestal in its tremendous fall from the sublime to the ridiculous, all over Bloomsbury the teacups rattled in their saucers amid an ever-swelling round of giggles. The *cognoscenti* smiled in anticipation when they read that 'the poor President would be playing blind man's bluff'; they sniggered when they saw how he was 'bamboozled' by Lloyd George; they wriggled with delight when they learned how it then proved impossible 'to debamboozle this old Presbyterian'. Louder and more homeric grew the laughter. Lloyd George himself was amused: after all, it was better to be immortalized as a knave than a fool; better Sir Toby Belch than Malvolio; better a Welsh Siren than a 'blind and deaf Don Quixote'; and better a live fox than a dead lion.

What the 'old Presbyterian' himself might feel was of no concern to Keynes. He was in the business of exposing wickedness and folly, not of sparing feelings, unless they were German feelings. 'My purpose in this book', he proclaimed, is to show that the Carthaginian peace is not practically right or possible.' There was thus no mockery of Brockdorff-Rantzau in *his* hour of distress, no thumbnail sketch of *his* physical discomfiture, no allusion, in the manner of Strachey's 'General Gordon', to his rumoured dependence on the brandy-bottle, in explanation of his gouty limp or his legendary failure to stand up. Like Mozart's Commendatore, the Count, in Keynes's scenario, represented the voice of destiny; of his terrible accusation levelled at the Big Three, Keynes wrote: 'I know of no adequate answer to these words.' In Germany, therefore, as was entirely predictable, the book was received with grim rapture as confirmation of the moral obliquity of the Allies and the 'unheard-of injustice' and sheer impossibility of the 'slave-treaty'.

Still less did it trouble Keynes that his attack on the President struck home at the very moment when Wilson was making his last desperate stand. It was a stand not merely for his own political survival – that might count for little in the scale of things – but for the survival of his policy and his ideals, for America's active involvement in the affairs of Europe: an involvement, by Keynes's own account, made all the more indispensable by the manifold defects of the Treaty. Would the Americans, as Keynes asked, 'complete the work that they began in saving Europe from the tyranny of organised force, by saving her from herself'? 'If we do not go in, my fellow-citizens,' warned Wilson himself in the last of his great appeals to the people before his final collapse, 'think of the tragedy of that result – the only sufficient guarantee to the peace of the world withheld!' That was what was at stake. While the outcome still hung in the balance, Keynes presented the Republicans with deadly ammunition. He made himself the ally of the Cabot Lodges and the Borahs and every backwoodsman in the Midwest who saw the chance to turn the great moral imperative to partisan gain. 'Every paper I saw', recalled Smuts, 'quoted the part about Wilson's bamboozlement.' When Senator Borah read excerpts aloud to the Foreign Relations Committee, the jaws of the isolationist senators hardened still further – for they were not amused – and the Democrats themselves were dismayed and dumbfounded. Who, as was said of Gibbon, can refute a sneer? Who, for that matter, can refute an economist? 'It helped to finish Wilson,' Smuts believed, 'and it strengthened the Americans against the League.' Here, if anywhere, was the 'stab in the back', the most unkindest cut of all. Whatever may have been the economic consequences of the peace, the political consequences of Maynard Keynes were wholly momentous.

Nowhere more so than in Britain. America, after all, as Clemenceau had often remarked, enjoyed a comfortable remoteness from the troubles of Europe. Isolationism, no less than idealism, lay within her range of permissible options. For Britain, however, the extent of freedom of choice in foreign policy, compared with that of the United States, stood in inverse proportion to the width of the Atlantic Ocean and the English Channel. Whatever dreams of continental disengagement might be indulged in London should have been tempered by the hard facts of physical proximity and recent memory. For four years, the rumble of the guns in Flanders had been audible in Kent, sometimes even in Whitehall. For four years the Germans had stood fast at Zeebrugge and Ostend, from where not even the supreme and terrible effort of Passchendaele came within sight of dislodging them. From there they had freely deployed their submarines, and in 1917 almost succeeded in severing the lifelines of their island-enemy. In 1918 they came close to breaking through to Calais and driving the

British into the sea, as 22 years later they duly did. Precisely because German national unity was on the whole so well respected at Versailles, at the relative expense of strategic considerations, the problem of German power had been answered only tentatively and conditionally by the peacemakers. They had scotched the snake, not killed it.

The German question remained the real problem of the peace as of the war, the more so now that America had washed its hands of Europe and withdrawn its decisive weight from the balance of power. The effectiveness of the Treaty having been predicated on American participation, the peace would now be what Britain and France chose to make of it. How opinion in Britain responded to the challenge, how people thought and felt about the peace, their readiness to justify and if need be to enforce it, were therefore quite literally questions of life and death. To the role of *The Economic Consequences of the Peace* in the formation of that opinion, the cliché 'epoch-making' may properly for once be applied.

More than any other single influence, it helped to brand Versailles as a *Diktat* long before the rise of Hitler, and to scourge the consciences of decent men. It made public the misgivings of the liberals at Paris; it articulated and crystallized the forebodings of the liberals in England. It provoked, as Keynes intended, 'a far-reaching revulsion of opinion on the part of the general public'. 'Your book has produced, as of course you know, an amazing impression,' wrote C.P. Scott; 'I think you have really set people on a new line of thought and, I hope, of action.'

The Economic Consequences of the Peace confirmed the feelings of literary subalterns in bitter alienation from the inadequacy of official patriotism; men who, in the fearsome lottery of the trenches, came to see the Germans as blood-brothers in suffering, fellow-victims of a monstrous, cosmic jest played out on their generation by fate and the old men, and whose hatred was reserved for incompetent generals behind the lines and for warmongers and profiteers at home. For such men, conventional images of Britain and Germany had already become blurred, even transposed during the war: Siegfried Sassoon had voiced the wish to 'clear those Junkers out of Parliament'. With the coming of peace, Commander Kenworthy, surveying the 'hard-faced' ranks of the Coalition from the Opposition back-benches, deplored 'the obvious Prussianization of the British governing class'.

By contrast, Germany in defeat became the counterpart of 'plucky little Belgium'. The army of occupation felt shame and pity at the sight of German children spindly with rickets, the Big Three still pontificating at Paris, the blockade still enforced to the hilt, terms profferred to the vanquished at bayonet-point. C.E. Montague wrote in *Disenchantment* of 'our press and our politicians parading at Paris in moral *Pickelhauben*. . . What a victory it might have been,' he lamented, invoking the lost spirit of 1914, 'the real, the Winged Victory, chivalric, whole and unstained.' To Kenworthy, likewise, the spectacle of the *Friedrich de Grosse* sliding majestically beneath the waves of Scapa Flow, was not the crowning proof of Prussian perfidy but the sportsmanlike gesture of a gallant loser. The extreme tensions of the war, the hopes and fears strained beyond bearing, deserved better than the petty spite of the war-guilt clause. Montague epitomized the obsessive, accusing theme of a generation betrayed by the terrible old men: 'Not a line,' he declared, 'not one line in your Treaty to show that those boys (our friends who were dead) had been any better than the emperors; not one line to stand for the kindliness of England; not one word to bring back some memory of the generosity of her sons.'

Like Strachey, Keynes as biographer held a special attraction for the younger generation, to whom his book was dedicated. If Austen Chamberlain himself, as he told him, 'chortled with joy over the Conference chapter', the 'people of the aftermath' responded with no less glee to his feline demolition of Father Figures and Great Men, his open contempt for the Old World of power politics and religiosity, vested interests and jingoism, the world of Kitchener and Haig, of Northcliffe and Bottomley, of Basil Zaharoff and Rudyard Kipling, which had dominated their adolescent years and against which their undergraduate spirits erupted in spontaneous and joyful rebellion. What fun to *épater les bourgeois*! Liberated from the prospect of the trenches, haunted by the slaughter of brothers and schoolfellows, even serious young men, like A.L.Rowse at Oxford or Kingsley Martin at Cambridge, took the caricatures for the real thing. 'It was wonderful for us', recalled Martin, 'to have such a high authority saying with inside knowledge of the Treaty what we felt emotionally.' In the topsy-turvydom of post-war Oxbridge and Bloomsbury, it was self-evident that if 'they' in England were fundamentally 'bogus', it followed that 'they' in Germany were probably all right. Keynes actually admitted of Dr Melchior: 'In a sort of way I was in love with him.' 'People in this country are really very funny,' pondered Hardinge of the reception accorded to the *Economic Consequences of the Peace*. 'Keynes is being treated as a sort of hero.' Meanwhile the hero himself was enthusiastically prophesying of the Treaty: 'It will just become absurd, irrelevant, inapplicable, and a time will soon arrive when no-one will pay the least attention to it.' Two years later, the President of the Cambridge Union stated as a fact that 'the Treaty of Versailles is null and void'.

The reaction sparked off by Keynes's book provides startling confirmation of the potency in history of ideas, of the incrustations of myth and half-truth which obscure and distort reality, and contribute in turn to the formation of a new reality. It was not only callow undergraduates who joined the chorus of denunciation. 'I am quite clear', wrote Cecil, after reading the book, 'that we shall have to begin a campaign for the revision of the Treaty as soon as possible.' Headlam-Morley, while deploring Keynes's tendency to caricature, could only confirm his searing account of reparations. As historical adviser to the Foreign Office, he produced his own meticulously impartial study of the question, in which he agreed that the British Cabinet had allowed itself 'to be diverted from the straight and narrow path of rectitude and integrity'. In similar vein, Lord Grey lamented that 'We have indeed lost the peace. And the cause of it is Lloyd George, who has some great qualities without being a great man and who is constitutionally incapable of understanding that straightforwardness is essential and "cleverness" fatal to success in the long run'.

Lloyd George himself began to question the thesis of German war-guilt within months of Versailles. The war, he admitted, was a terrible accident, desired by no single state, 'something into which they glided, or rather staggered and stumbled'. With the French in the Ruhr and himself out of office, he was calling for 'conciliation not vengeance'. The contrast with Versailles was too much for Margot Asquith, outspoken wife of the deposed Prime Minister. Her answer to that, as she told Geoffrey Dawson, was: 'You aren't in a position to criticize anything. But for your 1918 elections or "Make Germany pay the whole cost of the war," "hang the Kaiser", etc., France would not be in the Ruhr today.' Dawson agreed. He had just made the same point in a *Times* editorial: 'It was Mr Lloyd George who first demanded these huge amounts, who insisted, against the terms of Armistice, on the inclusion of pensions in the bill.'

Lloyd George out of office, his laurels faded, stripped of the power which alone gave him meaning, seemed increasingly to resemble the seedy, played-out conjurer of Northcliffe's jibe, treading the dusty boards of provincial music-hall, shuffling his grimy pack, trotting out his breezy, unconvincing patter. With the return of the Conservatives, who turned him out of Downing Street in 1922, he became the obvious scapegoat for Versailles, the Goat in the Wilderness, as he has been called, not least among the huge Government majority, for whom Bolshevism had replaced Prussia as the international bugbear and who branded Lloyd George as the bounder who kicked the Germans when they were down, 'that liar from Wales'. It was unfair – but not grossly unfair. Lloyd George was an occasional rather than a congenital liar. All things being equal, he would doubtless rather have told the truth in 1919. As it was, he had wanted, in Smuts's words 'to ride to heaven on the back of the devil'. In Garvin's description, he was 'the opportunist who has meant only temporary sin . . . With his genius for facility, he thinks that what he does wrong he can "some day" put right.' Thus when Lloyd George criticized Versailles, no doubt with genuine conviction, it was too much like Satan rebuking sin.

With general revulsion at a war sparked off by power-politics came a renunciation of power-politics altogether, a withdrawal into a spiritual nirvana, where the public conscience and the higher morality held sway. 'After all,' wrote C.P. Scott in the *Manchester Guardian* in February 1919, 'the organised opinion of the world is a tremendous weapon. It may well prove also to be a growing one. Where is the Power which dare in the long run expose itelf to universal obloquy?' In the light of the history of the previous five years, this might seem a signal instance of the triumph of hope over experience. It was, however, wholly characteristic of the period. It is no surprise to find Balfour assuring the worried Botha, with a complacency positively Panglossian, that with the creation of the League of Nations, 'all has been done that could be done to make war in the future difficult and peace easy'. By 1924, William Temple, Bishop of Manchester, was asserting 'the steadily growing sense that Machiavellian statecraft is bankrupt'.

The mirage of the League of Nations as an entity somehow different from the erring states which composed it, the myth of the actual efficacy of peaceful aspirations, was to prove among the most infectious and tenacious of the illusions born of the Peace Conference, even after the fresh tramp of jackboots and the trundle of heavy guns across the cobblestones of the Rhine bridges brought a belated reminder that Machiavellian statecraft was far from exhausted, that the lion was by no means ready to lie down peacefully with the lamb and that universal obloquy might not, after all, be a universal deterrent. By then, however, the Allied watch on the Rhine, the best guarantee of peace – but resented hardly less in England than in

Germany as a distasteful intrusion – had been discontinued, with the tacit abandonment of disarmament control and the withdrawal five years early as a gesture of goodwill of the last divisions of the Army of Occupation. But then, were not armies of occupation and disarmament commissions felt to be almost embarrassingly irrelevant and out of date? Had not Keynes lambasted the peacemakers for turning their attention 'to frontiers and nationalities, to the balance of power, to imperial aggrandisements, to the future enfeeblement of a strong and dangerous enemy', when it was common knowledge 'that the most serious of the problems which claimed their attention were not political or territorial but financial and economic, and that the perils of the future lay not in frontiers or sovereignties but in food, coal and transport?' 'Will France be safe,' he had asked rhetorically, 'because her sentries stand on the Rhine?'

Despite his personal aversion towards the President, Keynes's vision of regeneration was in its way as humane and inspiring as Wilson's. His book was conceived as an instrument of correction and enlightenment, a vehicle for 'the assertion of truth, the unveiling of illusion, the dissipation of hate'. Would that for the world's sake it had been informed by an understanding of history equal to such objectives, or illuminated by a grasp of the ineluctable dynamism of that balance of power which he so articulately denounced. If, as Colonel House had warned, 'we are so stupid as to let Germany train and arm a large army and again become a menace to the world, we would deserve the fate which such folly would bring upon us'. But the accepted wisdom of centuries was overturned, the sagacity of ripe practitioners set at naught, the deep policy and nice calculations of Clemenceau or Foch dismissed at a stroke of the pen by a Cambridge don 35 years old. *'Nous avons changé tout cela'*, he wrote in effect; and such was the national mood which he expressed, that his paradoxes passed for home-truths. But Clio is not lightly defied: and to those who flout her admonitions, she brings if not nemesis, then certainly consequences. In this case, they came with disconcerting, with devastating speed. Keynes had assured the world of Germany's utter prostration, her condemnation by the Treaty to decades of hopeless servitude and impoverishment – and now German, not French sentries, stood on the Rhine, armed to the hilt and not noticeably undernourished. Keynes awoke, dumbfounded at the spectacle, and, noted Nicolson, 'very defeatist', as well he might be. It would be a melancholy pastime to speculate, in terms of the balance of power, of armoured divisions, of acreage of territory, of bridgeheads secured, of tactical advances, of bloodless victories, on the value to the *Wehrmacht* of *The Economic Consequences of the Peace*.

The refusal to deal face to face with the Germans in 1919, it has often been said, was a political error of the first magnitude. They were spurned, in part, because they were supposed to be, in Nicolson's words, 'the representatives of a brutal militarism'. They probably represented in fact the best hope for the emergence of a liberal Germany. Leaving aside Brockdorff-Rantzau, a career diplomat of the old school, they included Schücking, a pacifist professor of international law and future judge of the International Court; Simons, later President of the German Supreme Court; and Melchior, the respected Hamburg financier – all of them men of decency, uprightness and sensibility, spokesmen of that other Germany which it *might*, perhaps, have been worthwhile to cultivate. Their counter-proposals might sensibly have been accepted for the most part or at least negotiated in the spirit of Churchill's called-for 'split-the-difference peace'. Certainly the sterile tussles over reparations, which wasted so much energy at Paris and which poisoned the international atmosphere for the next dozen years, could and should have been settled at Versailles. There is all the difference between paying off an agreed debt accepted only under duress; a difference between the Conference of victorious powers which took place at Paris and the Congress of all the powers, the 'peace between equals', which never took place.

Be that as it may, the shunning of the Germans appears in retrospect to have been a capital error of *British* psychology. In the final act of retribution in the Hall of Mirrors, Philip Kerr found the German delegates 'the most awful worms to look at'. A dozen years later, he was hobnobbing in the less exalted company of their successors, entertaining Von Ribbentrop at Blickling, quizzing the Führer himself at Berlin, and calling indefatigably in letters and articles to *The Times* and the *Observer*, in talks on the wireless and lectures at the Institute of International Affairs, for 'a new understanding' with Germany.

It was not, as was vulgarly supposed, that he had any sympathy for the new German regime or its leaders – 'They are nothing but a lot of gunmen,' he said after the Night of the Long Knives – but he also saw them as products of Versailles: and from the acceptance that Germany had been spurned as an outcast came the conviction that she must henceforth be welcomed as an equal. 'There would be no peace in Europe', he declared, 'until Germany is given effective equality.' Addressing the House of Lords as Marquess of Lothian, he cited as legitimate German grievances: the Rhineland, Austria, the Polish corridor, the lost colonies. 'My whole point', he explained to Lionel Curtis, 'is that you cannot deal with Nazi Germany until you give her justice.'

It was this belief that sent Kerr to Berlin in 1935, bypassing what he considered the narrow professionalism of the Foreign Office, to speak man to man to the Führer 'in a proper *Round Table* method'. The German language, German history, the German mind, were a closed book to this polished product of late Victorian classical humanism, as he shook hands with the former Bavarian corporal, now Chancellor of the Reich. 'I wonder if you would care to see a copy of an interview I had with Hitler,' he wrote to Baldwin on his return; to Colonel Hankey he added: 'There is no doubt Hitler wants to come to terms with us, and I think it is essential that the British Government should open up negotiations with him.' 'I have given copies to the Prime Minister, Sir John Simon and Mr Baldwin, as I promised,' he informed Ribbentrop. 'I have seen Sir John Simon and Mr Baldwin and pressed my view as to the importance of direct Anglo-German discussions as to how Europe should be stabilised upon them and the Führer's desire for such a discussion.' Six weeks later, Hitler reintroduced conscription, in open violation of the Treaty of Versailles.

Kerr was undeterred. The following year, addressing the Anglo-German Fellowship, recently founded with the genial assistance of Ribbentrop, he called on the British Government 'to abandon once and for all what is called in Germany the Versailles attitude of mind. . . . The peace was based on the assumption of the sole war-guilt of Germany. . . . The theory of sole war-guilt led to certain permanent and unilateral discriminations against Germany which are the root of all our troubles today'.

When the German army re-entered the Rhineland, Kerr remained unperturbed – except at the possibility of British retaliation. He had long since predicted, justified, invited almost, the event. 'After all,' he observed, in a celebrated metaphor, radiant with the parochial innocence of the Home Counties, 'they are only going into their own back garden.' Such was his view of this first overt military challenge to the peace: not as the destruction of the linchpin of the French defence system, the very contingency foreseen under the abortive Anglo-American guarantee and specified as the *casus belli*, at which Britain and the United States would leap to France's defence; not as the greatest westward thrust of German arms since the Ludendorff

Offensive, which if allowed to go unchecked, would enable them, as Clemenceau had predicted, to intervene at will in Austria and Bohemia; not even as the brazen violation of the Treaty of Locarno, freely negotiated by Germany, as Hitler himself admitted; certainly not as the 'hostile act . . . calculated to disturb the peace of the world', laid down in the Treaty of Versailles – but the homely suburban image of the back garden. He sharply rebuffed any suggestion of counter-measures. 'All this stuff about collective security', he wrote to Lloyd George, 'is simply "encirclement" in a new form. The only way to peace is justice for Germany; and justice for Germany means dropping encirclement and letting Germany become the leading power in Central Europe, and then dealing with the colonial and economic questions.'

The conversion of Philip Kerr is easier to record than to explain, except in terms of a fundamental British readiness always to think well of the world, and a personal anxiety to atone for the sins of 1919. The most promising of Milner's Young Men, his humanity, his informality, his winning smile, his good looks, preserved, enhanced even, in middle age – 'a regular Prince Charming,' recalls Dr Rowse, 'gifted, glamorous, and generous' – lent an almost saintly aura to this knight of the Round Table. 'He is the most Christ-like man I have ever known,' wrote Frances Stevenson, 'and he seems to shed his personality around and radiate happiness.' How was it that Kerr, who in 1919 denounced Smuts and Barnes as 'pro-Boche', and who, in his stingingly eloquent vindication of the war-guilt clause in the final Allied reply to Brockdorff-Rantzau, delivered what a German historian of today still regards as the harshest blow of all Versailles – came forth in the 1930s as the Sir Galahad of a new Grail, the elusive mission of a 'better understanding' with Hitler, 'Justice for Germany' emblazoned on his escutcheon? He was indeed, as Baldwin noted, 'a rum cove'.

It was not that he lacked intelligence. On the contrary, he suffered from a superabundance of bright ideas, a surfeit of imaginative utopianism, a too fluent pen and an infectious charm, which all too effectively concealed his underlying lack of insight. 'I think perhaps I ought to tell you,' warned Lionel Curtis, 'that when I read your speech in the House of Lords foretelling that Germany would not submit to the demilitarized zone, I had an instinctive fear that your speech might encourage Germany to earlier and more aggressive action than she might otherwise have taken.'

To regard Philip Kerr as an isolated example, however, to set him up as the Candide of the 1930s or deride him as a political Peter Pan, would be to exaggerate his singularity and to misconstrue his historical significance. Kerr is important, not because he was extraordinary, but because he was typical; not because he was different, but because, in that time of well-meaning confusion, he was Everyman. His views were by no means as exceptional as some people liked to suppose in their retrospective search for 'guilty men'. The ideas of the 'Cliveden set' and the Anglo-German Fellowship were not the subversive poison of some reactionary fifth column, some sinister nest of Nazi conspirators: they were the received wisdom, the commonplaces of 1936. They were shared by King Edward, by broad sections in Parliament, the Church, the army and the universities and by men and women of goodwill generally. 'Ninety out of every hundred people feel no anger against the Germans,' noted Balfour's niece. 'On all sides,' agreed Nicolson 'one hears sympathy for Germany.' Why should the Germans not regarrison Cologne or Mainz, ex-servicemen asked, with what E.M. Forster called 'the special generosity towards Germans which all decent people who fought with them seem to have'. How should we feel about a prohibition against stationing British troops in Colchester or Chatham?

'As to British opinion generally,' wrote Barrington Ward, deputy editor of *The Times*, 'our difficulty has been to find enough letters stating what might be crudely called the anti-German view to balance the correspondence.' In the Commons, Sir Archibald Sinclair, for the Liberals, agreeing that 'Germany is already breaking the shackles of Versailles', added, reprovingly, 'and we ought to have struck them off before now'. Dr Dalton confirmed that 'certainly the Labour Party would not support the taking of military sanctions or even economic sanctions against Germany'. As for the Conservatives, their reaction was laconically expressed by Baldwin – 'the boys won't have it'. Kerr was only voicing a widely held truth, when he wrote to impress on the Foreign Secretary that 'British public opinion, with its traditional sagacity, feels that Germany has not had justice'.

Kerr's image of the garden seems aptly to suggest a subliminal British vision of the Rhineland as a post-lapsarian Eden, where Britain and Germany, the one purged of guilt, the other of resentment, should shake hands in reconciliation and mutual remission of trespasses. The spirit of the time is well epitomized in the name and activities of the Anglo-German Fellowship, with its mixed evocation of Arthurian chivalry, Christmas Day 1914, and the beneficent influence of the Holy Ghost. On a conscious level, the friendly rivalry of the Olympic Games at Berlin suggested an actual opportunity for such symbolic and sportsmanlike catharsis. 'Forgive and forget' sums up the general feeling. There was much talk of square deals and fair dos, of motes and beams, of doing as we would be done by, and of judging not lest we be judged. 'Let him who is without sin cast the first stone,' a clergyman wrote to *The Times*, and was singled out for approval in the Commons by Lloyd George himself, once more attuned to the vagaries of popular sentiment. What Britain desired, scarcely less than Germany, was, not to enforce Versailles, but to let it disappear as soon as possible, and to pass the sponge of oblivion over its distasteful memory. Hitler's *démarche* might be deplored as melodramatic; but its outcome was positively welcome in so far as it put paid to one particularly outstanding German grievance, dished the vindictive French, and closed a shameful chapter in post-war history.

In the hearts and minds of the people, Versailles had long been written off. It had taken an unconscionable time a-dying, and as Bishop Bell of Chichester noted, 'the ordinary man almost breathed a sigh of relief when we heard that Hitler had entered the zone'. But now it was over. It only remained for *The Times* to pronounce the final exequies. 'The old structure of European peace,' wrote Barrington-Ward two days after the *Einmarsch*, 'one-sided and unbalanced, is nearly in ruins.' His tone was not of consternation or despair at the fast-crumbling edifice of European security, but of approbation, and of confidence that the final work of demolition would not be long delayed.

Ever since 1919, when he had witnessed something of the Peace Conference, Barrington-Ward, hag-ridden with guilt towards Germany, argued persistently for revision of the Treaty. He no more favoured Nazism than did Kerr, but, like Marley's ghost, he dragged the nation's self-forged fetters around with him and raised his voice in grief-stricken moans of self-reproach. It was Barrington-Ward whom Dawson entrusted with coverage of German affairs in *The Times*. 'It is hard to escape,' he lamented of the Rhineland dilemma, 'when we are, as the Prayer Book says, "*tied and bound by the chain of our sins,*" stretching all the way back to the General Election of 1918.' There spoke the High Anglican voice of Appeasement. It was inspired by no craven or unworthy motive – Barrington-Ward had won the D.S.O. in Flanders – but from the pangs of a conscience-stricken penitent, thirsting after righteousness and absolution. This agonizing high-mindedness, this spiritual self-flagellation reached its apogee at the time of Munich. 'Must there be resistance', he asked in an editorial, 'to demands which ought to have been granted when Germany was weak, merely because she is no longer weak?' There is an element almost of sublimity in this abnegation of worldliness, this willing sacrifice of national interest to the Christian ethic, until it is recalled that, in a world of flawed humanity and sovereign states, the task of Christian statesmanship must be to emerge with strong hands as well as clean hands.

Of all the blemishes of Versailles which Keynes held up for public reprobation, he made an exception, ironically enough, of the case of the war-guilt clause; partly, perhaps, because he himself had a hand in its formulation: 'It was', he said, 'only a matter of words, of virtuosity in draftsmanship, which does no-one any harm, and which probably seemed much more important at the time than it ever will again between now and Judgment Day.' In the cynical levity of this dismissal, he underestimated the formidable power of the Protestant conscience and the painful self-remembrance of a national Church which had too readily applauded the bloodletting of the war. 'It was the sin of us all,' confessed Temple, now Archbishop of York, preaching to the Disarmament Conference in 1932, 'it was the sin of us all that brought forth in those fearful years its flower and its fruit.' He denounced, 'in the name of Christian penitence', the war-guilt clause as a thing 'which offends in principle the Christian conscience and for the deletion of which . . . the voice of Christendom must be raised.' 'If the spirit that guides us is to be the spirit of the Gospel,' he declared, 'the war-guilt clause must go – struck out by those who framed it.' It was in the same almost magnificent spirit of reckless rectitude that Germany was allowed, in the name of equality, to rearm; and in the name of justice, to occupy first the Rhineland, then Austria, next the Sudetenland – 'not because it paid to do so', as Lord Astor said, 'but because it was right.'

The victory of 1918 was lost without a shot fired and with scarcely a voice raised in its defence; lost, not so much by the force of German arms as by the force of British sentiment, and more through virtue than through vice. Goodwill, chivalry, a sense of fair play, tolerance and sympathy for the supposed underdog: these were not least among the instruments of self-destruction. In this sense, and this sense alone, it is possible to agree with Mr A.J.P. Taylor that Munich 'was a triumph for all that was best and most enlightened in British life'. In France, Appeasement was seldom more than the squalid pursuit of supposed expediency; in England it was in considerable measure applauded as a crusade for the righting of former wrongs, a process at least as necessary for the sinner as the sinned, and for peace of mind as much as for peace on earth. 'Those grievances must go,' the Socialist Internationalist Lord Noel-Buxton wrote of Hitler's demands on Czechoslovakia, 'then we may have peace; and even if not, we shall have a clear conscience.' Neville Chamberlain, having conceded those demands in full, wrote that he had 'been terribly over-praised for having done no more than was my clear and obvious duty'. Was there not some truth in the cynical jibe that, considering their constant communion with the Almighty, the Appeasers were singularly ill-advised? Had they been less high-minded and more open-minded, had they not been blinded by tears of repentance, they might have distinguished, as others did, between the removal of grievances and the whetting of appetites; have perceived that their policy was leading inexorably to the catastrophe they sought to avoid; and that, so far and so recklessly had they allowed the balance of power to slide, that war, when it came, was likely to result in defeat for the United Kingdom. 'One has only to put the case in black and white to expose its absurdity,' Vansittart commented, when Kerr, after a second visit to Hitler, renewed his pleas for an 'understanding' with Germany.

> It means, to be quite precise, the conquest of Austria and
> Czechoslovakia, and the re-conquest of Danzig and Memel,
> followed by the reduction of the other states to the condition of
> satellites – *military* satellites when required. This is a quite clear
> and comprehensible programme, but it is quite incompatible
> with our interests. We fought the last war largely to prevent this.

The way to Munich was paved with good intentions; but the example of Geoffrey Dawson, that most pervasive spokesman of Appeasement, suggests that bending over backwards to see the other side's point of view was likely to produce an inverted perspective on reality and was not necessarily conducive to strength of spine. At the time of the Peace Conference, Dawson had resigned as editor of *The Times* rather than continue to tolerate Northcliffe's irresponsible Hun-baiting. As editor again after Northcliffe's death, when the paper came into the hands of Lord Astor, he sought to restore it to respectability as the purveyor of enlightened opinion, through a process of cross-pollination at various intersecting points of the ruling circles. Here, like an assiduous bee, he both imbibed and distilled the soporific nectar of Appeasement. From weekends at Cliveden, with the Astors and Philip Kerr, to Grillion's Dining Club, from the

Institute of International Affairs at Chatham House to the Common Room at All Souls, from meetings of the Round Table or the Rhodes Trust under Philip Kerr, he bumbled purposefully along to quiet tête-à-têtes with Baldwin, Chamberlain or Halifax, stealing and giving odour. 'I lunch with Edward Halifax today,' he told Barrington-Ward some months after the Rhineland crisis, 'and shall get the low-down on the Foreign Office. It is surprising how many converts there are in these days to what may be called *The Times* point of view about Foreign Policy.' Then back to Printing House Square, and honeyed words for the German Government. 'I spend my nights', he told Kerr, 'taking out anything which I think will hurt their susceptibilities, and dropping in little things which are intended to soothe them.'

With Lloyd George, still a force to be reckoned with in the thirties, there was never any question of repentance, since, though he agreed that Versailles was not 'Holy Writ', he did not admit to any personal error. Frances Stevenson noted his agility in defending the Treaty against criticism, as usual taking the offensive, his ability 'always to make out such a completely good case for everything – the instinct of the clever lawyer at all times.' With his kingfisher dartings, however, his lightning intuitions and native acumen, there were, if not changes of heart, at any rate reappraisals. Having conceded that Germany had not really caused the war, he wondered whether she had, militarily speaking, lost it. At work on his *War Memoirs*, he told Frances Stevenson of his bewilderment that the Germans ever signed the Armistice: 'They need only have withdrawn to the Rhine and stood there. . . . He cannot find any adequate explanation of why the Germans gave in so completely.' Miss Stevenson was not the only recipient of these reappraisals. Lloyd George made the same point to Ribbentrop, on his visit to Berchtesgaden in 1936, within a few months of the Rhineland coup.

The following day, he said as much to Hitler himself, when Lloyd George too made the journey to Canossa along the hairpin bends that led to the heights of the Berghof. There was Hitler, waiting to greet him at the foot of the steps. 'One seemed to be witnessing a symbolic act of reconciliation', we are told. Inside, over tea, Hitler presented Lloyd George with his signed photograph, set in a silver frame. Lloyd George received it with visible emotion. He shook Hitler's hand. Would the Führer mind if the photograph were to be placed side by side with those of Foch, Clemenceau and the other Great Men of 1918? Hitler smilingly agreed. As long as it was nowhere near the

'November Criminals', the German signatories to the Armistice.

Lloyd George's latest infatuation was something more than the momentary lapse of a failing dotard. To sup with the devil was completely in character for the man who, at the summit of affairs in 1919, had been drawn to power like a moth to a candle, who had come to worship success for its own sake and on its own terms and to make it the first and last determinant of his actions; and who, for his final appearance on the world stage, a few years after the Berchtesgaden visit, aspired to a role that would reconcile power with practical politics – that of a British counterpart to Marshal Pétain; in which capacity, let it be said, he would doubtless have pulled off a better 'deal' than most.

With Lloyd George himself paying homage, it was scarcely necessary for Hitler to simulate agitation over Versailles. Its iniquities had long been admitted in England. Germany had been branded with responsibility for a war which, to judge from her military prowess, she deserved to win and had not conclusively lost. As the leading continental power, she had been denied that influence over *Mitteleuropa* to which her position and strength entitled her. Versailles had been a bad show, of which British opinion was now heartily ashamed and was only too ready to atone for by yielding up, peacefully and in the name of right and justice, the victory of 1918. Vansittart, at his brother's graveside in France, amid the tiers of white marble headstones, railed at the vanity of things. 'The endless rows of these cemeteries, so lovingly tended, stifled forgiveness. "We are the dead," said each stone, "and for what?"'

Abbreviations

Note Places of publication are given only for works published outside the United Kingdom.

Burnett, *Reparation*	P.M. Burnett, *Reparation at the Paris Peace Conference*, vol. I (New York, 1940).
Calwell, *Henry Wilson*	*Field-Marshal Sir Henry Wilson. His Life and Diaries*, ed. C.E. Calwell, vol. II, (1927).
Floto, *Colonel House*	Inga Floto, *Colonel House in Paris. A Study of American Policy at the Paris Peace Conference 1919 (Aarhus, 1973).*
House, *Intimate Papers*, IV	*The Intimate Papers of Colonel House*, ed. Ch. Seymour, vol. IV (1928).
Keynes, *Economic Consequences*	*The Economic Consequences of the Peace. The Collected Writings of John Maynard Keynes* vol. II (1971).
Mantoux, *Délibérations*	P. Mantoux, *Les Délibérations du Conseil des Quatre. Notes de l'officier interprète*, vols. I–II (Paris, 1955).
Riddell, *Diary*	G. Riddell, *Lord Riddell's Intimate Diary of the Peace Conference and After* (1933).
Smuts Papers	*Selections from the Smuts Papers*, ed. W.K. Hancock and J. Van der Poel, vol. IV (1966).
Stevenson, *Diary*	Frances Stevenson, *Lloyd George. A Diary by Frances Stevenson*, ed. A.J.P. Taylor (1971).
Wilson, *Public Papers*	*The Public Papers of Woodrow Wilson*, ed. R.S. Baker and W.E. Dodd, II *War and Peace. Presidential Messages, Addresses and Public Papers* (New York, 1927).

156

References

INTRODUCTION

p.ix   1.13   'The greatest triumph in the history of the world.'
       Minutes of meeting of British Empire Delegation, 1 June
       1919, Cabinet Papers, CAB/29/28.

p.x   1.33   'An appeasement, and by degrees readjustments and modifica-
       tions.'
       Cecil, Diary, 26 May 1919, Cecil Papers; *Germany and the
       Rhineland*, suppl. to *International Affairs* (April 1936), 12;
       Fisher, Diary, 31 May 1919, Fisher Papers, 8A; Fisher to G.
       Murray, 11 June 1919, Fisher Papers, 7.

p.xi   1.4   'A terrible outcome of all our professions.'
       Cecil, Diary, 20 May 1919, Cecil Papers.

p.xii   1.19   'Guilty conscience . . . was undoubtedly the strongest factor.'
       Parliamentary Debates, 35 H.L. Deb. 5s, 170; T.E. Jessop,
       The Treaty of Versailles: Was it Just? (1942), v,. A.J.P. Taylor,
       English History 1914–1945, (1965), 417.

Chapter 1. ARMISTICE

p.2   1.35   'Let them keep their weapons.'
       *Papers Relating to the Foreign Relations of the United States,
       1918, Supplement 1* I (Washington, 1933), 358; W.S. Chur-
       chill, *The Gathering Storm* (1964), 4.

p.3   1.14   'A nation of seventy millions suffers, but it does not die.'
       H. Rudin, *Armistice 1918* (Yale, 1944), 383.

p.4   1.6   'We do not think the same thoughts or speak the same lan-
       guage.'
       Address to Congress, 2 Apr. 1917, Wilson, *Public Papers*, 7;
       Address, 27 Sept. 1918, *ibid.*, 255.

p.5   1.8   'And those to whom we do not wish to be just.'
       Address to Congress, 2 Apr. 1917 and 4 Dec. 1917, Wilson,
       Public Papers, 11, 130; Address at Baltimore, 6 Apr. 1918,
       ibid., 199. Address, 27 Sept. 1918, *ibid.*, 257.

p.5   1.31   'Diplomacy conducted "always frankly and in the public view"'
         Address to Congress, 8 Jan. 1918 (The Fourteen Points
         Speech), Wilson, *Public Papers*, 159–61.

p.6   1.5   'Whether they be strong or weak.'
         Address to Congress, 11 Feb. 1918, Wilson, *Public Papers*,
         180; message to Russia, 26 May 1917, *ibid.*, 51.

p.6   1.21   'Citizens of all modern states in their relations with one another.'
         Address at Mount Vernon, 4 July 1918, Wilson, *Public
         Papers*, 234.

p.6   1.35   'Fit for free men like ourselves to live in.'
         Address to Congress, 2 Mar. 1918, Wilson, *Public Papers*, 14.

p.7   1.24   'No mere peace of shreds and patches.'
         Address at Baltimore, 6 Apr. 1918, Wilson, *Public Papers*,
         202; Address to Congress, 11 Feb. 1918, *ibid.*, 179, 182–3.

p.8   1.33   'Agreeably, if we can; disagreeably, if we must.'
         J.T. Shotwell, *At the Paris Peace Conference* (New York,
         1937), 77.

p.9   1.26   'A temper of highminded justice.'
         R.S. Baker, *Woodrow Wilson. Life and Letters* (1939) VIII,
         442.

p.10   1.1   'Send Colonel House over at the earliest possible moment.'
         *Papers Relating to the Foreign Relations of the United States,
         1918, Supplement 1*, I (Washington, 1933), 344.

p.10   1.30   'Make a renewal of hostilities on the part of Germany im-
         possible.'
         The Intimate Papers of Colonel House, ed. Ch. Seymour, I
         (1926), 118; *Papers Relating to the Foreign Relations of the
         United States, 1918, supplement 1*, I (Washington, 1933), 382.

p.11   1.13   'Clemenceau too "agreed that this was the case".'
         House, *Intimate Papers*, IV, 167; notes of a conversation at the
         Quai d'Orsay, 29 Oct. 1918, Cabinet Papers, CAB/28/5.

p.12   1.10   'The aggression of Germany by land, by sea and from the air.'
         Minutes of meeting of Imperial War Cabinet, 4 Nov. 1918,
         Burnett, *Reparation*, 407.

p.12   1.24   'To make peace with the Government of Germany on the terms
         of peace laid down.'
         The Lansing note, 5 Nov. 1918, *Papers Relating to the Foreign
         Relations of the United States, 1918, supplement 1*, I, (Washing-
         ton, 1933), 468–9.

p.13   1.5   'Between a thousand and two thousand million pounds.'
         Burnett, *Reparation*, 108; minutes of meeting of Imperial
         War Cabinet, 6 Nov. 1918, Cabinet Papers, CAB 23/44.

p.13   1.15   'Not to demand an indemnity which would include the cost of
         prosecuting the war.'
         D. Lloyd George, *Memoirs of the Peace Conference*, I, (Yale,
         1939), 325.

p.13   1.39   'To give humble and reverent thanks for the deliverance of the
              world from its great peril.'
              Hankey, Diary, 4 Nov. 1918, Hankey Papers, HNKY 1/6;
              Davidson, Diary, 17 Nov. 1918, Davidson Papers, 13;
              Parliamentary Debates, 110 H.C. Deb. 5s 1463.
p.14   1.17   'I object to these terms of peace . . . because they do not provide
              for indemnities.'
              Morning Post, 8 Nov. 1918.
p.14   1.33   'To avoid the possibility of a misunderstanding from the outset.'
              Dawson, Diary, 2 Nov. 1918, Dawson Papers; L.S. Amery,
              My Political Life II (1953), 171; Lloyd George to Hughes, 11
              Nov. 1918, Lloyd George Papers, F/28/2/10; Lloyd George,
              Statement, Lloyd George Papers, F/28/2/10.
p.15   1.8   'The question must be left to the Government, which represents
              the nation.'
              Parliamentary Debates, 110 H.C. Deb. 5s 2633–4, 2511, 3190.
p.15   1.30   'Critics had compared him first with the Kaiser and then with
              Napoleon.'
              The History of the Times, IV, pt.1 (1952), 370.
p.15   1.41   'So that he may be present at the Peace Conference?'
              Parliamentary Debates, 110 H.C. Deb.5s, 2352.
p.16   1.12   'I told him to go to hell!'
              T. Clarke, *Northcliffe in History. An Intimate Study of Press
              Power* (1950), 145.
p.16   1.28   'In a dangerous mood and likely to make trouble.'
              Hankey, Diary, 24 Nov. 1918, Hankey papers, HNKY 1/5;
              Dawson, Diary, 2 Nov. 1918, Dawson Papers.
p.18   1.17   'Any Prime Minister in our political history.'
              S.Salvidge, Diary, Nov. 1918, *Salvidge of Liverpool. Behind
              the Political Scene, 1890–1928* (1934), 167; R. Blake, *The
              Unknown Prime Minister. The Life and Times of Andrew Bonar
              Law 1858–1923* (1955), 388.
p.18   1.37   'It must not . . . be dictated by extreme men.'
              D. Lloyd George, *The Great Crusade. Extracts from Speeches
              delivered during the War* (1918), 185, 180–1.
p.19   1.8   'It will be the business of every candidate to have regard to that.'
              Minutes of Liberal Party meeting, 12 Nov. 1918, Lothian
              Papers, GD40/17/1025/3.
p.19   1.22   'What . . . is the policy of the Coalition on this matter of
              indemnity?'
              Morning Post, 22 Nov. 1918.
p.20   1.24   'Report as to what might be imposed over and above repara-
              tions.'
              Minutes of meeting of Imperial War Cabinet, 26 Nov. 1918,
              Cabinet Papers, CAB/23/42; Foster, Diary, 28 Nov. 1918,
              The Memoirs of the Rt. Hon. Sir George Foster, ed. W.S.
              Wallace (Toronto, 1933), 193.

p.21　1.2　'"I think so", agreed Cunliffe.'
　　　　　　Minutes of meeting of Imperial War Cabinet, 24 Nov. 1918,
　　　　　　Cabinet Papers, CAB/23/42; Imperial War Cabinet Commit-
　　　　　　tee on Indemnity, Report, Minutes of meeting of 6 Dec. 1918,
　　　　　　Cabinet Papers, CAB/27/43.

p.21　1.23　'Proposals about which they know absolutely nothing.'
　　　　　　Imperial War Cabinet Committee on Indemnity, Report,
　　　　　　Minutes of meeting of 29 Nov. 1918, Cabinet Papers, CAB/
　　　　　　27/43; Foster, Diary, 30 Nov. 1918, 2 Dec. 1918, 11 Dec.
　　　　　　1918, Wallace (ed.), *op. cit.*, 193,194,195.

p.21　1.31　'Germany must pay the costs of the war up to the limit of her
　　　　　　capacity.'
　　　　　　The Times, 30 Nov. 1918.

p.22　1.6　'Don't be always making mischief.'
　　　　　　The Times, 30 Nov. 1918; Dawson, memoir of March 1919,
　　　　　　Dawson Papers; Lloyd George, *Memoirs of the Peace Confer-
　　　　　　ence* I, 311.

p.22　1.27　'You may find yourself committed to much more than you desire
　　　　　　to be.'
　　　　　　C.P. Scott to J.L. Hammond, 4 Dec. 1918, *The Political
　　　　　　Diaries of C.P. Scott 1911–1928*, ed. T. Wilson (1970), 362;
　　　　　　Notes of Allied Conversation, 2 Dec. 1918, Cabinet Papers,
　　　　　　CAB/28/5; *ibid.* 3 Dec. 1918, CAB/23/42; Smuts to Lloyd
　　　　　　George, 4 Dec. 1918, Lloyd George Papers, F/45/9/25.

p.23　1.10　'"It is impossible," echoed Cunliffe.'
　　　　　　A. Duff Cooper, Diary, *Old Men Forget* (1953), 93; Hankey,
　　　　　　Diary, 25 Dec. 1918, Hankey Papers, HNKY 1/5; Imperial
　　　　　　War Cabinet Committee on Indemnity, Report, Minutes of
　　　　　　meeting of 9 Dec. 1918, Cabinet Papers, CAB/27/43.

p.23　1.27　'The total cost of the war to the Allies.'
　　　　　　Imperial War Cabinet Committee on Indemnity, Report,
　　　　　　Minutes of meeting 10 Dec. 1918, Cabinet Papers, CAB/27/
　　　　　　43.

p.24　1.3　'We propose . . . to demand the whole cost of the war.'
　　　　　　The Times, 12 Dec. 1918.

p.24　1.26　'To squeeze Germany "until the pips squeak".'
　　　　　　Cambridge Chronicle, 11 Dec. 1918.

p.24　1.36　'A peace that did not contain in itself the seeds of future
　　　　　　quarrels.'
　　　　　　D. Lloyd George, *Memoirs of the Peace Conference* I, 310; *The
　　　　　　Times*, 10 Dec. 1918.

p.25　1.30　'If you take my advice, you won't touch it.'
　　　　　　Minutes of meeting of Imperial War Cabinet, 5 Nov. 1918.
　　　　　　Cabinet Papers, CAB/23/42; Diary, 11 Nov. 1918, Calwell,
　　　　　　Henry Wilson, 149; Curzon to Lloyd George, 13 Nov. 1918,
　　　　　　Beaverbrook, *Men and Power, 1917–1918* (1956), 387; M.
　　　　　　Hankey, *Politics, Trials and Errors*, (1950), 1.

p.26   1.16   'I am for hanging the Kaiser.'
           Stamfordham to George V, 5 Dec. 1918, H. Nicolson, *King George the Fifth* (1952), 337; *Cambridge Chronicle*, 6 Nov. 1918; *The Times*, 2 Dec. 1918.

p.26   1.32   'The country is not likely to . . . be tender towards the record of their failure.'
           Diary, 2 Dec. 1918, A. Fitzroy, *Memoirs*, II (1925), 688.

p.27   1.13   'No thoughtful people . . . who really advocate the trial of the Kaiser.'
           Bryce to A.V. Dicey, 31 Dec. 1918, Bryce Papers, 200; Diary, 13 Dec. 1918, Calwell, *Henry Wilson*, 155; Davidson, Diary, 8 Dec. 1918, Davidson Papers, 13; Buckmaster to A. Chamberlain, 7 Dec. 1918, Chamberlain Papers, AC 15/1/35A; *Manchester Guardian*, 11 Dec. 1918; F. Maurice, *Haldane. The Life of Viscount Haldane of Cloan* II, (1939), 64; Milner, Diary, 13 Dec. 1918, Milner Papers, Dep. 89; Davidson, Diary, 8 Dec. 1918, Davidson Papers, 13.

p.27   1.36   'These being the "controlling consideration".'
           Minutes of meeting of Imperial War Cabinet, 24 Dec. 1918, Cabinet Papers, CAB/23/42.

p.28   1.3   'Whatever the amount Germany does pay, we should get our fair share.'
           Amery to Smuts, 26 Dec. 1918, *Smuts Papers*, 33.

p.28   1.28   'Distrust of our Allies and a determination for swag.'
           Minutes of meeting of Imperial War Cabinet, 24 Dec. 1918, Cabinet Papers CAB/23/42; Montagu to Balfour, 20 Dec. 1918, Balfour Papers, FO 800/215.

p.28   1.38   'A man of clear, dispassionate judgment.'
           Nicolson, *op. cit.*, 331.

p.29   1.10   'For the good of Lloyd George himself, and to make for unity.'
           Hankey, Diary, 23 Nov. 1918 and 24 Nov. 1918, Hankey Papers, HNKY 1/5.

p.29   1.19   'Mumbled something about "considering the proposal".'
           R. Jenkins, *Asquith* (1964), 477.

p.29   1.34   '"That's the place for the Kaiser's trial!" he exclaimed.'
           M. Hankey, *Politics, Trials and Errors*, 3.

Chapter 2. PEACEMAKING

p.30   1.20   'They are the principles of mankind, and must prevail.'
           Address to Senate, 22 Jan. 1917, *The Public Papers of Woodrow Wilson.* II, ed. R.S. Baker and W.E. Dodd, *The New Democracy. Presidential Messages, Addresses and Other Papers* (New York 1926), 414.

p.31   1.23   'I believe we shall come to an early agreement.'
           Report by C.L. Swem, erroneously related to Wilson's

second crossing to France, H. Hoover, *The Ordeal of Wood-row Wilson*, (1958), 193–4.

p.32 1.10 'A really hard resistance from President Wilson.'
Minutes of meeting of Imperial War Cabinet, 30 Dec. 1918 and 31 Dec. 1918, Cabinet Papers, CAB/23/42.

p.32 1.26 'Expressive of the will of the American people.'
A. Walworth, *Woodrow Wilson*, II (2nd edn., Boston, 1965), 216–17.

p.33 1.2 'Part of the reparations that they owe us.'
L.S. Amery, *My Political Life* II (1953), 179; I. Malcolm, *Lord Balfour. A Memory* (1930), 67–8.

p.33 1.24 'Lord Birkenhead – "flanked by a bottle of champagne".'
Milner, Diary, 5 Feb. 1919, Milner Papers, dep. 90; Dawson, letter, 18 Jan. 1919 and 22 Jan. 1919, J.E. Wrench, *Geoffrey Dawson and Our Times* (1955), 193–4.

p.33 1.37 'They are "always summoned when some particularly nefarious act has to be committed.".'
Letter to Koppel, 30 June 1919, James Headlam-Morley, *A Memoir of the Paris Peace Conference 1919*, ed. A. Headlam-Morley (1972), 180.

p.34 1.19 'It remains only to give it a fair construction.'
Minutes of meeting 13 Feb. 1919, Commission on the Reparation of Damage, Paris, 1919, Keynes Papers, RT/12; Burnett, *Reparation*, 568, 574; A. Tardieu, *The Truth about the Treaty* (1921), 287; *La Paix de Versailles. La Commission de Réparations des Dommages* (Paris, 1932) I, 76.

p.34 1.33 'A matter of first-class importance.'
Minutes of meeting of War Cabinet, 25 Feb. 1919, Cabinet Papers CAB/23/9; Kerr to Lloyd George, 22 Feb. 1919, Lloyd George Papers, F/89/2/27.

p.36 1.8 'The delegates "should not recede from the attitude adopted".'
Sumner to I. Malcolm, 20 Feb. 1919, Balfour Papers, FO 800/215; Minutes of meeting of War Cabinet 25 Feb. 1919, Cabinet Papers, CAB/23/9.

p.36 1.14 'Mr. Hughes announced that he was not prepared to present any report which did not.'
Dudley Ward, memorandum to Hankey, 24 Feb. 1919, Keynes Papers, RT/12.

p.36 1.26 'With a view to some agreement on broad lines.'
Sumner to Kerr, 4 Mar. 1919, Lothian Papers, GD40/17/64/17–18; Hankey to Lloyd George, H. Elcock, *Portrait of a Decision. The Council of Four and the Treaty of Versailles* (1972), 124.

p.36 1.37 'We would absolutely refuse to ask for any indemnity from Germany.'
Papers Relating to the Foreign Relations of the United States. The Paris Peace Conference, 1919 (Washington, 1945) XI, 73.

p.37 1.8   'Cannot now honourably alter simply because we have the power.'
    Burnett, *Reparation*, 613–14.

p.37 1.19 'The question . . . "admitted of legitimate divergence of opinion".'
    A History of the Peace Conference of Paris, ed. H.W.V. Temperley VI, (1924) 353–4.

p.38 1.39 'It was the Tories that won the election, *and he will soon begin to find that out.*'
    Hardinge to Miss Bell, 6 Dec. 1918, Hardinge Papers, 39/278; Stevenson, *Diary*, 169; 5 Mar. 1919.

p.39 1.4   'The most uncontrolled and the most passion-driven.'
    J.M. Kenworthy, *Sailors, Statesmen and Others. An Autobiography* (1933), 157.

p.40 1.18 'Unscrupulous characters which are to be found in the present House.'
    Keynes, *Economic Consequences*, 91; Davidson to Stamfordham, H. Nicolson, *King George the Fifth* (1952), 333; *idem, Peacemaking 1919* (1933), 63.

p.41 1.13 'Evidently to the taste of a crowded house.'
    John Bull, 12 Oct. 1918; Kenworthy, *op. cit.*, 158; *Parliamentary Debates*, 112 H.C. Deb. 5s, 130; *The Times*, 13 Feb. 1919.

p.41 1.23 'Your presence has become indispensable.'
    D. Lloyd George, *Memoirs of the Peace Conference*, I (Yale, 1939), 305; B. Webb, 22 Feb. 1919, *Diaries 1912–1924*, ed. M. Cole (1952), 149; Kerr to Lloyd George, 3 Mar. 1919, Lloyd George Papers, F/89/2/39.

p.41 1.41 'French demands alone "would probably absorb the whole of the amount it was possible to obtain from Germany".'
    Minutes of meeting of War Cabinet, 19 Feb. 1919, Cabinet Papers, CAB 23/9.

p.42 1.23 'Lloyd George . . . "had had several conversations with Colonel House on the subject".'
    Minutes of meeting of War Cabinet; 19 Feb. 1919, Cabinet Papers CAB/23/9; House to Wilson, 7 Mar. 1919, Floto, *Colonel House*, 314; Minutes of meeting of British Empire Delegation, 13 Mar. 1919, Cabinet Papers, CAB/29/28.

p.43 1.7   'He did not want to let the Conservatives "throw him" on a question of such popular concern.'
    House, Diary, 6 Mar. 1919, Floto, *Colonel House*, 152; House, Diary, 27 Feb. 1919, *Intimate Papers*, IV, 355; House, Diary, 10 Mar. 1919, M. Trachtenberg, *Reparation in World Politics. France and European Economic Diplomacy 1916–1923* (New York, 1980), 360; Hankey to Lloyd George, 21 Feb. 1919, Lloyd George Papers, F/23/4/19; House, Diary, 27 Feb. 1919, Burnett, *Reparation*, 631.

p.43   1.32   'To include the capitalised cost of our pensions in our claim.'
House, Diary, 6 Mar. 1919, Floto, *Colonel House*, 152;
Minutes of meeting of British Empire Delegation, 13 Mar.
1919, Cabinet Papers, CAB/29/28.

p.44   1.10   *'Dans le plus grand secret.'*
Montagu to Lloyd George, 24 Feb. 1919, Lloyd George
Papers, F/40/2/38; L Loucheur, Diary, 10 Mar. 1919, *Carnets
Secrets 1908–1932*, ed. J. De Launey (Brussels, 1962), 71.

p.44   1.39   'I would as soon doubt your loyalty as his.'
Ch. Seymour, 'End of a friendship', *American Heritage*,
(August 1963), 80.

p.45   1.39   'I won't come back, till it's over, over there!'
Address, 4 Mar. 1919, Wilson, *Public Papers*, 444.

p.47   1.10   'Probably lead to another war.'
Stevenson, *Diary*, p. 175, 24 Mar. 1919.

p.48   1.16   'Quite willing to permit the Germans to default on it.'
Montagu, Memorandum, 4 Apr. 1919, Montagu Papers,
AS-I-12; House, Diary, 10 Mar. 1919, V. Czernin, *Versailles
1919* (New York, 1968), 288.

p.48   1.24   'Crucified at home if his original experts were not also brought
down to reasonable figures.'
Davis, Memorandum to Wilson, 25 Mar. 1919, Burnett,
Reparation, 711.

p.48   1.35   'The pressure of a state of war . . . will eventually bring them to
sign.'
Report by Sumner, Cunliffe and Hughes, 18 Mar. 1919,
Lloyd George Papers, F/213/2/1.

p.49   1.9   'Put their heads together, went off the deep end, and refused to
compromise at all.'
Sumner, Memorandum, 22 Mar.1919, Lloyd George Papers,
F/213/5/11; Davis, Memorandum to Wilson, 25 Mar. 1919,
Burnett, *Reparation*, 711.

p.49   1.23   'He agrees with me.'
T. Lamont, 'Reparations', *What Really Happened at Paris.
The Story of the Peace Conference 1918–1919*, ed. E.M. House
and Ch. Seymour (1921) 267–8; Smuts to M.C. Gillett, 29
Mar. 1919, *Smuts Papers*, 93; Smuts to Alice Clark, 28 Mar.
1919, *ibid.*, 90.

p.49   1.39   'To face the situation boldly and go under if necessary.'
Minutes of meeting of 26 Mar. 1919 and 27 Mar. 1919,
Mantoux, *Délibérations*, I, 27–8, 46; Smuts to M.C. Gillett,
27 Mar. 1919, *Smuts Papers*, 89.

p.50   1.22   'His want of courage and love of shooting from behind walls.'
F.S. Oliver to A. Chamberlain, 16 Mar. 1919, Chamberlain
Papers, AC 14/6/107.

p.51   1.13   'High authority.'
                Westminster Gazette, 31 March 1919; *Parliamentary Debates*,
                114 H.C. Deb. 5s, 1313.

p.51   1.30   'A struggle between Northcliffe and Wilson for the soul of
                Lloyd George – who has no soul.'
                Baker, Diary, 9 Apr. 1919, Floto, *Colonel House*, 197.

p.52   1.3   'Government has never recognised . . . a logical distinction
                between reparation and indemnity, including cost of war.'
                Lloyd George to Bonar Law, 2 Apr. 1919, Lloyd George
                Papers, F/30/3/41.

p.52   1.16   'Nine out of ten of the Unionist members at least were very
                disgusted.'
                R. Blake, *The Unknown Prime Minister. The Life and Times of
                Andrew Bonar Law 1858–1923* (1955), 407.

p.53   1.1   'A clever piece of electioneering legerdemain.'
                The Times, 19 May 1919.

Chapter 3. DRAFTSMANSHIP

p.55   1.9   'Wilson found "very legalistic" and rejected . . . "almost with
                contempt".'
                Sumner, Memorandum, 30 Mar. 1919, Lloyd George Papers,
                F/213/5/25; Lamont to Burnett, 25 June 1934, Burnett,
                Reparation, 63.

p.55   1.20   'In good conscience before God and the future.'
                Sumner to Lloyd George, 31 Mar. 1919, Lloyd George
                Papers, F/46/2/4.

p.55   1.31   'That is where the matter was left last night.'
                29 Mar. 1919, Mantoux, *Délibérations*, I, 83; Lloyd George to
                Bonar Law, 31 Mar. 1919, Lloyd George Papers, F/30/3/40.

p.56   1.7   'House has given away everything I had won before we left.'
                Edith Wilson, *Memoirs of Mrs. Woodrow Wilson* (1939), 293.

p.56   1.32   'You are a mere instrument, one among many.'
                A.J.P. Taylor, *Lloyd George. Rise and Fall* (1961), 9;
                B. Webb, *Diaries, 1912–1924*, ed. M. Cole (1952), 112.

p.57   1.16   'Valued his opinion more highly . . . "than that of any other
                person on the British delegation".'
                Nicolson, Diary, 11 Apr. 1919 and 24 June 1919, *Peace-
                making 1919* (1933) 311, 364; Smuts to Lloyd George, 26 Mar.
                1919, Lloyd George Papers, F/45/9/29; Smuts to M.C.
                Gillett, 19 May 1919, *Smuts Papers*, 171.

p.57   1.38   'A thing I had not done for more than twelve years.'
                L.F. Fitzhardinge, 'W.M. Hughes and the Treaty of Versail-
                les 1919'. *J. Commonwealth Political Studies*, V (1967) 137;
                A. Walworth, *Woodrow Wilson*, II (2nd edn., Boston, 1965),
                250; Smuts to M.C. Gillett, 31 Mar. 1919, *Smuts Papers*, 95.

p.58   1.18   'It is a farcical world.'
> Smuts to Alice Clark, 28 Mar. 1919, *Smuts Papers*, 90; Smuts
> to M.C. Gillett, 27 Mar. 1919 and 31 Mar. 1919, *ibid.*, 89, 95.

p.58   1.36   'Broad application of principles previously enunciated.'
> Burnett, *Reparation*, 776, 777.

p.60   1.14   'Establishment of just democracy throughout the world.'
> *Papers Relating to the Foreign Relations of the United States.*
> *The Paris Peace Conference 1919*, I (Washington, 1942), 1.

p.61   1.1   'Not a compromise of principle, but a compromise of detail.'
> House, Diary, 14 Feb. 1919, *Intimate Papers*, IV, 341.

p.61   1.20   'The essential justice of that particular case.'
> Address to Congress, 11 Feb. 1918, Wilson, *Public Papers*,
> 182.

p.61   1.27   'Tell me what's right, and I'll fight for it.'
> J.T. Shotwell, *At the Paris Peace Conference* (New York,
> 1937), 78.

p.62   1.4   'Our unlimited right to compensation for all damages suffered.'
> Minutes of meeting of 1 Apr. 1919, Mantoux, *Délibérations*, I,
> 109.

p.62   1.32   'Very important to mention that our right is unlimited.'
> Minutes of meeting of 29 Mar. 1919 and 31 Mar. 1919,
> Mantoux, *Délibérations*, I, 83–4, 85.

p.63   1.11   'We disagreed about everything.'
> House, Diary, 20 Mar. 1919, *Intimate Papers*, IV, 405.

p.63   1.30   'I really pitied him.'
> Baker, Diary, 2 Apr. 1919, Floto, *Colonel House*, 203;
> V. McCormick, Diary, 3 Apr. 1919, H. Hoover, *The Ordeal
> of Woodrow Wilson* (1958), 199.

p.64   1.20   'Bottled-up wrath at Lloyd George.'
> G. Smith, *When the Cheering Stopped* (1964), 47–48.

p.65   1.14   'He conciliates . . . into the solid flesh of principle.'
> House, Diary, 2 Apr. 1919, *Intimate Papers*, IV, 412; Baker,
> Diary, 3 Apr. 1919, Floto, *Colonel House*, 192.

p.65   1.24   'A good American . . . very nearly as good as a Frenchman.'
> A. Walworth, *Woodrow Wilson*, II (2nd edn., 1965), 282.

p.66   1.2   'His wretched, hypocritical Fourteen Points.'
> R. Lansing, *The Big Four and Others of the Peace Conference*
> (1922), 60; Hankey to his wife, 25 Apr. 1919, Hankey Papers,
> HNKY 3/25.

p.66   1.19   'To settle all subjects necessary for a peace.'
> Baker, Diary, 3 Apr. 1919, Floto, *Colonel House*, 192; House,
> Diary, 4 Apr. 1919, *ibid.*, 332.

p.66   1.31   'The war imposed upon them by the aggression of the enemy
states.'
> Stevenson, *Diary*, 178; Burnett, *Reparation*, 817.

p.67   1.5   'The text must be drafted so as not to constitute a violation of our
engagements.'

Burnett, *Reparation*, 817, 825–6.

p.67 1.16 '*I am getting my own way!*'
Mantoux, *Délibérations*, I, 152; Stevenson, *Diary*, 178.

p.67 1.39 'You are far and away ahead of the whole lot.'
Cecil to Lloyd George, 4 Apr. 1919, Lloyd George Papers,
F/6/6/25; Stevenson, *Diary*, 178.

p.68 1.19 'To conform to the principles of the Fourteen Points.'
House, Diary, 6 Apr. 1919, *Intimate Papers*, IV, 417.

p.68 1.28 '*As soon as you think it is safe for me to make the trip.*'
Edith Wilson, *op. cit.*, 297.

p.69 1.37 'We are gambling each day with the situation.'
House, Diary, 22 Mar. 1919, *Intimate Papers*, IV, 405.

p.70 1.11 'Lest they should mar more than they mend.'
W. Wilson, *When a Man comes to Himself* (New York, 1915),
30–1.

p.70 1.32 'The business of the League to set such matters right.'
J.S. Barnes, *Half a Life* (1933), 323.

p.72 1.35 'A great deal of give and take.'
Barnes, *op. cit.*, 323.

p.73 1.24 'The things for which the heart of mankind has longed.'
Address at Manchester, 30 Dec. 1918, Wilson, *Public Papers*,
351.

p.74 1.3 'A puckish grin to crease the face of Lloyd George.'
W. Wilson, *When a Man comes to Himself*, 30–1; Barnes, *op.
cit.*, 323.

p.74 1.24 'We saw in him no more than a presbyterian dominie.'
Baker, Diary, 30 Apr. 1919, R.S. Baker, *Woodrow Wilson and
World Settlement*, II (1923), 266; Nicolson, *op. cit.*, 164.

p.75 1.3 'President Wilson has a very elastic mind.'
Address to Congress, 11 Dec. 1918, Wilson, *Public Papers*,
182; Hankey, Diary, 13 May 1919, Hankey Papers, HNKY
1/5.

p.75 1.27 'I absolutely can.'
J.C. Smuts, *Jan Christian Smuts* (1952), 222.

p.76 1.2 '*Se refaire une virginité* at the expense of Italy'.
Nicolson, Diary, 30 Apr. 1919, *op. cit.*, 319.

p.76 1.19 'To fulfil, *at least in words*, the expectations of their constituents.'
Burnett, *Reparation*, 27.

p.76 1.42 'Urged "Lloyd George to return to England for a few days".'
Riddell, *Diary*, 50, 11 Apr. 1919.

p.77 1.9 'The ineffable Hughes.'
Cecil, Diary, 27 Feb. 1919, Cecil Papers.

p.77 1.32 'Heads I win, tails you lose.'
Minutes of meeting of Imperial War Cabinet, 11 Apr. 1919,
Lloyd George Papers, F/28/3/26; Hankey to his wife, 12 Apr.
1919, Hankey Papers, HNKY 3/25; Hughes to Lloyd

George, 11 Apr. 1919, Lloyd George Papers, F/28/3/26;
Lloyd George to Hughes, 14 Apr. 1919, *ibid.*, F/28/3/27.

p.78 1.8 'To attack Northcliffe and declare war to the knife.'
Stevenson, *Diary*, 179–180, 14 Apr. 1919.

p.78 1.28 'The House of Commons . . . would have been free to take its own action.'
The Times, 17 Apr. 1919.

p.80 1.2 'A threepenny edition of the *Daily Mail*.'
Parliamentary debates, H.C. 114 Deb. 5s, 2953.

p.80 1.12 'I would as soon as rely on a grasshopper.'
Parliamentary Debates, H.C. 114 Deb. 5s, 2952.

p.80 1.18 'There are many eligible offers.'
Parliamentary Debates, H.C. 114 Deb. 5s, 2950; *The Times*, 17 Apr. 1919.

p.80 1.39 'A wonderful performance – one of his very best.'
Observer, 20 Apr. 1919; Stevenson, *Diary*, 180.

Chapter 4. VERSAILLES

p.81 1.8 'Until we had seen all we could endure.'
Simons to his wife, 30 Apr. 1919, *The German Delegation at the Paris Peace Conference*, ed. A. Luckau (New York, 1941), 115.

p.82 1.3 'The force of circumstances . . . determined the matter.'
Kerr to Headlam-Morley, 20 Dec. 1921, Lothian Papers.

p.83 1.18 'We are to present the terms . . . tomorrow.'
Diary 5 May 1919 and 6 May 1919, Calwell, *Henry Wilson*, 189.

p.84 1.2 'What worse fate have we . . . in the event of refusal?'
Keynes to Bradbury, 4 May 1919, Keynes Papers, PT/1/.

p.84 1.12 'It has taken adroitness to lead us in.'
H. Hoover, *The Ordeal of Woodrow Wilson* (New York, 1958), 234; Keynes to Bradbury, 4 May 1919, Keynes Papers, PT/1/.

p.84 1.40 'Received it with a stiff little bow.'
La Paix de Versailles, I. Les Conditions de l'Entente (Paris, 1930), 3; Riddell, *Diary*, 72: 7 May 1919.

p.85 1.25 'Almost anxious to recommence the war.'
Hankey to his wife, 8 May 1919, Hankey Papers, HNKY 3/25; Kerr to his mother, 13 May 1919, Lothian Papers, GD40/17/466/25.

p.87 1.12 'If the agreed bases of the peace remain unshaken.'
Brockdorff-Rantzau, *Dokumente* (Charlottenburg, 1920), 113, 114–16, 118.

p.87 1.38 'The manner in which they said it.'
Stevenson, *Diary*, 183: 7 May 1919; Headlam-Morley to P. Koppel, 8 May 1919, Headlam-Morley Papers.

p.88 1.2 'The most tactless speech I have ever heard.'
   Riddell, *Diary*, 74: 7 May 1919.

p.89 1.3 'Something which the conditions did not justify.'
   Parliamentary Debates, 33 H.L., Deb. 5s 124.

p.89 1.27 'The reconciling and enduring peace.'
   New Statesman, 19 Apr. 1919; *Spectator*, 19 Apr. 1919;
   Observer, 13 Apr. 1919.

p.90 1.1 'Anything of that kind . . . must be bad.'
   Bonar Law to Lloyd George, 9 May 1919, Lloyd George
   Papers, F/30/3/54.

p.90 1.8 'A peace of appeasement or a peace of violence.'
   Diary, 10 May 1919, B. Webb, *Diaries 1912–1924*, ed.
   M. Cole (1952), 159; *Manchester Guardian*, 10 May 1919.

p.90 1.38 'The duty of man to man.'
   Davidson to Brent, 11 Dec. 1918, Davidson Papers, War
   Boxes, 28; Davidson, Notes, Jan. 1919, *ibid.*, 9/56, 9/57;
   Davidson to his wife, 12 Jan. 1919, *ibid.*, 9/57.

p.91 1.18 'A peace of finality.'
   Alice Clark to Smuts, 15 May 1919, *Smuts Papers*, 159,160.
   The Times, 19 May 1919.

p.92 1.3 'Rely upon the support of your countrymen.'
   Nicolson, Diary, 9 Apr. 1919, *Peacemaking 1919* (1933),308;
   Alice Clark to Smuts 15 May 1919, *Smuts Papers* 159; T.
   Jones, Diary, 14 Apr. 1919, *Whitehall Diary*, ed. K. Middle-
   mas I (1969), 84; Long to Lloyd George, 29 Apr. 1919, Ch.
   Petrie, *Walter Long and his Times* (1936), 220.

p.92 1.38 'Such that we can ask God's blessing upon it.'
   Cecil, Diary, 22 May 1919, Cecil Papers; *New Statesman*, 31
   May 1919; Davidson to Lloyd George, 24 May 1919, David-
   son Papers, War Boxes, 27.

p.93 1.6 'We shall not . . . ever be able to get all that is owed to us.'
   Spectator, 19 Apr. 1919.

p.93 1.32 'We shall get a genuine German acceptance.'
   Barnes to Lloyd George, 16 May 1919, Lloyd George Papers,
   F/4/3/15; Cecil to Lloyd George, 14 May 1919, *ibid.*, F/6/6/45;
   Smuts to Lloyd George, 22 May 1919, *ibid.*, F/45/9/35; Cecil
   to Lloyd George, 27 May 1919, *ibid.*, F/45/9/35; Churchill,
   Memorandum to Lloyd George, 21 May 1919, Keynes Pap-
   ers, PT/32.

p.94 1.11 'Unless important alterations are made in it.'
   Bonar Law to Lloyd George, 31 May 1919, Lloyd George
   Papers, F/30/3/71; Wilson, Diary, 30 May 1919, Calwell,
   Henry Wilson, 195; Smuts to Lloyd George, 30 May 1919,
   Smuts Papers, 207; to his mother, 20 May 1919, *ibid.*, 179.

p.94 1.28 'A case requiring considerable modification of the Treaty.'
   Montagu, note, 4 June 1919, S.D. Waley, *Edwin Montagu*
   (1964), 211.

p.94 1.38 'Very much impressed.'
Diary, 31 May 1919, Calwell, *Henry Wilson*, 196; Fisher, Diary, 31 May 1919, Fisher Papers, 8A; Montagu, note, 4 June 1919, Waley, *op. cit.* 211.

p.95 1.14 'A "split-the-difference peace".'
Montagu, note, 4 June 1919, Waley, *op. cit.*, 211; Minutes of meeting of British Empire Delegation, 1 June 1919, Cabinet Papers, CAB/29/28.

p.95 1.20 'The French would give up nothing unless they were forced.'
Minutes of meeting of British Empire Delegation, 1 June 1919, Cabinet Papers, CAB/29/28.

p.95 1.36 'It would be moderation which would save the world.'
Minutes of meeting of British Empire Delegation, 1 June 1919, Cabinet Papers, CAB/29/28.

p.96 1.2 'Barnes and Smuts were actually "refusing to sign".'
Minutes of meeting of 2 June 1919, *Papers Relating to the Foreign Relations of the United States. The Paris Peace Conference 1919* (Washington, 1946), VI, 139.

p.96 1.27 'He would give up a good deal to get a signature.'
Cecil, Diary, 31 May 1919, Cecil Papers; Minutes of meeting of 2 June 1919, *Papers Relating to the Foreign Relations of the United States. The Paris Peace Conference, 1919, (Washington 1946)*, VI, 146; Montagu, note, 4 June 1919, Waley, *op. cit.*, 212; Minutes of meeting of British Empire Delegation, 1 June 1919, Cabinet Papers, CAB/29/28.

p.96 1.41 'Monstrous to put Germans under Polish rule.'
Lloyd George to Davidson, 30 May 1919, Davidson Papers, War Boxes, 27; Minutes of meeting of British Empire Delegation, 1 June 1919, Cabinet Papers, CAB/29/28.

p.97 1.15 'Without nearly as much interference in her economic life as she so richly merits.'
Sumner, Memorandum, 31 May 1919, Lloyd George Papers, F/213/5/36; Cunliffe, Memorandum, 1 June 1919, Lothian Papers, GD40/17/62, 11–15.

p.97 1.30 'Not of a corner of France, but of Europe.'
Smuts to Lloyd George, 4 June 1919, Lloyd George Papers, F/45/9/41

p.97 1.39 'The Treaty . . . must be signed.'
Sumner, Memorandum, 3 June 1919, Lloyd George Papers, F/46/2/4, and Memorandum 5 June 1919, *ibid.* F/46/2/10.

p.98 1.17 'Really weighty and trustworthy people.'
Minutes of meeting of 9 June 1919, *Papers relating to the Foreign Relations of the United States, The Paris Peace Conference, 1919*, VI, 261, 262; Davidson to Lloyd George, 24 May 1919, Davidson Papers, War Boxes, 27.

p.98 1.26 'No longer any time for dodges and subterfuges.'
Smuts to M.C. Gillett, 3 June 1919, *Smuts Papers*, 219.

p.98 1.40 'I do not want to do anything to break the spirit of our people.'
Minutes of meeting of 13 June 1919, Mantoux, *Déliberations*,
II, 410.

p.99 1.24 'A chance of improving the thing and he won't take it.'
Minutes of meeting of American Commissioners, 3 June
1919, *Papers Relating to the Foreign Relations of the United
States. The Paris Peace Conference, 1919* (Washington, 1945),
XI, 222; Minutes of meeting of 3 June 1919, Mantoux,
Déliberations, II, 278; Nicolson, Diary, 5 June 1919, *op. cit.*, 358.

p.100 1.4 'You make me sick!'
B. Baruch, *The Public Years*, (1961), 118.

p.100 1.27 'Is it right? Is it just?'
Edith G. Reid, *Woodrow Wilson. The Caricature, the Myth and
the Man* (1934), 160; Address of 27 Sept. 1918, Wilson, *Public
Papers*, 257; Wilson to Smuts, 16 May 1919, *Smuts Papers*,
161; 30 May 1919, Wilson, *Public Papers*, 505.

p.101 1.13 'Justice had shown itself overwhelmingly against Germany.'
Lansing, 'The mentality of Woodrow Wilson', diary entry 20
Nov. 1921, J. Braeman (ed.) *Wilson* (Englewood Cliffs, N.J.,
1972), 87; Minutes of meeting of 2 June 1919, in Mantoux,
Déliberations, II, 273; Minutes of meeting of 3 June 1919,
*Papers Relating to the Foreign Relations of the United States.
The Paris Peace Conference, 1919*, VI, 159.

p.102 1.19 'Such things can lead only to the most severe punishment.'
Wilson to Smuts, 16 May 1919, *Smuts Papers*, 160–1.

p.102 1.37 'We are entirely convinced of her guilt.'
Minutes of meeting of 12 June 1919, Mantoux, *Déliberations*,
II, 391.

p.103 1.8 'Any nation, calling itself civilised.'
*Papers Relating to the Foreign Relations of the United States.
The Paris Peace Conference, 1919.* VI, 926–7.

p.103 1.16 'To stir up public opinion again to a cértain extent.'
Minutes of meeting of 12 June 1919, *Papers Relating to the
Foreign Relations of the United States. The Paris Peace Confer-
ence, 1919*, VI, 327.

p.103 1.29 'To sign or not to sign.'
Minutes of meeting of 22 June, 1919, *Papers Relating to the
Foreign Relations of the United States. The Paris Peace Confer-
ence, 1919*, VI, 605–6.

p.103 1.39 'Unheard-of injustice of the conditions of peace.'
*Papers Relating to the Foreign Relations of the United States.
The Paris Peace Conference, 1919*, VI, 644.

p.104 1.9 '"En êtes-vous sûr"?'
Nicolson, Diary, 28 June 1919, *op.cit.*, 370.

p.104 1.26 'Milner "impassive"; and Barnes "benign".'
Nicolson Diary, 28 June 1919, *op. cit.*, 368; H.W. Harris, *The
Peace in the Making*, (1920), 194.

Chapter 5. THE PEACEMAKERS

p.105　1.18　'Men come together at such a time and for such a purpose.'
House, Diary, 29 June 1919, *Intimate Papers*, IV, 504.

p.107　1.31　'Bring home something which would pass muster for a week.'
H. Nicolson, to his wife, 28 May 1919, *Peacemaking 1919*
(1933), 350; Keynes, *Economic Consequences*, 143.

p.108　1.14　'If that acknowledgment is repudiated . . . the Treaty is destroyed.'
Report of London Conference, 3 Mar. 1921, J. Headlam-
Morley, Responsibility for the War and the Treaty of Versailles. Confidential Foreign Office memorandum, 30 Oct. 1925,
12837/c/13831/1085/18, Headlam-Morley Papers.

p.109　1.10　'They will seek only the chance to obtain revenge.'
House to Seymour, 7 Apr. 1928, House, *Intimate Papers*, IV,
197; 28 Mar. 1919, Mantoux, *Déliberations*, I, 70.

p.110　1.20　'He became as common clay.'
House, Diary, 29 June 1919, *Intimate Papers*, IV, 503.

p.111　1.25　'Here I have dug in.'
'A. Walworth, *Woodrow Wilson* (2nd edn, Boston, 1965), II,
323.

p.112　1.3　'By birth, instinct and upbringing, a liberal.'
House, Diary, 6 Mar. 1919, Floto, *Colonel House*, 314.

p.112　1.24　'Advice tendered on such high authority?'
Lloyd George to Barnes, 2 June 1919, Lloyd George Papers,
F/4/3/20; cf. Minutes of meeting of British Empire Delega-
tion, 1 June 1919, Cabinet Papers, CAB/29/28; Chamberlain
to Keynes, *The Life and Letters of the Rt. Hon. Sir Austen
Chamberlain*, ed. Ch. Petrie, II (1940) 145

p.113　1.5　'A discussion with a person in that state of mind is not much use.'
26 Mar. 1919, Mantoux, *Déliberations*, I, 31.

p.113　1.21　'Some very able lawyers can be very cruel men.'
Sumner, Memorandum, 27 June 1919, Keynes Papers, RT/
15; T. Jones, Diary, 12 Feb. 1929, *Whitehall Diary*, ed. K.
Middlemas II (1969), 170.

p.114　1.2　'Trained to listen to arguments.'
Fisher to G. Murray, 11 June 1919, Fisher Papers, Box 7;
R.F.Harrod, *The Life of John Maynard Keynes* (1971), 237.

p.114　1.18　'Pressed to arrive at it between a Saturday and a Monday.'
Keynes to A. Chamberlain, 28 Dec. 1919, Chamberlain
Papers, AC35/1/10; Minutes of meeting of British Empire
Delegation, 11 Apr. 1919, Lloyd George Papers, F/28/3/26.

p.115　1.4　'I never believed in costly frontal attacks . . . if there were a way
round.'
Keynes, Memorandum, 25 Mar. 1919, Lothian Papers,
GD40/17/1303; D. Lloyd George, *War Memoirs* IV (1934),
2274.

p.115 1.26 'Whether any British statesman then alive could . . . have
avoided so much.'
Nicolson, *op. cit.*, 20, 63–4.

p.115 1.37 'Demanding that the cost of the war should be paid by
Germany.'
House, Diary, 10 Mar. 1919, Floto, *Colonel House*, 158.

p.116 1.6 'An ethical level compatible with his own genuine moderation.'
S.P. Tillman, *Anglo-American Relations at the Paris Peace
Conference of 1919* (Princeton, 1961), 64.

p.116 1.33 'The too fierce ardour of an expectant public.'
D. Lloyd George, *The Truth about Reparations and War-Debts*
(1932) 11.

p.118 1.31 'Wild men screaming through the keyholes.'
Parliamentary Debates, 114 H.C. Deb. 5s, 2938.

p.119 1.20 'Got to keep afloat in order to give effect to his principles.'
Riddell, *Diary*, 57: 23 Apr. 1919.

p.120 1.3 'One never knows the orbits of minds like his.'
'Mr. Lloyd George: a Fragment', *The Collected Writings of
John Maynard Keynes*, X (1972), 24; Smuts to M.C. Gillett,
27 Mar. 1919, *Smuts Papers*, 89.

p.120 1.22 'Looks at things from the standpoint of expediency.'
Beaverbrook, *The Decline and Fall of Lloyd George* (1963), 72;
House, Diary, 6 Mar. 1919, Floto, *Colonel House*, 314.

p.120 1.31 'Anything that will lead Germany to suppose that we want a war
indemnity.'
Burnett, *Reparation*, 208..

p.121 1.9 'According to Dr Wilson . . . a policy of premeditated guile.'
Burnett, *Reparation*, 208; T. Wilson, *The Downfall of the
Liberal Party 1914–1935* (1966), 135–57.

p.121 1.35 'The arbiter of all Europe.'
Riddell, *Diary*, 45: 3 Apr. 1919, and 101: 29 June 1919; A.
Walworth, *Woodrow Wilson* (2nd edn, Boston, 1965), II, 329;
Beaverbrook, *Men and Power 1917–1918* (1956), 325.

p.122 1.30 'Final purposelessness, inner irresponsibility.'
B. Webb, *Diaries, 1912–1924*, ed. M. Cole (1952), 111; E.
Holt, *The Tiger. The Life of Georges Clemenceau 1841–1929*
(1976), 235; L.S. Amery, *My Political Life* II (1953), 95; 'Mr.
Lloyd George: a Fragment', *The Collected Writings of John
Maynard Keynes* X (1972), 23.

p.122 1.34 'He clung to the wheel.'
Beaverbrook, *The Decline and Fall of Lloyd George*, 11.

p.123 1.3 'Oh vanity!'
K.O. Morgan, *Lloyd George* (1974), 26.

p.124 1.34 'He was greeted with a howl of derision, even from Hughes.'
L. Mosley, *Curzon. The End of an Epoch* (1960), 206; Smuts
to M.C. Gillett, 22 May 1919, *Smuts Papers*, 182; Cecil,
Diary, 26 May 1919, Cecil Papers; Montagu, note, 4 June

1919, S.D. Waley, *Edwin Montagu* (1964), 212.

p.125 1.1 'A contract between two litigants.'
Minutes of meeting of British Empire Delegation, 1 June 1919, Cabinet Papers, CAB/29/28.

p.125 1.23 'AJB makes the whole of Paris seem vulgar.'
Nicolson, Diary, 8 May 1919, *op. cit.*, 329–30.

p.126 1.10 'Just like the scent on a pocket handkerchief.'
Vansittart, *The Mist Procession* (1958), 218; Diary, 5 May 1919, Calwell, *Henry Wilson*, 195; C.P. Scott, Diary, 5 July 1919, *The Political Diaries of C.P. Scott*, ed. T. Wilson, (1970), 357; Montagu, notes of 4 June 1919, Waley, *op. cit.*, 212; Jones, 9 June 1922, *op. cit.*, I, 201.

p.126 1.29 'He would not be afraid to face the House.'
Riddell, *Diary*, 87: 8 June 1919; Minutes of meeting of British Empire Delegation, 11 Apr. 1919, Lloyd George Papers, F/28/3/26.

p.127 1.3 'I have complete confidence in your doing the best possible.'
Minutes of meeting of 9 June 1919, *Papers Relating to the Foreign Relations of the United States. The Paris Peace Conference 1919*, VI (Washington 1946), 261–2; Jones, Diary, 14 Apr. 1919, *op. cit.*, I, 84; Bonar Law to Lloyd George, 31 May 1919, Lloyd George Papers, F/30/3/71.

p.127 1.28 'More glad than ever that I am going away.'
Cecil, Diary, 1 June 1919 and 9 June 1919, Cecil Papers.

p.128 1.25 'I am not in the disposition to use it with the Prime Minister.'
J. Marlowe, *Milner, Apostle of Empire* (1967), 325; L.Amery, *Diaries. Volume I: 1896–1927*, ed. J. Barnes and D. Nicolson (1981), 247; J.E. Wrench, *Lord Milner* (1958), 250.

p.129 1.7 'More damage to his reputation than any other document that he ever produced in his whole life.'
W.K. Hancock, *Smuts. The Sanguine Years 1870–1919* (1962), 515.

p.129 1.31 'Leave this Treaty to its own devices, and it will soon come to an end.'
Smuts to Keynes, Hancock, *op. cit.*, 533.

p.130 1.11 'If David could have listened to him in 1919, it would have been well.'
Stevenson, *Diary*, 284.

p.131 1.2 'Discontented but admiring colleagues who cling to his shirt.'
Montagu to E. Drummond, 30 Apr. 1919, Montagu Papers, AS-VI-9.

Chapter 6. THE CARTHAGINIAN PEACE

p.132 1.14 'Versailles was "too mild for its severity".'
J. Bainville, *Action Française*, 8 May 1919.

p.132 l.17　'The most reactionary since Scipio Africanus dealt with
　　　　　　Carthage.'
　　　　　　Smuts to M.C. Gillett, 19 May 1919, *Smuts Papers*, 171.
p.133 l.28　'I leave the Twins to gloat over the devastation of Europe.'
　　　　　　Keynes to his mother, 14 May 1919, *The Collected Writings of
　　　　　　John Maynard Keynes* XVI, (1971) 458; Nicolson to his father,
　　　　　　8 June 1919, and to his wife, 28 May 1919, *Peacemaking 1919*
　　　　　　(1933), 350, 359; Keynes to Lloyd George, 5 June 1919,
　　　　　　Collected writings, XVI, 469.
p.133 l.39　'One little word from Clemenceau or George or Wilson would
　　　　　　have meant so much.'
　　　　　　Smuts to M.C. Gillett, 28 June 1919, *Smuts Papers*, 255.
p.134 l.10　'No right to accuse the Germans of want of good faith.'
　　　　　　E. Abraham to Kerr, 3 June 1919, Lothian Papers, GD40/17/
　　　　　　62/21; Nicolson, *op. cit.*, 187; J. Headlam-Morley, *A Memoir
　　　　　　of the Paris Peace Conference 1919*, ed. A. Headlam-Morley
　　　　　　(1972), 162.
p.134 l.29　'God be merciful to us poor sinners.'
　　　　　　Nicolson, Diary, 28 June 1919, *op. cit.*, 370; Keynes to his
　　　　　　mother, 14 May 1919, *Collected writings*, XVI, 458; Smuts to
　　　　　　Alice Clark, W.K. Hancock, *Smuts. The Sanguine years
　　　　　　1870–1919.* (1962), 544.
p.134 l.41　'Our intention to endeavour to get the Treaty revised.'
　　　　　　Vansittart, *The Mist Procession* (1958), 220; B. Webb, *Diaries
　　　　　　1912–1924*, ed. M. Cole (1952), 162; Letter to G. Murray,
　　　　　　4 June 1919, Gilbert Murray Papers, 181.
p.135 l.19　'Our disappointment is an excellent symptom: let us perpetuate
　　　　　　it.'
　　　　　　Nicolson, Diary, 30 May 1919, *op. cit.*, 353.
p.135 l.31　'The day may not be far distant when they will be sensibly
　　　　　　modified.'
　　　　　　A. Luckau, *The German Delegation* (New York, 1941), 418,
　　　　　　419; *Observer*, 29 June 1919; *Manchester Guardian*, 24 June
　　　　　　1919.
p.135 l.36　'A temporary measure of a nature to satisfy public opinion.'
　　　　　　H. Nicolson, *Diaries and Letters 1930–1939*, ed. N. Nicolson
　　　　　　(1966), 82.
p.137 l.5　'The fictitious energy shown in demanding his surrender.'
　　　　　　W.S. Churchill, 'The Ex-Kaiser', *Great Contemporaries*
　　　　　　(1937), 25; Davidson, Diary, 6 July 1919, Davidson Papers,
　　　　　　13; Hardinge to R. Graham, 10 Apr. 1920, Hardinge papers,
　　　　　　42/150.
p.137 l.21　'One of the most outrageous acts of a cruel victor in civilised
　　　　　　history.'
　　　　　　Smuts to Keynes, Sarah Millin, *General Smuts*, II (1936), 256;
　　　　　　Keynes to A. Chamberlain, 8 Dec. 1919, Keynes Papers,
　　　　　　EC/11; Keynes, *Economic Consequences*, 56.

p.137 l.33 'The death sentence of many millions of German men, women and children.'
Keynes, *Economic Consequences*, 146.

p.138 l.19 'How they jeered and hooted at his name.'
B.M. Baruch, *The Public Years* (1961), 127; W.A. White to R.S. Baker, 3 June 1919, A.J. Mayer, *Politics and Diplomacy of Peacemaking. Containment and Counterrevolution at Versailles 1918–1919* (1968), 877.

p.139 l.2 'The President looked wiser when he was seated.'
Keynes, *Economic Consequences*, 25, 26, 32.

p.139 l.21 'Better a live fox than a dead lion.'
J.C. Smuts, *Jan Christian Smuts* (1952), 222; Keynes, *Economic Consequences*, 26. J.C. Stamp wrote to Keynes (8 Feb. 1920): 'Davidson told me the other day that while parts of it [*The Economic Consequences of the Peace – A.L.*] made the P.M. wild, on the whole he liked it, "for it showed he was a cleverer man than Wilson," which after all is the thing that matters.' (Keynes Papers, EC/12).

p.139 l.34 'I know of no adequate answer to these words.'
Keynes, *Economic Consequences*, 23, 146.

p.140 l.22 'It strengthened the Americans against the League.'
Keynes, *Economic Consequences*, 181; Address at Pueblo, Colorado, 25 Sept. 1919, Wilson, *Public Papers*, 412; Millin, *op. cit.*, II (1936), 257.

p.141 l.26 'A new line of thought and . . . action.'
Keynes to Davis, 18 Mar. 1920, Keynes Papers, EC/12; C.P. Scott to Keynes, 11 Jan. 1920, *ibid.*, EC/12.

p.141 l.39 'The obvious Prussianization of the British governing class.'
J.M. Kenworthy, *Sailors, Statesmen and Others. An Autobiography.* (1933), 148.

p.142 l.17 'Not one word to bring back some memory of the generosity of her sons.'
C.E. Montague, *Disenchantment* (1922), 172, 180, 182.

p.143 l.4 'The Treaty of Versailles is null and void.'
A. Chamberlain to Keynes, 22 Dec. 1919, Chamberlain Papers, AC35/1/9; K. Martin, *Father Figures* (1966), 103; 'Dr. Melchior: a defeated enemy,' *Collected Writings*, X, 415; Hardinge to R. Graham, 12 Feb. 1920, Hardinge Papers, 42/149; Keynes to Davis, 18 Mar. 1919, Keynes Papers EC/12; A. Ebray, *A Frenchman looks at the Peace* (1927), 249.

p.143 l.21 '"Cleverness" fatal to success in the long run.'
Cecil to G. Murray, M. Gilbert, *The Roots of Appeasement* (1966), 64; Headlam-Morley, 'Reparation. A Chapter of a History of the Peace Conference', Confidential Foreign Office memorandum, 27 June 1922. 11984, Headlam-Morley Papers; T. Wilson, *The Downfall of the Liberal Party 1914–1935* (1966), 202–3.

p.143 l.35 'The inclusion of pensions in the bill.'
             The Times, 12 March 1923; *The Times*, 23 Dec. 1920.

p.144 l.12 'He thinks that what he does wrong he can "some day" put
             right.'
             Smuts, 28 May 1919, W.K. Hancock, *op. cit.*, 527; Garvin to
             Kerr, 10 Sept. 1928, Lothian Papers, GD40/17/240, 238.

p.144 l.30 'Machiavellian statecraft is bankrupt.'
             Manchester Guardian, 15 Feb. 1919; Balfour to Botha, 27 May
             1919, Balfour Papers, FO 800/216; F.A. Iremonger, *William
             Temple, Archbishop of Canterbury* (1948), 335.

p.145 l.14 'Will France be safe . . . because her sentries stand on the
             Rhine?'
             Keynes, *Economic Consequences*, 35, 92; English text of
             French preface, *ibid.*, xxi.

p.145 l.26 'We would deserve the fate which such folly would bring upon
             us.'
             Keynes, *Economic Consequences*, 188; House, Diary, 9 Feb.
             1919, *Intimate Papers*, IV, 356.

p.147 l.4   'You cannot deal with Nazi Germany until you give her justice.'
             A.L. Rowse, *All Souls and Appeasement* (1961), 31; speech at
             Nottingham, 11 Nov. 1933, J.R.M. Butler, *Lord Lothian
             (Philip Kerr) 1882–1940*, (1960), 197; Kerr to Curtis, 25 July
             1936, Lothian Papers, GD40/17/319.

p.147 l.20 'The Führer's desire for such a discussion.'
             Kerr, Memorandum, Lothian Papers, GD40/17/319/217;
             Kerr to Baldwin, 30 Jan. 1935, *ibid.*, GD40/17/201/69; Kerr
             to Hankey, 1 Feb. 1935, Hankey Papers, HNKY 8/32–33/1;
             Kerr to Ribbentrop, 31 Jan. 1935, Lothian Papers, GD40/17/
             202/97.

p.147 l.30 'Discriminations against Germany which are the root of all our
             troubles today.'
             Kerr, Address to Anglo-German Fellowship, 14 July 1936,
             Lothian Papers, GD40/17/317/32–33.

p.148 l.13 'Dealing with the colonial and economic questions.'
             W.S. Churchill, *The Gathering Storm* (1964), 172; Kerr to
             Lloyd George, 23 May 1936, Lothian Papers GD40/17/319/
             207.

p.148 l.27 'What a German historian of today still regards as the harshest
             blow of all Versailles.'
             Rowse, *op. cit.*, 31, and letter to author, 19 Oct. 1980;
             Stevenson, *Diary*, 214; F. Dickmann, *Die Kriegsschuldfrage
             auf der Friedenskonferenz von Paris 1919* (Munich, 1964),
             91–2.

p.148 l.40 'More aggressive action than she might otherwise have taken.'
             L. Curtis to Kerr, 19 July 1936, Lothian Papers, GD40/17/
             319.

p.149 1.19 'Generosity towards Germans which all decent people . . . seem
to have.'
Baffy, The Diaries of Blanche Dugdale, 1936–1947, ed. N.A.
Rose (1973), 8; Nicolson, Diary, 10 March 1936, ed. N.
Nicolson, op.cit., 249; E.M. Forster to E. Blunden, 1 May
1937, Forster Papers.

p.149 1.29 'Economic sanctions against Germany.'
F.R. Gannon, The British Press and Germany 1936–1939
(1971), 99; Parliamentary Debates, 310 H.C. Deb. 5s, 1462,
1454.

p.150 1.6   'Let him who is without sin cast the first stone.'
Kerr to Eden, June 1936, Lothian Papers, GD40/17/445/37;
The Times, 16 Mar. 1936.

p.150 1.23 'The old structure of European peace . . . is nearly in ruins.'
Rose (ed.) op. cit., 8; The Times, 6 Mar. 1936.

p.151 1.3   'Merely because she is no longer weak.'
Barrington Ward, Note, 24 March 1936, The History of The
Times, IV pt.2 (1952), 901; The Times, 7 Nov. 1938.

p.151 1.31 'Not because it paid to do so . . . but because it was right.'
Keynes, Economic Consequences, 96; The Times, 1 Feb. 1932;
Germany and the Rhineland. Supplement to International
Affairs (April 1936), 20.

p.152 1.26 'We fought the last war largely to prevent this.'
A.J.P. Taylor, The Origins of the Second World War (2nd edn,
1964), 235; M. Anderson, Noel Buxton. A Life (1952), 167;
N. Chamberlain to Derby, 12 Oct. 1938, Derby Papers, 920
(DER); Vansittart, Memorandum, 22 Jan. 1936, Vansittart
Papers, VNST 1/12; Commentary on compte rendu of Kerr's
interview with Hitler (4 May 1937), 28 May 1937, Vansittart
Papers, VNST 2/31.

p.153 1.13 'Dropping in little things which are intended to soothe them.'
Dawson to Barrington-Ward, 11 Aug. 1936, Dawson Papers;
Gilbert, op. cit., 143–4.

p.153 1.28 'He cannot find any adequate explanation of why the Germans
gave in so completely.'
Stevenson, Diary, 261, 286–7.

p.153 1.36 'A symbolic act of reconciliation.'
T.P. Conwell-Evans, notes of a conversation between Lloyd
George and Hitler, 4 Sept. 1936, Gilbert, op. cit., 208.

p.154 1.26 'We are the dead . . . and for what?'
Vansittart, The Mist Procession 366.

Bibliography

PRINCIPAL SOURCES

Cabinet Papers 1918–1919, Public Record Office
Cabinet Records
War Cabinet Records
Imperial War Cabinet Records
Imperial War Cabinet Committee on Indemnity. Report, Proceedings and
    Memoranda. 1918.
British Empire Delegation to the Paris Peace Conference Records

MANUSCRIPT COLLECTIONS

Balfour Papers, Public Record Office
Bell Papers, Lambeth Palace
Bryce Papers, Bodleian Library
Cecil Papers, British Library
Chamberlain Papers, University of Birmingham
Davidson Papers, Lambeth Palace
Dawson Papers, Bodleian Library
Derby Papers, Liverpool City Library
Fisher Papers, Bodleian Library
Hankey Papers, Churchill College, Cambridge
Hardinge Papers, University Library, Cambridge.
Headlam-Morley Papers, in the possession of Professor Agnes Headlam-
    Morley
Keynes Papers, Marshall Library, Cambridge
Lloyd George Papers, House of Lords Record Office
Lothian Papers, Scottish Record Office, Edinburgh
Milner Papers, Bodleian Library
Montagu Papers, Trinity College, Cambridge
Murray Papers, Bodleian Library
Vansittart Papers, Churchill College, Cambridge

DOCUMENTARY COLLECTIONS

Brockdorff-Rantzau, *Dokumente* (Charlottenburg, 1920).

P.M. Burnett, *Reparation at the Paris Peace Conference* (2 vols, New York, 1940).

A. Luckau, *The German Delegation at the Paris Peace Conference* (New York, 1941).

P.J. Mantoux, *Les Délibérations du Conseil des Quatre: Notes de l' Officier Interprète* (2 vols, Paris 1955). See also *Proceedings of the Council of Four*, trans. J.B. Whitton (Geneva, 1964).

La Paix de Versailles, Vol. I: *Les Conditions de paix de l'Entente à l'Allemagne* (Paris, 1930).

La Paix de Versailles. La Commission de Réparations des Dommages, vol. I (Paris, 1932).

Papers Relating to the Foreign Relations of the United States. The Paris Peace Conference, 1919 (13 vols., Washington, 1942–7).

Papers Relating to the Foreign Relations of the United States, 1918, Supplement 1, vol. I (Washington, 1933).

The Treaty of Versailles and After. Annotations of the Text of the Treaty (Washington, 1947).

DIARIES, MEMOIRS AND CONTEMPORARY SOURCES

Note Places of publication are given only for works published outside the United Kingdom.

L.S. Amery, *My Political Life* (3 vols., 1953).

— *Diaries, Volume I: 1896–1927*, ed. J. Barnes and D. Nicholson (1980).

M. Asquith, *Autobiography*, ed. M. Bonham Carter (1962).

J. Bainville, *Les Conséquences Politiques de la Paix* (Paris, 1920).

R.S. Baker, *Woodrow Wilson and World Settlement*, vol.II (1923).

— *Woodrow Wilson. Life and Letters*, vol. VIII (1939).

— *American Chronicle* (New York, 1945).

J.S. Barnes, *Half a Life* (1933).

B.M. Baruch, *The Public Years* (1961).

R.H. Beadon, *Some Memories of the Peace Conference* (1933).

S. Bonsal, *Unfinished Business* (1944).

R.L. Borden, *Memoirs*, ed. H. Borden (1938).

Cambridge Chronicle

R. Cecil, *All the Way* (1949).

A. Chamberlain, *Life and Letters*, ed. Ch. Petrie (2 vols., 1940).

T. Clarke, *My Lloyd George Diary* (1939).

G. Clemenceau, *Grandeur and Misery of a Victory* (1930).

Daily Mail

A. Duff Cooper, *Old Men Forget* (1953).

Esher, Lord, *Journal and Letters* (4 vols., 1934–8).

A. Fitzroy, *Memoirs*, vol. II (1925).

G. Foster, *The Memoirs of the Rt. Hon. Sir George Foster*, ed. W.S. Wallace (Toronto, 1933).

Germany and the Rhineland. A record of addresses delivered at meetings held at Chatham House, supplement to *International Affairs* (April 1936).

C.T. Grayson, *Woodrow Wilson. An Intimate Memoir* (New York, 1960).

E. Halévy, 'Après les elections anglaises', *Revue de Paris* (Mar.–Apr. 1919).

G. Hanotaux, *Le Traité de Versailles* (Paris, 1919).

Hansard, *Parliamentary Debates*.

H.W. Harris, *The Peace in the Making* (1920).

J. Headlam-Morley, *A Memoir of the Paris Peace Conference 1919*, (ed.) Agnes Headlam-Morley (1972).

The Intimate Papers of Colonel House, (ed.) Ch. Seymour, vol. IV (1928).

E.M. House and Ch. Seymour (eds.) *What Really Happened at Paris. The Story of the Peace Conference 1918–1919* (1921).

D. Houston, *Eight Years with Woodrow Wilson* (New York, 1926).

W.M. Hughes, *Policies and Potentates* (1950).

T.E. Jessop, *The Treaty of Versailles: Was it Just?* (1942).

John Bull

T. Jones, *A Diary with Letters 1931–1950* (1954).

— *Whitehall Diary*, (ed.) K. Middlemas, vols I and II (1969).

J.M. Kenworthy, *Soldiers, Statesmen and Others. An Autobiography* (1933).

J.M. Keynes, *The Economic Consequences of the Peace* (1919).

— *Essays in Biography* (1933).

— *Two Memoirs* (1949).

R. Lansing, *The Peace Negotiations. A Personal Narrative.* (1921).

— *The Big Four and Others of the Peace Conference* (1922).

L. Loucheur, *Carnets Secrets 1908–1932*, ed. J. de Launey (Brussels, 1962).

D. Lloyd George, *The Great Crusade. Extracts from Speeches delivered during the War* (1918).

— *The Truth about Reparations and War Debts* (1932).

— *Memoirs of the Peace Conference* (2 vols., Yale, 1939).

I. Malcolm, *Lord Balfour. A Memory* (1930).

Manchester Guardian

K. Martin, *Father Figures* (1966).

F. Maurice, *Haldane. The Life of Viscount Haldane of Cloan*, vol. II (London, 1939).

Mermeix, (G. Terrail), *Le Combat des Trois* (Paris, 1922).

C.E. Montague, *Disenchantment* (1922).

H. Mordacq, *Le Ministère Clemenceau: Journal d'un Témoin* (Paris, 1930).

Morning Post

New Statesman

H. Nicolson, *Peacemaking 1919* (1933).

— *Diaries and Letters 1930–1939*, ed. N. Nicolson (1966).

Observer

V.E. Orlando, *Memorie*, ed. R. Mosca (Milan, 1960).

C. Repington, *The First World War 1949–1918. Personal Reminiscences*, vol. II (1920).

G. Riddell, *Lord Riddell's Intimate Diary of the Peace Conference and After* (1933).

N.A. Rose (ed.), *Baffy, The Diaries of Blanche Dugdale 1936–1947* (1973).

A.L. Rowse, *A Cornishman at Oxford* (1965).

S. Salvidge, *Salvidge of Liverpool. Behind the Political Scene 1890–1928* (1934).

C.P. Scott, *The Political Diaries of C.P. Scott 1911–1928*, ed. T. Wilson (1970).

B. Shaw, *Peace Conference Hints* (1919).

J.T. Shotwell, *At the Paris Peace Conference* (New York, 1937).

J.C. Smuts, *Selections from the Smuts Papers*,ed. W.K. Hancock and J.Van Der Poel, vol. IV (1966).

Spectator

F. Lloyd George (Stevenson), *The Years that are Past* (1967).

F. Stevenson, *Lloyd George. A Diary by Frances Stevenson*, ed. A.J.P. Taylor (1971).

A.J. Sylvester, *Life with Lloyd George*, ed. C. Cross (1975).

A. Tardieu, *The Truth about the Treaty* (1921).

The Times

Vansittart, Lord, *The Mist Procession* (1958).

B.Webb, *Diaries 1912–1924*, ed. M. Cole, (1952).

E. Wilson, *Memoirs of Mrs. Woodrow Wilson* (1939).

Sir H. Wilson, *Life and Diaries*, ed. C.E. Calwell, 2 vols., 1927).

W. Wilson, *Presidential Messages, Addresses and Public Papers*, vols I and II, ed. R.S. Baker and W.E. Dodd (New York, 1926, 1927).

— *When a Man comes to Himself* (New York, 1915).

SECONDARY STUDIES

P. Addison, 'Lloyd George and compromise peace in the Second World War', in *Lloyd George: Twelve Essays*, ed. A.J.P. Taylor (1971).

M. Anderson, *Noel Buxton. A Life* (1952).

C. Barnet, *The Collapse of British Power* (1972).

Beaverbrook, Lord, *Men and Power, 1917–1918* (1956).

— *The Decline and Fall of Lloyd George* (1963).

E.W. Bennett, *German Rearmament and the West 1932–1933* (Princeton, 1979).

M. Bentley, *The Liberal Mind, 1914–1929* (1977).

P. Birdsall, *Versailles. Twenty Years After* (New York, 1941).

R. Blake, *The Unknown Prime Minister. The Life and Times of Andrew Bonar Law 1858–1923* (1955).

J. Braeman (ed.), *Wilson* (Englewood Cliffs, N.J., 1972).

G. Bruun, *Clemenceau* (Cambridge, Mass. 1943).

E.H. Buehrig (ed.), *Wilson's Foreign Policy in Perspective*, (Gloucester, Mass. 1970).

R.E Bunselmeyer, *The Cost of the War 1914–1919. British Economic War Aims and the Origins of Reparations* (Hamden, Conn. 1975).

J.R.M. Butler, *Lord Lothian (Philip Kerr) 1882–1940* (1960).

J.C. Cairns, 'A nation of shopkeepers in search of a suitable France', *The American Historical Rev.*, LXXIX (1974).

W.S. Churchill, *The Aftermath* (1929).

— *Great Contemporaries* (1937).

— *The Second World War. Volume I. The Gathering Storm* (1948).

T. Clarke, *Northcliffe in History. An Intimate Study of Press Power* (1950).

C. Coote, *Editorial* (1965).

G.M. Curry, 'Woodrow Wilson, Jan Smuts and the Versailles settlement', *American Historical Rev.*, LXVI (1961).

V. Czernin, *Versailles 1919* (New York, 1968).

E. David, 'The Liberal Party divided 1916–1918', *Historical J.*, XIII (1970).

J.T. Davies, *The Prime Minister's Secretariat 1916–1920* (Newport, Conn., 1951).

F. Dickmann, *Die Kriegsschuldfrage auf der Friedenskonferenz von Paris 1919* (Munich, 1964).

M.L. Dockrill and J.D. Goold, *Peace without Promise. Britain and the Peace Conference 1919–23* (1981).

M.L. Dockrill and Z. Steiner, 'The Foreign Office at the Paris Peace Conference in 1919', *International History Rev.* (Jan.1980).

B. Dugdale, *Arthur James Balfour, First Earl of Balfour* (1936).

M. Egremont, *Balfour* (1980).

H. Elcock, *Portrait of a Decision. The Council of Four and the Treaty of Versailles*, (1972).

J.T. Emmerson, *The Rhineland Crisis* (1977).

L.F. Fitzhardinge, 'W.M. Hughes and the Treaty of Versailles 1919', *J. Commonwealth Studies*, V.2, (1967).

I. Floto, *Colonel House in Paris. A Study of American Policy at the Paris Peace Conference 1919* (Aarhus, 1973).

W.B. Fowler, *British-American Relations 1917–1918. The role of Sir William Wiseman* (Princeton, 1969).

F.R. Gannon, *The British Press and Germany 1936–1939*) (1971).

M. Gilbert, *The Roots of Appeasement* (1966).

M. Green, *Children of the Sun. A Narrative of 'Decadence' in England after 1918*, (1977).

R. Griffiths, *Fellow Travellers of the Right. British Enthusiasts for Nazi Germany 1933–39*, (1980).

J.L. Hammond, *C.P. Scott of the Manchester Guardian*, (1934).

W.K. Hancock, *Smuts. The Sanguine Years 1870–1919*. (1962).

M. Hankey, *Politics, Trials and Errors* (1950).

— *The Supreme Control at the Paris Peace Conference 1919* (1963).

Hardinge, Lord, *The Old Diplomacy*, (1947).

R.F. Harrod, *The Life of John Maynard Keynes* (1953).

Q. Hogg, *The Left was Never Right* (1945).

E. Holt, *The Tiger. The Life of Georges Clemenceau* (1976).

H. Hoover, *The Ordeal of Woodrow Wilson* (New York, 1958).

M. Howard, *War and the Liberal Conscience* (1978).

F.A. Iremonger, *William Temple, Archbishop of Canterbury* (1948).

R. Jenkins, *Asquith* (1963)

T. Jones, *Lloyd George* (1951).

S.J. Kernet, 'Distractions of peace during war. The Lloyd George Government's reaction to Woodrow Wilson, December 1916–November 1918', *Trans. American Philosophical Soc.* (April 1975).

S. Koss, 'Asquith versus Lloyd George: the last phase and beyond', in *Crisis and Controversy. Essays in Honour of A.J.P. Taylor*, ed. A. Sked and C. Cook (1976).

P. Krüger, *Deutschland und die Reparationen 1918–19* (Stuttgart, 1973).

J. Lees-Milne, *Harold Nicolson. A Biography 1886–1929.* (1980).

A. Lentin, 'Philip Kerr e "l'aggressione della Germania"', *Lord Lothian. Una vita per la pace* (Florence, 1984).

R.B. McCallum, *Public Opinion and the Last Peace* (1944).

J.M. McEwen, 'The Coupon Election of 1918 and Unionist Members of Parliament', *J. Modern History*, XXXIV (1962).

— 'Northcliffe and Lloyd George at War, 1914–1918', *Historical J.*, XXIV (1981).

D. MacLachlan, *In the Chair: Barrington-Ward of the Times* (1971).

E. Mantoux, *The Carthaginian Peace* (1946).

J. Marlowe, *Milner, Apostle of Empire* (1967).

L.W. Martin, *Peace without Victory. Woodrow Wilson and the British Liberals* (Yale, 1958).

A. Marwick, *The Deluge: British Society and the First World War* (1965).

A.J. Mayer, *The Politics and Diplomacy of Peacemaking. Containment and Counterrevolution at Versailles 1918–1919* (1968).

N. Medlicott, 'Britain and Germany: the search for agreement 1930–37', in *Retreat from Power. Studies in Britain's Foreign Policy of the Twentieth Century*, vol. I, ed. D. Dilks (1981).

S. Millin, *General Smuts* (2 vols., 1936).

K.O. Morgan, *David Lloyd George. Welsh Radical as World Statesman* (2nd edn, 1964).

— *Lloyd George* (1974).

— 'David Lloyd George', in J.P. Mackintosh (ed.), *British Prime Ministers in the Twentieth Century*, vol. I (1977).

— *Consensus and Disunity. The Lloyd George Coalition Government 1918–1922* (1979).

L. Mosley, *Curzon. The End of an Epoch* (1960).

C.L. Mowat, *Lloyd George* (1964).

H.I. Nelson, *Land and Power. British and Allied Policy on Germany's Frontiers 1916–19* (1963).

H. Nicolson, *King George the Fifth* (1952).

F.S. Northedge, *The Troubled Giant. Britain among the Great Powers 1916–1939* (1966).

D. Ogg, *Herbert Fisher 1865–1940* (1947).

T.H. O'Brien, *Milner* (1979).

G.A. Panichas (ed.), *Promise of Greatness. The War of 1914–1918*, foreword by Herbert Read (1968).

Ch. Petrie, *Walter Long and his Times* (1936).

R. Pound and G. Harmsworth, *Northcliffe* (1960).

P. Renouvin and C. Bloch, 'L'article 231 du traité de Versailles: sa genèse et sa signification', *Revue d'histoire de la guerre mondiale*, X (1932).

E.G. Reid, *Woodrow Wilson. The Caricature, the Myth and the Man* (1939).

K. Rose, *The Later Cecils* (1975).

N. Rose, *Vansittart. Study of a Diplomat* (1978).

S. Roskill, *Hankey, Man of Secrets*, vol. II (London, 1972).

A.L. Rowse, *All Souls and Appeasement* (1961).

H. Rudin, *Armistice 1918* (Yale, 1944).

Ch. Seymour, *Geography, Justice and Politics at the Paris Conference of 1919* (New York, 1951).

— 'Policy and personality at the Paris Peace Conference', *Virginia Q. Rev.* (1945).

— 'End of a friendship', *American Heritage* (August 1963).

R. Skidelsky, *John Maynard Keynes*, vol. I (1983).

G. Smith, *When the Cheering Stopped* (1966).

J.C. Smuts, *Jan Christian Smuts* (1952).

J.A. Spender and C. Asquith, *Life of Herbert Henry Asquith, Lord Oxford and Asquith* (1932).

D. Stevenson, *French War Aims against Germany 1914–1919* (1982).

A.J.P. Taylor, 'The war aims of the Allies in the First World War', in *Essays presented to Sir Lewis Namier*, ed. R. Pares and A.J.P. Taylor (1956).

— *Lloyd George. Rise and Fall* (1961).

— *The Origins of the Second World War* (2nd edn 1964).

— *English History 1914–1945* (1965).

H.W.V. Temperley (ed.), *A History of the Peace Conference of Paris*, (6 vols., 1920–4).

S.P. Tillman, *Anglo–American Relations at the Paris Peace Conference of 1919* (Princeton, 1961).

— *The History of the Times*, vol. IV (1952).

M. Trachtenberg, *Reparation in World Politics. France and European Economic Diplomacy 1916–1923* (New York, 1980).

— 'Versailles after sixty years', *J. Contemporary History*, XVII (1982).

J. Turner, *Lloyd George's Secretariat* (1980).

S.D. Waley, *Edwin Montagu* (1964).

A. Walworth, *Woodrow Wilson*, (2nd edn, Boston, 1965).

D. Watt, 'The historiography of Appeasement', in *Crisis and Controversy. Essays in honour of A.J.P. Taylor*, ed. A. Sked and C. Cook (1976).

E. Weill-Raynal, *Les Réparations Allemandes et la France*, vol. I (Paris, 1938).

T. Wilson, *The Downfall of the Liberal Party 1914–1935* (1966).

F. Wilson, *Eglantyne Jebb* (1967).

R. Wohl, *The Generation of 1914* (1980).

J.E. Wrench, *Geoffrey Dawson and Our Times* (1955).
— *Lord Milner* (1958).
K. Young, *Arthur James Balfour* (1963).

Index

INDEX OF PERSONS

Amery, Leopold (1873–1955), Assistant Secretary to War Cabinet and Imperial War Cabinet, Parliamentary Under-Secretary, Colonial Office, 1919–21, 14, 28, 122, 128

Asquith, Herbert Henry (1852–1928), Prime Minster 1908–16, 17, 18, 19, 24, 26, 28–9, 52–3, 88, 89, 91, 113, 121, 143

Asquith, Margot (1862–1945), second wife of H.H. Asquith, 143

Astbury, Frederick, Lt.-Commander, Conservative M.P., 117

Astor, Waldorf, Viscount (1879–1952), 151, 152

Baker, Ray Stannard (1870–1946), journalist, Director of American Press Bureau at Peace Conference, 51, 65, 110

Baldwin, Stanley (1867–1947), Prime Minister 1923, 1924–9 and 1935–7, 40, 119, 147, 148, 149, 153

Balfour, Arthur James (1848–1930), Conservative elder statesman and former Prime Minster, Foreign Secretary 1916–1919 and member British Delegation to Peace Conference, 4, 9, 10, 11, 13, 27, 28, 30, 32, 33, 93, 104, 105, 123–6, 127, 130, 144, 149

Barnes, George Nicholl (1859–1940), Socialist politician, member of War Cabinet 1917–19 and British delegation to Peace Conference, 26, 27, 33, 92, 93, 94, 95, 96, 97, 104, 130, 148

Barrington-Ward, Robert (1891–1948), deputy editor of *The Times* 1927–41, ix, 149, 150–1, 153

Beaverbrook, Lord, 120, 121, 122

Bell, George (1883–1958), Bishop of Chichester 1929–58, 150

Bell, Johannes (1868–1949), German Minister of Colonies and Transport 1919–20, co-signatory of Treaty of Versailles, 104, 133, 146

Borah, William Edgar (1865–1940), isolationist republican Senator, 118, 140

Borden, Sir Robert Laird (1854–1937), Canadian Prime Minister 1911–1920, member of Imperial War Cabinet, chief Canadian representative on British Empire Delegation at Peace Conference, 25, 27

Botha, General Louis (1862–1919), South African Prime Minister 1910–19, chief South African representative on British Empire Delegation at Peace Conference, 33, 93, 95, 97, 129, 144

Bottomley, Horatio (1860–1933), Independent M.P., editor of *John Bull*, 40–1, 50, 69, 89, 90–1, 98, 107, 122, 142

Brockdorff-Rantzau, Count Ulrich von (1869–1928), German Foreign Minister 1918–19 and Head of German Delegation at Peace Conference, 84–8, 101, 103, 105, 125, 129, 130, 133, 137, 139, 146, 148

Bryce, Lord (1838–1922), Liberal peer, 26, 136

Buckmaster, Lord (1861–1934), Liberal Lord Chancellor 1915–16, 26, 88–9, 113, 136

Carson, Sir Edward (1854–1935), Conservative member of War Cabinet 1917–18, 15

Cecil, Lord Robert (1864–1958), Minister of Blockade 1916–18, Assistant Secretary of State, Foreign Office, 1918, member of British Delegation at Peace Conference, x, 33, 67, 77, 92, 93, 94, 96, 97, 105, 113, 122, 124, 127, 129, 130, 135, 143

Chamberlain, Sir Austen (1863–1937), Chancellor of Exchequer 1919–21, 94, 95, 96, 112, 142

Chamberlain, Neville (1869–1940), Prime Minister 1937–40, 152, 153

Churchill, Winston (1875–1965), Secretary of State for War 1918–21, ix, 19, 24, 25, 27, 28, 90, 91, 93, 94, 95, 118, 130, 136, 146

Clark, Alice, correspondent of Smuts, 91, 126

Clemenceau, Georges (1841–1929), French Prime Minister 1917–20, 'President' of the Paris Peace Conference, x, xii, xiii, 10, 11, 12, 25, 29, 31, 34, 37, 38, 41, 42, 43, 44, 45, 46, 47, 48, 49, 56, 58, 62, 63, 64, 65, 66, 67, 68–9, 70–2, 73, 74, 75, 76, 82,

INDEX OF PLACES AND TOPICS